# Value
# Engineering

# Value
# Engineering

## A SYSTEMATIC APPROACH

Arthur E. Mudge

**Senior Associate**
*Value Associates*

## j.pohl associates

Published By
**J. POHL ASSOCIATES**
**1706 Berkwood Drive**
**Pittsburgh, PA 15243**
**(412) 279-5000**


**ISBN 0-939332-17-5**

9th printing, 1996

# Contents

*Student*
*Value Instructor*
*Value Specialist*
*Value Management*
*Executive*

This Contents incorporates a "Reader's Guide." This Reader's Guide has been developed based on "Interest" and "Need to Know."

In order to provide the greatest assistance, it has been divided into five specific levels of interest. Within each of these levels, three different depths of study are indicated on a "need-to-know" basis.

The three depths of study are symbolized and described as follows:

X — to be read and studied for complete understanding
/ — to be read for familiarization and general understanding
* — to be scanned for basic understanding of content for future reference

|  | Executive | Value Management | Value Specialist | Value Instructor | Student |
|---|---|---|---|---|---|

| | Executive | Value Management | Value Specialist | Value Instructor | Student |
|---|---|---|---|---|---|
| **Chapter 6. Information Phase 45** | * | * | / | / | X |
| General 45 | * | * | / | / | X |
| Information Phase 46 | * | * | / | / | X |
| Secure the Facts 46 | * | * | / | / | X |
| Worksheets—General 48 | * | / | / | X | X |
| Project Number 48 | * | / | / | X | X |
| Product 48 | * | / | / | X | X |
| Project 48 | * | / | / | X | X |
| Quantity Required 48 | * | / | / | X | X |
| Information Worksheet 48 | * | * | / | / | X |
| Application and Marketing Background 48 | * | * | / | / | X |
| Engineering Background 49 | * | * | / | / | X |
| Manufacturing and Procurement 50 | * | * | / | / | X |
| Consultation Summary 51 | * | * | / | / | X |
| Determine the Costs 52 | * | * | / | / | X |
| Definition of Costs 53 | * | * | / | X | X |
| Prime Costs 53 | * | * | / | X | X |
| Overhead Costs 54 | * | * | / | X | X |
| Conversion Costs 54 | * | * | / | X | X |
| The 20-80 Rules 56 | / | / | X | X | X |
| Rule 1: Cost of Goods Manufactured (General Cost Structure) 56 | / | / | X | X | X |
| Rule 2: Factory Cost (Modified Cost Structure) 56 | / | / | X | X | X |
| Rule 3: Basic and Secondary Function (To Be Explained in Chapter 7) 56 | / | / | X | X | X |
| Fix Costs on Specifications and Requirements 56 | * | * | / | X | X |
| Specifications and Requirements 57 | * | * | / | / | X |
| **Chapter 7. Function Phase 59** | * | / | X | X | X |
| Functional Approach 59 | * | / | X | X | X |
| Define the Function 60 | * | / | X | X | X |
| Rules of Function Definition 61 | * | / | X | X | X |
| Evaluate Functional Relationships 66 | * | / | X | X | X |
| Numerical Evaluation of Functional Relationships 68 | * | X | X | X | X |
| **Chapter 8. Creation Phase 75** | * | * | / | X | X |
| Establish Positive Thinking 79 | * | * | / | X | X |
| Develop Creative Ideas 81 | * | * | / | X | X |
| Idea Activators 83 | * | * | / | X | X |
| Idea Needlers 84 | * | * | / | X | X |

# Preface

The Systematic Approach of Value Engineering, as described in this book, is a plan which provides a positive course of action to remove the unwanted and unnecessary. It is described herein in theory, application, and case-study forms.

We must use a plan which will not only provide us with the management of change but one which will also ensure that this constant change is used to our advantage. The major advantage to us is the removal of unwanted and unnecessary factors from our environment.

Change and modification, like death and taxes, are items with which each of us will be confronted every day of his life; for change and modification are both constant and important parts of our environment and are unalterable facts of life.

These are facts which we cannot shun or sidestep. They are facts with which we must deal in both our personal and business lives. The facts of change and modification are normally felt to a lesser extent in our personal lives because they are subtle. They are recognized and felt to the strongest degree in our business lives, primarily because they are forced on us by the actions of other individuals or groups.

Therefore, if we are to survive, it is vital for each of us, when encountering these facts of life, to learn the *management of change*. This is vital whether we are concerned with our personal or business environment. For, if each of us does not learn the management of change, there is most surely going to be a change of management.

In order to fully understand the basic significance of the term *management of change* we must understand the definition of the word *management*. *Management* is defined as follows:

> —*the act, art, or manner of managing*
> —*skillful managing, executive ability*

In reviewing these definitions, it is found that we have progressed no further toward understanding than when we started. In order to gain the needed understanding we must go back to the base of the word *management*; i.e., *manage*. This word then is defined as follows:

> —*to control, guide, or work*
> —*to have charge of, direct, conduct, administer*

If, therefore, each of us is to manage change—to control, guide, direct or administer it—he cannot do it in a hit-or-miss manner. This can only be accomplished through the application of a distinct plan, a positive course of action.

Because of the necessity for complete understanding, this book has been written in plain "kitchen English" to provide you with understandable recipes for the management of change. These recipes not only describe for you the theory but explain the methodology of applying the principles of Value Engineering to a wide variety of situations by means of specific techniques. These techniques are designed to assure the greatest possible benefit from successful application of the basic principles as well as to reduce the possibility of failure to a minimum.

Throughout this book, the application of the Value Engineering Systematic Approach to all types of "productive" and "nonproductive" activities is shown. Through these applications, you will see and learn that this Systematic Approach is applicable to any product. This remains true even under the broadest definition of the term *product*; i.e., anything which is the result of someone's labor.

If you as an individual or as a member of a group desire to learn the management of change and are not afraid of the consequences of such knowledge, it is recommended that you read the material in this book. If, however, it is your desire to remain complacent and have others control your destiny, it is recommended that you read no further.

*A. E. Mudge*

Part One

# Fundamentals and Theory

# Chapter One

# Fundamentals

## A Type of Magic

The Value Engineering Approach is a type of magic!

The "magic" acts which we have seen performed on stage over the years are not achieved through sorcery or miracles. Instead, these acts are based on the application of a systematic, planned approach to obtain a desired effect. In the case of the magician, this desired effect is illusion, or the seeming accomplishment of the impossible, the results of which are amusing and nonproductive.

The Value Engineering Approach is likewise neither sorcery nor miracle. It, like the magician's approach, involves the application of a systematic, planned procedure to obtain a desired effect. It is in their desired effects, however, that the two approaches differ. The desired effect of the Value Engineering Approach is positive; its result is "the same or better performance at lower total costs."

We find in business and industry a number of approaches whose basic objective is cost reduction. These include:

Competitive cost comparison
Manufacturing systems analysis

Motion analysis
Make or buy
Standardization

These programs are quite effective in their spheres of application. The Value Engineering Systematic Approach is such that its application, coupled with these other approaches, increases the effectiveness of the latter. Value Engineering is designed to supplement these approaches, not to replace them in any way.

## Value Analysis to Value Management

In 1947, in the General Electric Company, the fundamentals of the Systematic Approach were conceived and brought together. The approach was called *value analysis* and was applied within the purchasing area of the industry.

As more was learned about the Systematic Approach and as it was refined, it was realized that it had a broader application. This broader application was in the engineering and manufacturing spheres of influence. In other words, the Systematic Approach could, it was found, be applied in all the areas that generated and influenced the costs of a physical product.

With growing use and continual refinement and development, the Systematic Approach has evolved to the point where it has been found to be applicable to all business areas; i.e., hardware and software, systems and procedures, processes and services—indeed, to anything that affects a product's total cost. It has further been determined that this Systematic Approach—its objectives and purpose, its creeds and philosophy—is applicable by anyone to anything that affects the profits of business or industry.

Over the years since its inception, this growth and refinement has stimulated the thought and served as the goal of those who have applied and continued the development of the Systematic Approach. This growth has characterized not only the range of problems to which the approach has been applied but also the approach itself, for its developers have realized that a growing, improving approach is a useful approach, one that will never become obsolete.

## Objective of Value Engeering

The objective of the Value Engineering Systematic Approach is to provide a means of total cost control anywhere within a product's life cycle. It stresses *only* the reduction or elimination of cost. This is done while maintaining the required quality and reliability of the product to which the systematic approach is applied.

An implied objective is *not* to cheapen or degrade the product. For when it is said that a product has been cheapened, it is implied that the product's quality and reliability have been impaired while its cost was being reduced.

The specific objective of the Value Engineering Systematic Approach is stated in its definition by the Society of American Value Engineers:

> *Value Engineering is the systematic application*
> *of recognized techniques which identify the*
> *function of a product or service, establish a*
> *monetary value for that function, and provide*
> *the necessary function reliably at the lowest*
> *overall cost.*

NOTE: The terms *value analysis, value control, value assurance, value management,* and all other similar terms are considered to be synonymous. They are so considered because they apply the same basic methodology and techniques and have the same basic objective.

## Purpose of Value Engineering

The purpose of the Value Engineering Systematic Approach is to provide each individual with a means of skillfully, deliberately, and systematically analyzing and controlling the total cost of a product. This total cost control is accomplished, in the main, by the systematic analysis and development of alternative means of achieving the functions that are desired and required.

The application of the technology of this systematic approach provides a means of isolating the necessary from the unnecessary. This is accomplished in the areas of both function and cost.

> *The inquiring mind is never satisfied with*
> *things as they are. It is always seeking ways*
> *to make things better and do things better.*
> *It assumes that everything and anything can*
> *be improved.* — HARLOW H. CURTIS

The purpose of the Value Engineering Systematic Approach is well served when the user is able to define and segregate the necessary from the unnecessary and thereby develop alternate means of accomplishing the necessary at a lower total cost.

## Cost

As can be determined from the discussions of the purpose and objectives of this Systematic Approach, one of its major focal points is *total cost.*

*Total Cost: The sum of all efforts and
expenditures made in the development,
production, and application of the product.*

This is a fine definition, but as is the case with most definitions, further definition is required to establish complete understanding.

Total cost as defined contains three basic areas of cost which must be analyzed and related to each other at all times; i.e., development cost, production cost, and application cost.  Starting with the latter, the producer of the item must constantly evaluate effects on quality, reliability, and maintainability.  This is necessary because any effect on any of these will have a distinct effect on the user's total cost.  The first area, development cost, should be looked at next.  The efforts and expenditures made in this area also have a telling effect on the item's total cost.  Because they must be spread over every item produced, they further affect the item's production and application costs.  The final area of the total cost that is to be considered is the production cost.  This area of the total cost must be given the greatest consideration because it normally contains the greatest amount of unnecessary cost.

The area of production cost can, in itself, be broken down into three distinct areas of cost: material, labor, and overhead.  A simile can best be used at this point to show the relationship of these three costs to each other as well as to the whole.  Since this discussion deals with costs, or money, the simile used here will involve money.

The production cost of the item being considered is represented by the twenty pennies shown.

Figure 1-1

These can be divided into the three areas of production cost.

Figure 1-2

These three piles represent material, overhead, and labor respectively.  Looking at it another way, if the total production cost, not including profit, is represented by the 20 cents and equals 100 percent, then the material,

11½ cents, equals 57.5 percent; the overhead, 6½ cents, equals 32½ percent; and the labor, 2 cents, equals 10 percent.

These percentages and amounts are quite significant when viewed from the standpoint that most cost reduction or cost control efforts are directed at the reduction of the labor content of the production cost. As can be seen from the above, even a complete elimination of the labor would result in only a 10 percent reduction of the product cost.

The Value Engineering Systematic Approach, on the other hand, directs its primary efforts at the material content of the product cost. It is important to note that this does not mean just the physical material but that it also considers the function or functions to be performed by the material and the effect that these functions have on all other cost factors.

Because of this functional approach and the area of cost to which it is applied, the resultant cost improvement normally amounts to 20 to 35 percent, even, at times, 100 percent. This is accomplished through the elimination of the unnecessary costs.

## Unnecessary Costs

Unnecessary costs are those costs which do not meaningfully contribute to the product to which they accrue. This in itself is an understandable statement, but unnecessary costs are best understood if their causes are established, interpreted, and analyzed. The establishment of the reasons for unnecessary costs is not an easy task, for they are many and varied. They can, however, be grouped into three basic categories: *mental conditioning, mental roadblocks,* and *faulty communications.*

**Mental Conditioning**    Mental conditioning is a category of unnecessary cost which must further be broken down to be fully understood. This category can be subdivided into five basic conditions: lack of information, lack of ideas, honest wrong beliefs, temporary circumstances, and habits and attitudes. These individual conditions are best interpreted and analyzed when explained in further detail.

*Lack of Information:* This is caused by the nonaccumulation of accurate and detailed facts regarding, for instance, costs and specifications. It may also result from misinterpretation or misunderstanding of the requirements or from inaccurate definition of the problem.

*Lack of Ideas:* This is caused by insufficient use and application of background knowledge, industrial knowledge, the skills of company and industrial specialists, standards, specialty products, creative thinking, and time.

*Honest Wrong Beliefs:* These may result from the above conditions as well as from the ready acceptance of opinion, hearsay, half truths, speculation, and theories for whole facts without justification or verification.

These beliefs, although honest, are incorrect and not in accord with existing facts.

*Temporary Circumstances:* These cause the continued application of solutions which are applicable to a temporary condition or set of conditions after that condition has disappeared. This improper application of solutions is occasioned by the presence of one or more of the first three conditions.

*Habits and Attitudes:* These are established as a result of the acceptance of the first four conditions, basically because the human individual is a creature of habit. The individual's past experiences, beliefs, and traditions cause him to establish a particular habit pattern in what he does and thinks, and habits cause him to solve similar problems in similar ways. Because of this, a new solution, being different from the normal pattern, causes the attitude of "resistance to change." It has been said that "Habits take us where we were yesterday, and our attitudes tend to keep us there."

Analysis of the above five conditions indicates that unnecessary costs exist as a rule rather than as the exception. Decisions made in solving a problem will cause unnecessary costs to occur when one or more of the above conditions is present.

Further analysis reveals a deeper and more fundamental cause of these mental conditions. This cause is human nature. When these five categories are analyzed in depth, we find that each is a distinct part of human nature and that each of us is subject to them.

On the surface, these appear to be conditions that could, with a special effort, be avoided, and thus their effect on cost could be avoided. However, since they concern human nature as well as the technical and organizational aspects of a solution, the problem is much more complex. With these thoughts in mind, it is worthwhile to note that because everyone is subject to these conditions, no one individual or group of individuals can be blamed for the existence of unnecessary costs caused by them. Hence the thought: *Point not your finger at any man, for in so doing you point three at yourself.*

Figure 1-3

The unnecessary costs developed by these five conditions are not the total extra costs. The second category, mental roadblocks, expands and multiplies the effects of these five conditions.

**Mental Roadblocks**    Mental roadblocks constitute the second major category of the causes of unnecessary costs. This category is, again, the result of human nature and one to which every individual is subject to a degree dependent on the conditions at a particular time.

Another name for this cause of unnecessary costs is the *single-solution fixation.* This single-solution fixation is akin to the above habits-and-attitudes condition, but it is also quite different.

What happens here is that a problem is presented, the mind assimilates that problem, finds a solution, and then immediately shuts itself off. When this reaction is carried to its full extent, one reaches the state in which habits and attitudes play their part. It has been found that when a similar problem occurs, the mind goes back through its memory system and seeks out the original solution and applies it to the current problem without any modification or deviation. Hence, the single-solution fixation.

Figure 1-4

This mental roadblock or single-solution fixation is best understood through example. What do you see in the drawing above? A pretty girl? An old lady? Actually both an old lady and a young girl are in the picture. If you don't see both, you, like most individuals, are subject to the single-solution fixation or to possible mental roadblocks. Look at the drawing again.

The pretty girl is facing away from you, toward the right background, and she wears a big hat and a decorative choker around her neck. Looking again, you will see another face. Instead of the pretty girl's chin, see an old woman's nose; instead of the girl's ear, the old woman's eye; a toothless mouth for the choker; and a jutting chin for the shoulder.

When this drawing is viewed by a group, there is a fairly even distribution of the individuals who see one or the other of the women in the picture. There are, however, very few who see both women. It has further been found that if the same group is shown the picture again after a period of time, each of its members sees the same woman he saw the first time.

We see this same phenomenon daily in business and industry. Its occurrence causes problems similar to others that were encountered in the past, and these problems are often solved with the same old remedies. This is done while taking no account of the constantly changing technology, experiences, or ideas. This is not a rare condition; rather, it is commonplace.

When this category of the causes of unnecessary costs is recognized, a major step has been taken to overcoming it. There remains, however, the third category of the causes of unnecessary costs.

This third category, *faulty communications*, both aids and abets the first two major categories. It is one which we constantly talk about but which is difficult to deal with single-handedly or in a short period of time.

**Faulty Communications**    Communications, or rather the lack thereof, make up the third category of causes of unnecessary costs. Furthermore, this category is not merely additive but is a multiplier of the effects of the previous two categories.

Each individual's ability to communicate is undeniably and permanently linked to his background, education, and training. In the case of communications, the old saying, "As the twig is bent, so is the tree inclined," holds true.

In business and industry, this is a vital and costly point, especially when viewed in terms of the results obtained in a study conducted within a major company. This study showed that the average manager spends 90 percent of his working time in the act of communication. This study further showed the following breakdown of these acts of communication:

Writing . . . . . . . . . . . . .  9%
Reading . . . . . . . . . . . . . 16%
Talking . . . . . . . . . . . . . 30%
Listening. . . . . . . . . . . . . 35%
Other activities . . . . . . . . 10%

As in the case of the first category, the problem involved here may be divided into two conditions; i.e., *lack of communications* and *multiple meanings.*

*Lack of Communications:*    From the above, it is readily recognized that faulty communication is not only expensive in itself but also extremely time-consuming.

When, from the standpoint of the faulty communications, one looks at the previous two categories which cause unnecessary costs, it can readily be seen how this third category compounds effects of the former two. Communications in all four areas, as mentioned above, are subject to varied misinterpretations and misunderstandings based on the individual's background, training, and experience. This being so, they are a major source of poor actions and wrong decisions.

Such misunderstandings and misinterpretations are behind the following statements:

*What we thought he said was. . . .*
*I understood him to say. . . .*
*The way I read it was. . . .*
*What I meant was. . . .*

Again, this condition is not one which can be simply isolated, as it at first might seem to be, for we must add to it the condition of multiple meanings.

*Multiple Meanings:*  The multiple-meaning condition of the communications category is where the individual's background, education, and training play the greatest and ofttimes the deadliest part.  These parts of each individual's personality have the most telling effect on his ability to understand the spoken and written word as well as his ability to make himself understood.

This effect can most graphically be illustrated by the use of a simple and fundamental example.  The magnitude of the multiple-meaning problem graphically takes shape when the following word is studied for its meaning.  The word is *cat.*  This is one of the first words that we learn to read, write, and speak.  *What does it mean?*

It is a simple yet complex word.  It is one that has specific definitions as well as implied definitions, universal as well as local definitions.  *What does it mean?*  The following are some common dictionary definitions:

1. A carnivorous mammal long domesticated and kept by man as a pet (tomcat, alley cat)
2. A person, as a spiteful woman, likened to a cat
3. Short for catfish or cat-o'-nine-tails
4. A name for numerous games
5. A strong tackle used to hoist a ship's anchor
6. A hepcat

In addition to these six definitions, both specific and slang, there are at least two more uses of the word in business and industry.  The word is used in the oil-drilling industry to specify a part of the drilling equipment.  In the construction field, it is used as another name for a bulldozer.

Here then is a simple, three-letter word that, when spoken or written, can be used to mean any one of eight different things to the user and can be understood to mean the same thing or any one of seven other things by the listener or reader.

When these difficulties, caused by the problems of communications, are multiplied by the effects of mental conditioning and mental roadblocks, steps must be taken to overcome, alleviate, or reduce them.  Thus arises the need for the application of a type of magic, the application of the Systematic Approach of Value Engineering!

# Chapter Two

# Basic Terms

In the preceding chapter, one of the basic problem areas outlined was that of communications. Within that chapter, also, a number of common, frequently expounded basic words were used.

With the recognized problem in communications and the aforementioned case of misunderstanding, it is best that, at this early stage, we come to common definitions of the basic terms to be used in our discussion of the Value Engineering Systematic Approach. These basic terms include *value, function,* and *product.*

These words, although in common everyday use, are, like the word *cat,* readily misunderstood because of their many possible meanings and connotations. Therefore, each will be discussed in detail to fully explain its use within the Systematic Approach.

## Value

In the preceding chapter, the terms *value engineering, value analysis,* and *value management* have been used and in specific cases have been defined, but the initial word *value* has not been defined.

*Value* means many things to many people because the term is used in a variety of ways. Also, all too often, it is confused with the terms *cost* and *price*. *Value* is a difficult word to define because it is applied to both subjective qualities (those determined by the emotions) and objective qualities (those determined by external characteristics). The wide scope of definitions is evidenced by the wide usage and misunderstanding of this term.

This misunderstanding is not a recent thing; in actuality, it has been with us for thousands of years. When we trace its history, we find that Aristotle spent time considering this very problem about the year 350 B.C. At that time, he named seven classes of value, a classification that is still recognized today. These are:

1. Economic
2. Moral
3. Aesthetic
4. Social
5. Political
6. Religious
7. Judicial

Of these, however, only the *economic* classification can be considered to be objective. It is the only one that can be measured in external units. All the other classes must be evaluated subjectively.

The Value Engineering Systematic Approach is concerned primarily with the economic value. Therefore, *value* as used in the Systematic Approach is defined as:

> *The lowest cost to reliably provide the required*
> *functions or service at the desired time and*
> *place and with the essential quality.*

This is, however, only a broad definition of economic value, and this individual class of value must, itself, be further subdivided to be fully understood.

Within the class *economic value* there are also found subjective and objective qualities. Economic value in fact comprises four specific kinds of value, each of which is describable. They are:

1. Use value—properties that accomplish a use, work, or service
2. Esteem value—properties that make ownership of an object desirable
3. Cost value—properties which are the sum of the labor, material, overhead, and other costs required to produce something
4. Exchange value—properties of an object that make it possible to procure other items by trading

It can be seen from these definitions that only *use value* is wholly objective. This is quite significant when, in the end, monetary ratings are to be associated with a product's value, both to the user and the supplier.

From the foregoing definitions, it can readily be seen how a single outlook on value could be misleading or completely off the track. The quotation which follows is an example of this:

*Nothing can have value without being an object*
*of utility.  If it be useless, the labor contained in*
*it is useless, cannot be reckoned as labor, and*
*cannot therefore create value.* — KARL MARX (1818–1883)

Such a statement, in the light of today's understanding of value, would not stand unchallenged, for it looks only at a small segment of the full meaning and takes this as the whole.

In order to fully understand and rationalize the import of value, all parts of economic value must be taken into account. The subjective areas of economic value, i.e., esteem, cost, and exchange value, can be grouped into one category of personal value or prestige value for the individual.

The difference between use value and prestige value can best be visualized by the study of the simple example shown below.

Figure 2-1

If we study this gold tie clip and ask why it was made, we shall, of necessity have to determine its intended use. When we ask "What is its use?" we find that it was developed to provide location or to locate the tie; i.e., to prevent the individual's tie from falling into the soup or coffee.

This function or value, however, could also be accomplished by the common paper clip or fastener shown below, at a cost of between 1 cent and $\frac{1}{10}$ cent.

Figure 2-2

Yet the gold tie clip would cost at least several hundred times as much as the paper clip. What is the reason for this extreme difference in cost? Is it founded on each item's relative use value?

No! The use value can be accomplished equally well for 1 cent or a fraction thereof. The difference comes in the area of personal or prestige value. As a matter of fact, the common paper clip can have prestige added to it to a considerable degree, so that it can be used as a tie clip. This is shown by the fact that gold-plated paper-clip tie clips have been advertised for sale at $10 each.

From this it can readily be seen that when the value of an item is to be studied or determined, it is essential to determine its use or *function*.

## Function

The term *function*, as used in the Systematic Approach, must be recognized to denote both an individual characteristic and also the Functional Approach system; i.e., within discussion of the approach there are references to both *functions* and to the *functional approach*. These are very closely knit together and are basically inseparable. In later chapters, the Functional Approach will be explained and described in detail. However, in this portion of our discussion, the two will be considered to be synonymous.

The term *function*, like *value*, means many things to many people. It can mean *province, role, duty, office,* or *faculty*. To the user of the Value Engineering Systematic Approach, it must mean all these and more.

The *province* of the Functional Approach is to intermesh and meld together all the parts, knowledge, and technology of the Systematic Approach into one dynamic and successful plan. Function is the controlling factor within the overall approach.

The *role* of the Functional Approach is that of converting the complex to the simple, the entangled to the straightforward, and the unsolvable to the solvable. In essence, it is the understanding of function which establishes and maintains an organized method of thinking.

The *duty* of the Functional Approach is to provide a useful tool to the user. Value-oriented individuals work with functions in the same way that mathematicians work with numbers and carpenters work with wood. Function, like the numbers and wood, is the main ingredient of the value-oriented individual's product.

It is the *office* of the Functional Approach to provide a means by which the user can establish a ranking or order of importance for the various and sundry needs of a given product. This ranking or order of importance is necessary for the simplification of design, the elimination of components or elements, and the improvement of quality and reliability.

It is the *faculty* of the Functional Approach to form the intermeshing web that knits the systematic approach into one dynamic and successful plan. Function is the key to the Systematic Approach of Value Engineering, the tool which makes this approach different from all other cost reduction approaches and the ingredient which makes this Systematic Approach both compatible with and usable by all other business and industrial disciplines.

The term *function* as we will use it in the Systematic Approach is defined as "that which makes a product work or sell." From this definition, two important realizations can be determined. The first concerns the relationship between value and function. It can readily be seen that in this definition the word *work* directly relates to the use value and the word *sell* relates to the personal or prestige value. This direct relationship between value and function starts to show us the magnitude of the importance of function.

The second important realization is the significance of the word *or* in the basic definition of *function*. In business and industry, it has been found that, as a general rule, we say that "This is what makes a product work and sell." The use of the word *and* in this statement indicates that the costs of what makes a product work and sell are run together so that there is no clear delineation of the cost of either. The use of the word *or* in the definition of function assures us that these two costs and the specifications and requirements causing them will be segregated from each other. This definite segregation provides a means by which they can be analyzed and fully evaluated.

## Product

*Product*, like so many other terms that we encounter in the written and spoken language, has a multiplicity of meanings. These meanings are dependent upon circumstances as well as on the user's and listener's backgrounds. This term can mean the result of a mathematical computation; the result of a chemical change; the output of a farm; or any tangible result of industrial, artistic, or literary labor. This term, for our purposes, can best be defined as "anything produced or obtained as a result of some operation or work, as by generation, growth, labor, study or skill." More simply put, a product is *anything which is the result of someone's effort.*

A complete understanding of this term is vital to those of us who intend to use or administer the Value Engineering Systematic Approach. It has been established over many years and many experiences that this Systematic Approach can be successfully applied to *any product;* i.e., a piece of hardware, a system, a process, or a procedure.

In other words, the Systematic Approach, which is to be explained in detail and in specific terms in the following chapters, can be applied to anything. Anything, whether it be thought, word, or deed!

## Other Definitions

VALUE OBJECTIVE:   The same or better performance at lower costs.

VALUE IMPROVEMENT:   The improved function-to-cost ratio resulting from applying the Value Engineering Methodology to all phases of a product or service and their development.

TOTAL COST:   The total cost is to be considered as the combined direct and supporting costs.

CUSTOMER COST:   The estimated amount of monies to be paid by the user for the operation, installation, supply, and maintenance of the equipment during its useful life.

UNNECESSARY COST:   The total cost of items that do not contribute to the essential functions, reliability, quality, or maintainability.

COST PREVENTION:   The elimination of unnecessary costs during the development stages of designs or operations.

COST TARGETS:   Cost models generated in conjunction with the functional chart establishing cost goals for the system and subsystems.   These cost targets also serve as a measurement tool to the systems management.

TASK FORCE:   A team of value-oriented personnel with a defined short-term task to develop, recommend, and implement solutions for a cost or value problem.   The effort may be related to any phase of the total problem.

VALUE ENGINEERING PROPOSAL:   A document which clearly describes a recommended change that will lead to an overall cost improvement, that is, a change in procedure, design, or equipment.   Such a proposal will state the effect, direct or indirect, that this change will have (as improved reliability or maintainability, or lower support costs) without detrimental effect on the essential characteristics.

SAVINGS:   The difference between original cost and cost after a change or improvement.

FUNCTIONAL CHART:   A chart of the system developed on the "family tree" concept, depicting the basic and secondary functions to be provided by the system.

COST-TO-FUNCTION CHART:   A refinement of the function chart arrived at by adding the actual or estimated costs required to perform the functions depicted on the chart.

WORKSHEETS:   Thought guides for difficult problems and training aids to develop proficiency in the application of the Value Engineering Methodology.

Chapter Three

# Personal Aims
# and Philosophy

Before attempting to apply the vital concepts and techniques of the Systematic Approach, it is important that we have as clear a definition and understanding of the personal aims and philosophy of this approach as we have of the basic terms. We will find that these personal aims and philosophies help us correlate the basic terms, the objectives, and the purpose of the Systematic Approach.

## Personal Aims

Every individual, no matter what his walk of life, position, or profession, is governed and directed in his activities by an aim or set of aims. Likewise, every profession or undertaking devised by man is governed and directed by an aim or aims.

These aims which govern and direct the thoughts of the individual and his activities are multifaceted: they contain both positive and negative aspects. A dictionary definition of the verb *aim* is "to direct one's efforts;" a definition of the noun is "purpose or intention."

The aims which govern and direct the Value Engineering Systematic

Approach are also multifaceted, containing numerous individual yet inter-locking points. These points, covering both the positive and negative aspects, are: *equal performance–lower cost, multiple solutions,* and *constructive discontent.*

An individual examination of each of these aspects will show their distinct yet interlocking characteristics.

**Equal Performance–Lower Cost**    This is the fundamental aim of the Value Engineering Systematic Approach. The most important part of it is *equal performance.* For if, in the application of the Systematic Approach, reliability, quality, or maintainability are reduced, then overall performance is also reduced. Such a reduction is in actuality a cheapening of the product, and this is *not* within the principles of Value Engineering. It must be noted, however, that this aim does not connote excess performance; i.e., performance over and above that which is required to make the product work and/or sell.

This fundamental aim can be stated and more easily remembered as follows: "The same or better performance at lower cost."

A close examination of the statement of the total aim will show that the only thing to be lowered or reduced in the product under analysis is the cost. By keeping this point constantly in the forefront, the fundamental beliefs and principles of the Value Engineering Systematic Approach will never be violated.

**Multiple Solutions**    It has been proved throughout the development and use of the Systematic Approach that the most positive means of accomplishing both parts of the equal performance–lower cost creed is by strict adherence to this second aim—multiple solutions. Experience has shown that when the mind is forced to remain open and creative in order to find more than a single solution, some of the solutions developed are of a higher quality than others. This occurs because parts of each of the multiple solutions are applicable to the improvement of the other solutions.

In addition to the definite improvement of some solutions, this creed also deals with the basic laws of probability and with human nature. Both of these must be considered when dealing with the development of new approaches and solutions to a problem and with the individual's fear of change or his reluctance to face it.

When considering the area of probability, it is readily recognized that as the number of possible solutions is increased, the probability of success is increased as well. Likewise, the probability of the development of a completely new or revolutionary solution to the problem is also increased many-fold. This particular aspect will be discussed in greater depth in a later chapter on creativity.

Multiple solutions are just as important when reviewed from the stand-point of human nature. It is a recognized fact that, because of the individual's fear of change, his first reaction to the suggestion of a change is to reject it.  It is, however, a less known fact that once a rejection has been made, a guilty feeling occurs.  This guilty feeling is overcome through acceptance.  Thus arises another advantage of multiple solutions.

A final area to be considered in the creed of multiple solutions is the types of solutions to be developed; i.e., minor changes and major changes. Every time the Systematic Approach is applied to a problem, it should include the development of both minor and major changes.  This is because minor changes can readily and rapidly be put into effect, thereby immediately securing the benefits of lower cost while the major changes are being proved and verified.  This development of both minor and major changes also allows that flexibility in the creative and developmental aspects which is so necessary to the finding of superior solutions.

**Constructive Discontent**    There is within every individual a natural feeling of discontent with things as they are—a dissatisfaction with the status quo.

The statement below, a play on the words of a famous quotation, can channel this natural discontent and dissatisfaction into the first phase of constructive discontent:

> *Ours not to do or die,*
> *Ours but to reason why.*

Once the individual has started to question everything, constantly asking "why" in order to determine a better way of accomplishing things, he is well on the road to the establishment of a *constructive* discontent.

This question leads the individual to ask the remaining five questions of constructive discontent: *what, when, where, how,* and *who.*  The individual who is seasoned in constructive discontent uses these six questions as servants, as so aptly stated in Kipling's poem:

> *I keep six honest serving men*
> *(They taught me all I knew);*
> *Their names are What and Why and When*
> *And How and Where and Who.*

These two statements, one a direct and the other a reversed quotation, form the basis of the methodology's creed of constructive discontent.


## Philosophy

As the individual establishes, throughout his lifetime, the aims by which he governs himself, he also develops specific philosophies which modify and strengthen those aims.  These philosophies are developed over a period of time, as are the aims, as the result of successful experiences.  For it is successful experience which moves a man's mind and in time moves the man.

A better and further understanding of this occurrence can be achieved by looking at definitions of *philosophy.* The following are such definitions:

*—a study of the processes governing thought*
*and conduct*
*—the general principles of a field of knowledge*
*—a particular system of principles for the*
*conduct of life*

The philosophies which govern the thought and conduct of the Value Engineering Methodology, the general principles of the Systematic Approach, form a particular system of principles for the conduct of the individual's life. These thoughts, principles, and systems are, once established, used by the individual in all the areas of his life.

The philosophies of this systematic, planned approach are only three in number, but they are dynamic and far-reaching in their application and significance. Simply stated, they are: have a positive approach, develop and practice teamwork, and do a better job.

An examination of each of these in more detail will highlight their individual yet interlocking characteristics as well as their relationship to aims.

**Have a Positive Approach**    No one has ever seen, heard, touched, or tasted an approach. In reality, an approach is the result of motivation, and today's motivations must come from within, not from without.

A positive approach or positive motivation is something that each individual must develop within himself as a way of life. When the individual works toward the establishment of a *constructive* discontent, he is at the same time establishing a positive approach. For as one element is developed and refined, another is similarly developed and refined.

It has been said: "It is only the minds of men that make the mind of man."

Any job can be done better if it is approached positively and systematically. It has been found that when a job or problem is undertaken with a negative approach, it is either accomplished after a long period of time or not accomplished at all.

The positive approach, the feeling that a job *can* be done, is the greatest motivating force that the individual can use—not only for himself but for motivating others. In reality, inner-motivated people march to the beat of their own drum—they even march when the band doesn't play.

However, no matter how simple or complex the job or problem, other individuals must be called upon for assistance. A positive approach combined with an understanding and application of teamwork is most likely to lead the individual to a successful outcome.

**Teamwork**    *Teamwork* is a term that is constantly used in our daily conversations; however, it is one that is often grossly misused and misunderstood. If this seems like a harsh statement, take but a moment to look back to the time when you undertook the simple act of determining what this word meant.

If you are like the majority, you have never even looked the word up in the dictionary or thumbed through the thesaurus to determine its synonyms and antonyms.

Wait! Before you go off to secure your dictionary or thesaurus and search out this oh-so-common word, we may save time by defining it here.

First, among the synonyms for the word *teamwork* are *cooperation, collaboration, coaction, concurrence, joint effort, common effort,* and *union in action.*

Second, and more to the point, is the dictionary definition: "Work done by a number of associates, all subordinating personal prominence to the efficiency of the whole." It has been determined, by survey over the years, that very few have ever taken the time to search out the meaning of this vital word. Most individuals have simply established their own definition.

The key to the difficulty lies within the last part of the dictionary definition, i.e., "... *all subordinating personal prominence to the efficiency of the whole.*" Looking at and understanding this brings on the realization that this is not a part of human nature; as a matter of fact, it is in direct opposition to human nature and human desires.

The perfect example of real teamwork is shown in the field of sports where one group of individuals is pitted against another group of individuals. In these sports, football, baseball, soccer, basketball, rugby, etc., a number of *individuals* are selected for a team. These individuals then spend weeks, months, even years training to react as a team, i.e., as a whole. It has been determined that the better they learn this lesson, the greater is their proficiency as a winning team.

Teamwork is not a God-given gift, rather it is something that must be implanted, nurtured, developed, and constantly practiced. Teamwork, like constructive discontent and having a positive approach, is a philosophy which must first be searched out, then diligently and constantly practiced and applied. The philosophies of a positive approach coupled with an understanding and use of teamwork are the major steps toward the accomplishment of the third philosophy or attitude, that of doing a better job.

> *They found that even the Belly, in its dull quiet*
> *way, was doing necessary work for the Body,*
> *and that all must work together or the Body*
> *will go to pieces.* — AESOP (550 B.C.)

**Do a Better Job** At first glance, this part of the three-step philosophy might look as if it were directed at other individuals, but it is not. Doing a better job is a major part of the Systematic Approach's philosophy—a philosophy which is aimed directly at the practitioner.

Again, this phrase, like the term *teamwork*, is one which does not fit with the general attitudes of human nature. Each individual, in his own way, tends to defend that which he is doing as *the* very best. However, if the individual will diligently and honestly analyze the job being done, he will find that a different situation really exists.

The situation that exists is that he is doing the best job he can with the information, knowledge, and experience he has at his disposal at that given time and place. This realization, coupled with the indisputable fact that his information, knowledge, and experience amount to only a minute portion of what is available in any given field, brings a rapid realization that he *can* do a better job. This realization then emphasizes the vital importance and interrelationship of the philosophies of a positive approach and teamwork.

Without the positive approach and the individual's realization that he indeed *can* do a better job, it would be impossible for him to learn from the cooperative teamwork of others. Likewise, it would be impossible for him to convey his knowledge and experience to others. This philosophy, like the previous two, is not one that can simply be stated and thereby accomplished—it is one that must be worked at, striven for, and diligently pursued!

None of the aims and philosophies discussed in this chapter will come easily, for nothing that is of universal application and value will ever be found easy to achieve! Each of these aims and philosophies, each in its own way, outlines to the individual who is to master it a difficult and arduous journey. It will be found that these different journeys at times diverge while at other times they converge. They do, in the last instance, converge in the greatest pot of gold, the ultimate reward—*success.*

The task may seem difficult; the journey may seem extremely long. However, the great Chinese proverb "The longest journey starts with but a single step" is quite apropos. Since you are undertaking this systematic approach to one degree or another, you must also take the first step. For without these personal aims and philosophies as a foundation, the application of this methodology is doomed to failure.

Since human nature does not acquiesce in failure, now is the time to start toward the successful application of these personal aims and philosophies.

*The mind of man grows from the day he is born*
*to the day he dies.*

Chapter Four

# Overview of
# the Systematic Approach

## Development of the Approach

"Timber!"

This cry resounds throughout the forests and industry of today—in the forests as the trees are cut, in industry as product improvement and cost reduction timber is felled. In both areas, this cry is being heard with ever-increasing frequency.

But why this increase in the tempo of thundering trees and cost improvement timber? Because of the introduction of better working tools in both instances. For a clearer answer, it is necessary that we study a bit of the history and development of the tools used.

In the forests, this history and development had its start when man entered the Stone Age.

At that time in man's development, the ax was conceived. The head was chipped from stone and a handle of wood was affixed. With this tool, man could cut trees rather than wait for them to be blown down. This cutting took hours, even days to accomplish.

Then the Bronze Age dawned and the stone ax head was replaced by one of bronze. Thus, the felling of timber for Solomon's temple and other structures was accomplished at a more rapid rate.

Centuries later, man discovered iron, and with it came the inevitable improvement of his basic cutting tool, the ax.

Following in swift progression came steel, a better head shape, an improved handle, and each time a better ax. With each improvement, the cutting ability of the ax improved.

Finally, the ax attained its ultimate development in the double-bladed steel ax used by lumbermen. This the woodsman treasured above all his possessions. He prided himself on being able to cut more wood with this ax than anyone within miles.

Yet today, even after this long and arduous refinement, the ax—at least in the forests—is rapidly being replaced.

What has transpired? What is causing this to happen?

In the not-too-distant past, it was realized that this straight-line progression of improvement had attained its basic peak and that further improvement would be excessively time-consuming in relation to the rewards to be gained. It was further realized that if the desired further improvement in cutting ability was to be attained, a new tool had to be developed.

For this new tool knowledge was sought in many fields—from the gasoline-engine industry, knowledge of a power source; from the saw industry, knowledge of cutting edges; and from the chain industry, knowledge of power-transmission techniques. These bits and pieces of knowledge were modified, rearranged, built on, and combined with new knowledge into a new cutting tool, the chain saw—a dynamic cutting tool which outperforms the double-bladed steel ax many times over.

In the product improvement and cost reduction areas of industry, we find a direct parallel. The history and development of these areas first began when man entered the industrial age. However, in these areas, there are many historical and developmental paths to follow.

In industry, throughout the years, the Management, Engineering, Manufacturing, Purchasing, and Finance Departments have developed and refined their individual product improvement and cost reduction axes to a fine degree. In most instances, however, this history and development, like that of the ax, has been a straight-line progression within each individual department, with little if any overlap or cross-pollination of information.

Similarly, as in the cutting of timber, these programs are rapidly being replaced after long and zealous refinement.

Today, many industries, companies, groups, and individuals are felling their product improvement and cost reduction timber at an ever-increasing rate. What has happened? What is causing this to transpire? As in the history of the ax, it was realized that these individual progressions had attained their basic peaks. It was further realized that if the necessary drastic improvement in results was to be attained, a new tool, program, or methodology would have to be developed. Here again, the need prompted the seeking of knowledge from many sources. This development was not, as with the chain saw, quite as simple to accomplish. Detailed knowledge and quantities of data were first required.

The present programs of Management, Engineering, Manufacturing, Purchasing, and Finance were analyzed and dissected as the source of this data. Bits and pieces, whole techniques and programs were culled out of these vast bodies of knowledge. These bits were then rearranged, built on, and combined with new knowledge into a new, systematic product improvement tool, the Value Engineering Systematic Approach. Known specifically as the Value Engineering Job Plan, this dynamic approach outperforms all others many times over.

## Value Tests

The first step in the development of this systematic approach was the establishment of a set of value tests. These tests comprise ten basic questions which aid in the determination of satisfactory or unsatisfactory value. These ten question tests for determination of value are:

1. Does its use contribute value?

2. Is its cost proportionate to its usefulness?

3. Does it need all its features?

4. Is there anything better for the intended use?

5. Is anyone buying it for less?

6. Can a usable part be made by a lower-cost method?

7. Will another dependable supplier provide it for less?

8. Do material, reasonable labor, overhead, and profit total its cost?

9. Is it made on proper tooling—considering quantities used?

10. Can a standard product be found which will be usable?

It has been found in 99 percent of the cases that, when these questions are answered honestly, there is unsatisfactory value—with considerable room for improvement. This being the case, it became necessary to develop a systematic approach to the problems of value improvement.

This was accomplished, and the Value Engineering Job Plan was born. Over the years, this basic Job Plan has been applied and constantly improved. At this point in time, we have available to us a powerful tool, a positive Job Plan capable of solving our product improvement and cost reduction problems.

## Value Engineering Job Plan

In this plan there are seven phases, corresponding in part to the chain saw's course of development. The specific phases of the Job Plan are:

General Phase
Information Phase
Function Phase
Creation Phase
Evaluation Phase
Investigation Phase
Recommendation Phase

Each of these phases, in turn, comprises or is supported by one or more techniques. Before analyzing these phases and techniques, even in an overview, it must again be stipulated that many are not new. Rather, these older techniques have been used intuitively by good management, engineering, manufacturing, purchasing, finance, and service personnel singly or in various combinations. The developers and users of the Job Plan, recognizing the worth of these older techniques, organized them along with new ones into a systematic plan which takes the best advantage of each. Analyzing each phase of the Job Plan in turn, it is found that some twenty-two individual techniques are employed.

These techniques will be briefly discussed in the remainder of this chapter within the phase of the Job Plan in which they are most specifically employed. They will be treated in detail in subsequent chapters, both as theory and by application.

**General Phase**    Throughout the application of the entire Job Plan, the techniques of each phase must be diligently applied; therefore, the success or failure of the complete undertaking depends on their proper application.

*Use Good Human Relations:*    It will be seen that considerable personal contact is necessary throughout the subsequent Job Plan. The use of good human relations means the difference between assistance or resistance.

*Inspire Teamwork:* This is one of the easiest things to talk about, yet one of the hardest to accomplish. Only by constantly and consciously working toward it can teamwork be accomplished.

*Work on Specifics:* Concrete data and information on specific problems must be secured. Only opinions and hearsay can be expected when talking in generalities.

*Overcome Roadblocks:* In any organization or group, dissenters can be found. These individuals, knowingly or unknowingly, will use every means at their command to resist change. It is important to be able to recognize roadblocks and then take steps to overcome them.

*Apply Good Business Judgment:* Business decisions and judgment must be based on facts. Poor business decisions and poor judgment become prevalent when personal opinions and feelings take control.

These techniques of the General Phase, it will be recognized, must be the foundation techniques of any plan used in industry. Likewise, in the Job Plan, they must be used conscientiously throughout the entire Systematic Approach.

With the General Phase as the base or foundation of the Job Plan, this overview can be continued into the Information Phase. The techniques included in this second phase, though seemingly simple, incorporate some of the most difficult portions of the approach.

**Information Phase**    This phase of the Job Plan contains only three techniques. They will, however, be found to be among the most difficult and time-consuming to apply.

*Secure the Facts:* One of the most arduous tasks is to secure *all* the facts—making sure that the information and data gathered are not hearsay or half-truths.

*Determine the Costs:* In order that efforts can be directed toward those areas containing the greatest return on the invested time, complete, concise, and accurate costs must be secured.

*Fix Costs on Specifications and Requirements:* By establishing a relationship between the costs and the specifications and requirements, a means is presented by which the latter two can be quantitatively evaluated.

Extreme care must be used during this phase to be sure that true facts are gathered, that accurate costs are secured, and that these costs are truly related to the specifications and requirements before any progression is made toward the next phase of the Job Plan.

Once the techniques of the Information Phase have been used to secure all the pertinent and available data, the Function Phase and its included techniques can be employed.

**Function Phase**    The two techniques of this phase are a major part of the Functional Approach—the Functional Approach being that group of techniques which, when combined with the other techniques of the Job Plan, produces a systematic approach different and vastly more productive than any other product improvement or cost reduction approach.

*Define the Function:*   Within this technique lies the keystone of the Value Engineering Systematic Approach.   It sounds quite simple, but in reality it is not easy to accomplish.   Each function must be defined in two words, one verb and one noun.

*Evaluate Function Relationships:*   This is accomplished by taking the functions as defined in the above technique and the information and data secured in the Information Phase and establishing a relationship between them.   Through this technique, a descending order of importance of the functions is established along with the relative value of their importance.

These techniques not only establish which functions are basic, secondary, and dependent but also which functions are present because of specifications and requirements or because of the existing design.

Having thus defined and evaluated all the functions, the techniques of the Creation Phase can be applied.

**Creation Phase**   The subject of creativity or brainstorming is not new; as a matter of fact, there are many books written on this specific subject. The two techniques of this phase simply point up the vital areas of this subject.

*Establish Positive Thinking:*   When dealing with the subject of creativity, it must be recognized that your mind comprises two parts: the judicial and the creative.   This technique establishes the necessity of turning off the judicial part during the Creation Phase.

*Develop Creative Ideas:*   This is done by cultivating uninhibited thinking and developing a multitude of ideas and approaches for accomplishing the defined functions.   The desired thing at this point is a large quantity of ideas.

This phase basically involves the two mental processes; i.e., the creative and the judicial.   It requires the inhibition of the latter and the stimulation of the former.   When the desired quantity of ideas, providing for the defined functions, has been achieved (no matter how ridiculous they may seem) through the Creation Phase, the next phase of the Job Plan — evaluation — is undertaken.

**Evaluation Phase**   This phase and its supporting techniques must be undertaken with both care and diligence.   For it is here that the judicial part of the mind is brought into active use.

*Refine and Combine Ideas:*   The generation of a quantity of ideas does not, in itself, accomplish a thing if these ideas are not put to use.   Before they can be put to use, continued creativity and refinement must be applied. This is done on a single idea or a combination of ideas.

*Establish Cost on All Ideas:*   As a device or process applying an idea or combination of ideas is being refined, an estimated cost should be calculated; i.e., what is the potential cost of applying this idea and what are the resultant savings implied?

*Develop Function Alternatives:*   This is a continuation and combination of the first two techniques of this phase.   It makes further use of the information developed in the evaluation of functional relationships to meld the individual functional solutions into total solutions of the product problem.

*Evaluate by Comparison:*   When these rough total solutions and their related estimated costs have been established, they are compared to determine which one will provide the greatest possibility of attaining the value-level goal.   At this point, the selection of the idea or ideas which are to be carried through further development is made.

As this judgment is carefully applied to the creative ideas, they are refined to basic workable solutions, *not eliminated.*   In this refinement and combination of the ideas and the establishment of estimated cost on them through additional creative thinking, it is quite easy to either eliminate them or have them slip into a low-quality process.   This must be guarded against, again because of human nature, for it is human nature to choose one solution and shy away from the unusual way or new approach.

The combined creative ideas that have been refined to basically workable solutions and have the greatest potential return on further invested time are subjected to the techniques of the Investigation Phase.

**Investigation Phase**   The three techniques of this phase further refine the selected ideas into workable and salable solutions, providing lower-cost methods of performing the required and desired functions through the application of additional, vast resources of knowledge.

*Use Company and Industrial Standards:*   Within a standard lies a tried and proved solution to a problem.   This type of solution is applied if it is also the lowest total-cost approach.

*Consult Vendors and Specialists:*   These people should always be consulted because of their specialized knowledge.   Such knowledge can pinpoint problems in their specialized field and bring new information to bear on the solution of the problem.

*Use Specialty Products, Processes, and Procedures:*   These in many cases provide a lower-cost way of accomplishing the function or functions.   These are to be evaluated and used when they provide a lower total cost than standard products, processes, and procedures would.

As the ideas are thus evolved through the foregoing approach into reasonable and salable lower-cost solutions, the completion step of the Job Plan —the Recommendation Phase—is put into effect.

**Recommendation Phase**   This phase and its included techniques are the culmination and wrap-up of all the previous efforts exerted throughout the

Job Plan. Upon these techniques and their diligent fulfillment hinges the success or failure of all the foregoing work.

*Present Facts:* Just as it was important to start with facts, it is doubly important to conclude with facts. Facts, in most instances, speak for themselves.

*Present Costs:* Accurate costs, whether estimated or factual, must be presented as part of the final recommendation. Again, costs, like facts, speak for themselves.

*Motivate Positive Action:* The proper presentation of accurate, specific, and detailed facts and costs will motivate positive action. This technique also requires the follow-through to make sure that action is taken and that complete implementation is accomplished.

The presentation of these facts and costs and the motivation of positive action is accomplished in one of three ways: in verbal form, in written form, or in a combination of both written and verbal form. The final, combined form is recognized as the best.

The final recommendation need not, in fact should not, contain all the data accumulated. It should, however, contain sufficient data for the decision makers to determine the course of action to be taken.

## Conclusion

The Job Plan of the Value Engineering Systematic Approach can realistically be compared to the construction of a building, the General Phase forming the foundation. The Information Phase through the Investigation Phase form the individual floors of the building, each founded on the strength and completeness of the preceding steps. The Recommendation Phase is the wrap-up of the finished structure.

It must be recognized that in order to have this Job Plan function as it should, the efforts of the total industrial management team must be employed. Without the aid and support of every part and individual of industry, very little can be accomplished. For, just as with the chain saw, if any part does not work, the entire tool is useless or will very rapidly become so.

In the next seven chapters, the technical theory of each phase of the Job Plan and the included techniques will be discussed in detail. The last chapter of Part 1 will, through charts and discussion, show the application of the Job Plan in actual practice.

# Chapter Five

# General Phase

Only upon a strong foundation can a strong structure be built.  The five techniques of the General Phase, when applied correctly, form the strong foundation necessary for the Value Engineering Job Plan.  For that matter, these techniques form a strong foundation for any job or task we undertake.  The importance of these techniques is emphasized by the realization that they deal with the individual and his subjective judgment.

From a study of these techniques and of the reasons for their application, we soon discover that life is a mixture of good and bad days, victory and defeat, give and take.  We learn that it doesn't pay to be a sensitive soul, that we should let some things go past like water over a dam.

We learn that he who loses his temper usually loses everything.  We learn that any man may have a bad breakfast now and then, and that we shouldn't take the other fellow's grouch too seriously.  We learn that carrying a chip on your shoulder is the easiest way to get into a fight, and that the surest way to become unpopular is to be carrying tales and gossip about others.

We learn that buck-passing always returns as a boomerang and in the end never pays.  We learn that school keeps fairly well without us.  Also that it doesn't really matter so much who gets the credit as long as the job gets done.

We find out that all people are human and that it doesn't do any harm to smile and be pleasant even if it is raining.   We discover that most of the other fellows are as ambitious as we are, that they have brains that are as good as or better than ours, and that hard work and not cleverness is the secret of success.   We learn to help the youngsters coming into the profession because we remember how bewildered we were at first.

We acquire the ability to avoid worry when we make a blunder because experience has shown us that if we always do our best, our average will break pretty well.   We learn that no man ever succeeds alone, and that it is only through cooperative effort that we move on to greater successes.

We discover that folks are not any harder to get along with in one place than another, and that the "getting along" depends 99 percent upon our own behavior.

By our acquisition of knowledge, we soon determine that judgment is not a gift but an ability based on facts and not on personal opinion, and that one of the greatest satisfactions in life is the knowledge that we have made good use of our judicial abilities to make a required decision.

The strong foundation of this Job Plan is composed of the five techniques of using good human relations, inspiring teamwork, working on specifics, overcoming roadblocks, and using good business judgment.   Although there are numerous books which to some extent cover these vital subjects, a definition of each follows.

## Use Good Human Relations

*Everybody is a bit right; nobody is completely*
*right or completely wrong.*

The successful application of this Job Plan is based on human relations. More important than working techniques, approaches to cost improvement programs and the ultimate success of any business reside in the know-how of understanding and working with people.   Without establishing a good background in the field of human relations, conducting a successful Value Engineering program is impossible.

Everywhere we go, in everything we do, we come into contact with people.   We know, or soon learn, that no man lives or works alone; that we are always with others, agreeing, disagreeing, cooperating, and competing.   As far back as history goes, man has always had someone with whom to live and cooperate in order to survive.   Our complicated, fast-moving society leaves us so very dependent upon one another.   It is sometimes astonishing to us to realize that we are dependent upon multitudes of individuals whom we neither know nor have ever contacted.   We seldom consider the endless quantity of things we would have to do without if we chose, as the hermit does, to be independent of all other human beings.

Yes, we take all this for granted because it is what we have come to accept; it has become a way of life.   Our greatest task is that of getting others to help and understand us as well as learning to help and understand them. From the beginning of our lives, we seek the aid of someone — our parents, our teachers, our friends, and our associates.   From our first cry to our last breath, we are learning the most important lesson of all: mastery of the best techniques for securing as well as giving help and encouragement.

From the beginning, we learn how to smile, how to plead, how to command, and how to obey.   With all this, we are most flexible in order that we may adjust to others.   The people that we like the most are those who are most skilled in dealing with us and with whom we can most easily deal. Our association with them brings out the better qualities in us.   The successful person is one who can inspire loyalty and enthusiastic work from those who work with him.   Therefore, it becomes our prime purpose to investigate and master the abilities and skills of working with people and utilizing these skills to the best of our ability.

In looking at this problem of human relations, we must treat each individual as an individual.   We must, however, think not only of the individual but also the group.   If our lives, our industries, and our businesses are to expand and flourish, we must work as a group or team and do what is best for the majority.

## Inspire Teamwork

*Teamwork: Work done by a number of*
*associates, all subordinating personal*
*prominence to the efficiency of the whole.*

By the nature of our society, we are born to families, clans, or groups and progress into clubs, fraternities, and company groups.   Since this is the beginning and the end, we learn the human way of doing things.   We learn this by the contacts we make and have and by the experiences of others. From our home environment, we learn the correct way of life; from our parents, we gather some of our habits and attitudes.   From experience and conditioning, we decipher how to be human beings.   Every individual we meet, no matter how big or small, important or insignificant, has an effect on us. Only through these contacts and relationships do we learn the vital lessons of how to act, think, feel, and get along with others.   These associations, experiences, and lessons are part of our selves.   Without taking all these into account, can we really and fully know ourselves?

It is most important to realize, at this point, that everyone, including ourselves, has shortcomings; but quite often these can be explained and understood if the background and human contacts of the individual are studied. It is of the utmost importance for each of us to find the best means of working successfully with *all* people in relationships which bring out the best in everyone.

In order to become part of a good working group, we must first learn togetherness: we must be cohesive. An office or industry whose groups lack cohesion is comprised of individualists, persons who do not help one another, whose attitudes are poor, and whose morale is low. The group that does have togetherness, that works as a team, is one in which there is a strong "we-ness." Its members have become congenial—loyal to one another and to the group as a whole. They, together, share the responsibility of the group. When this state exists, the team members freely participate and readily subordinate personal prominence to the efficiency of the whole. This type of reaction and togetherness is only accomplished when the members of the team are able to achieve their individual goals through the activities of the team.

In such a team, there will develop, over a period of time, a code of ethics to which all members will readily conform. Such ethics will be as strong or as weak as the team is tightly or loosely knit. A team which is highly active will be tightly knit; an inactive team will have little holding power.

It must be clear that when a job is to be done by a group of people, it is best accomplished when they feel themselves firmly united in a team striving for a common goal. Work done in this manner leads to self-respect and a sense of mutual responsibility.

When a man is asked to participate with others in the achievement of a plan, his task appears in a new light. He develops *esprit de corps* and the feeling of belonging to the plan rather than the feeling of one standing on the outside looking in. If he is consulted, he becomes aware of a mutual dependence.

Let us look at the team members as they support and assist one another. On occasion, it has been said, "If I give you a dollar and you give me a dollar, we shall each have one dollar. If, however, I give you an idea and you give me an idea, we shall each have two ideas." In the latter instance, each individual has gained a second idea; each shared idea tends to become a strong one because it is shared. It is a band of union, and union contributes to strength.

When all things are taken into consideration, all people have the same basic needs, but it behooves us to realize that each person is, to a great degree, the end product or goal of his overall environment. If we can understand that the reason the other fellow does not behave and act as we do is largely because his environment, contacts, and experiences have not been the same as ours, we have taken a major step in human understanding. This will help us to comprehend the vital concepts and wants that are common to all mankind. It will give us an insight into the actions and behavior of others and help us to work more harmoniously together.

The mutual sharing of responsibility and flexibility and the mutual sacrifice, at least in part, of authority are among the significant conditions producing good teamwork. The individual who recognizes and creates such conditions changes his status from that of one looking in from the outside to that of one working for and supporting the team on the inside.

In discussing the necessity of a unified effort, we are not promoting the achievement of the goal through "overcoming by force or subjugation." Rather, each problem must be conquered through the mutual and cooperative efforts of all. In this endeavor, the word *conquer* holds the vital key. It is used as derived from the original Latin, i.e., from *conquaerere*, which when broken down gives *con*, meaning "together," and *quaerere*, meaning "to seek." The literal translation then is *"to seek together,"* or in a more liberal translation, "teamwork." Without teamwork, any energies expended would most likely be wasted.

Teamwork, however, is not the action of a group attacking all things at once but an organized dividing and subdividing of a particular problem into its specific parts and then a systematic appraisal and solution of each part of the problem.

## Work on Specifics

*Divide and conquer.*

Down through the ages, from Biblical times to the present, man has found that he is unable to conquer until he first divides. If we look back into our own lives, we find that those difficult problems which we finally solved or overcame were those which we divided into specific smaller parts. We also find that those problems which we failed to solve were those which we approached on a broad front, the ones on which we dealt in generalities.

A specific, like a specification, is something *particular*. As such, it can be dealt with in a specific way and with the application of detailed knowledge. This use of specific knowledge with specific techniques of application provides a course of action which ensures the development of alternatives of outstanding merit.

In our daily work as well as in our work in the field of Value Engineering, we must avoid the trap of using generalities. For, all too often, a valuable solution is swept aside by a good-sounding generality.

It has also been found, over the years, that the uncritical use of generalities often has the effect of causing us to defer action or decisions. Such inaction or indecision rapidly leads us down the primrose path and in the end to oblivion.

The vital importance of dealing with specifics can be seen by the ever-increasing specialization of individuals in their chosen fields of work: the doctor who is now an internist; the lawyer, now a corporate counsel; and the industrial specialist. These men are called upon to handle specific problems in their particular fields.

The problem for us, however, is to know when to call upon these specialists. We can only know this when we have brought all the individual parts of the problem into distinct and sharp focus.

In retrospect all these points look simple, and the reasons for them appear obvious. The problem, however, lies in the fact that we, as human beings, are involved; and, more specifically, human attitudes are involved. Unfortunately, many actions are taken and many decisions are made with much of the necessary information lacking.

In essence, the tendency to generalize is one of the major roadblocks which we must learn to overcome both in ourselves and in others.

## Overcome Roadblocks

*Roadblocks are one form of objection.*
*Objections are forms of request for more*
*information.*

Progress and change are things that each of us resists. You don't think so? Don't be too sure. Human beings who don't resist change and progress to some degree are rare exceptions. The plain, simple fact is that most of us do.

Change and progress are wonderful things — as long as they involve somebody else. But when a new idea crops up in *your* area, affecting *your* job, how fast and in what way do you react? Do you take the idea and appraise it on its merits with an open mind? Or do you draw back, even unconsciously, and reach for a roadblock to stave it off or kill it?

Resistance to progress and change are almost instinctive. Doing things differently would upset our comfortable habits and attitudes of thought and action. It would create the need for thinking, planning, and new decision making. And decisions imply risk — the risk of failure, the risk that things won't be as much to our liking as they are now.

Are you still sure you don't resist change and progress?

In reality, there are two types of roadblocks: those imposed on us by others and those imposed on us by ourselves. Here are some of the more common ones from both categories:

1. We tried that before.
2. Our place is different.
3. It would cost too much.

4. That's beyond our responsibility.
5. That's not my job.
6. We're all too busy to do that.
7. It's too radical a change.
8. We don't have the time.
9. There's not enough help.
10. That will make other equipment obsolete.
11. Let's make a market-research test of it first.
12. We're too small for it.
13. It's not practical for operating people.
14. The men will never buy it.
15. The union will scream.
16. We've never done it before.
17. It's against company policy.
18. It will run up our overhead.
19. We don't have the authority.
20. That's too ivory tower.
21. Let's get back to reality.
22. That's not our problem.
23. Why change?  It's still working OK.
24. The executive committee will never go for it.
25. What do they do in our competitor's plant?
26. I don't like the ideas.
27. We're not ready for that.
28. It isn't in the budget.
29. You can't teach an old dog new tricks.
30. It's a good thought, but impractical.
31. Let's hold it in abeyance.
32. Let's give it more thought.
33. Top management would never go for it.
34. Let's put it in writing.
35. We'll be a laughing stock.
36. Not that again!
37. We'd lose money in the long run.
38. Where'd you dig that one up?
39. We did all right without it.
40. That's what we can expect from staff.
41. It's never been tried before.
42. Let's shelve it for the time being.
43. Let's form a committee.
44. Has anyone else ever tried it?
45. What's the use?
46. Customers won't like it.

47. It will be too hard to sell.
48. I don't see the connection.
49. It won't work in our industry.
50. What you are really saying is . . . .
51. Maybe that will work in your department, but not in mine.
52. Don't you think we should look into it further before we act?
53. Let's all sleep on it.
54. You're right—but . . . .
55. You're two years ahead of your time.
56. We don't have the money, equipment, room, personnel.

These are killer phrases which chloroform ideas and put our minds to sleep. Under certain circumstances, some of the statements quoted above make excellent sense. This is precisely what makes them so dangerous and damaging. Used wrongly, they stop change and progress dead in their tracks.

Habits, attitudes, and the resulting roadblocks, upon the deepest study, are found to dominate human nature with the strength of natural laws. The process of habitual thinking is more constant and works with greater force than the creative process. In fact, it will be found that the creative mind, of which we so glowingly speak, is in reality an emergency unit— a unit which takes over only when our habits cannot cope with a given situation.

When you find yourself or someone else using one of these roadblocks or a reasonable facsimile, stop and ask yourself a few basic questions:

Is there a good reason for saying this?
Is this really what is meant?
Is this really a way to kill an idea or avoid action?

We, you or I, can't stop change or progress. All we can do is stop it for ourselves. If an idea is a good one, someone, somewhere, sometime, is going to think of it and put it to use. Why shouldn't it be you?

The biggest step in overcoming roadblocks, both our own and those of others, is to recognize them as such. For once we recognize them, we can determine what additional information is being sought and then go and dig it out.

The recognition, overcoming, and removal of roadblocks is only one part of the application of good business judgment.

## Apply Good Business Judgment

*Overeagerness to please ruins the effectiveness*
*of more individuals' judgment than does the lack*
*of zeal. The individual who tries too hard to*

*please usually succeeds only in creating*
*problems where none existed before.*

One of the most important ingredients that we must bring to our cultivation of good business judgment is an open mind. This is so vitally important because it has been found that the more successful an individual becomes, the more difficult he finds it to deviate from the formula and methods that made him successful. Thus, when conditions change, it is the newcomers who are most adept at wresting success from the hands of the incumbents.

The interactions between the desire to please, personal opinion, and the guarding of "sacred cows" have undermined more business judgments than any other group of conditions. The application of good business judgment requires action, a delicate evaluation of all the facts, and the elimination of concern about "sacred cows."

There is at least one "sacred cow" skulking around in every situation. And for every individual who wants to eliminate it, you'll find a half-dozen other individuals feeding the animal on the sly and keeping it alive. One denies such an unwritten rule or a hallowed article of business dogma at one's peril. It is the ultimate veto or roadblock produced by the opposition when all other generalities fail. These dogmas batten and fatten on human inertia. None of them could stay alive for a day if people weren't fundamentally lazy or afraid of change.

Getting rid of the menace of the "sacred cow" is a simple operation as soon as you realize that not one of them can stand up to facts or questioning. Therefore, good business judgment demands the elimination of personal prejudices and the strong desire to please, followed by the application of an open mind dealing only with facts and specific questions.

The application of good business judgment requires straight thinking. Or, to put it another way, we must think straight to succeed. Every successful action rests on suitable plans and decisions. Whenever the objective is to promote beneficial change, the decisions must be based on specifics. Generalities serve only to prevent change and protect the status quo.

If we are to apply good business judgment, we must be resourceful. We must know how to think. Equally important, we must continuously pursue new knowledge, new understanding. We must be creative! We must be sensitive but at the same time strong. We must be flexible but tenacious. We must apply our talents and efforts at all times, accepting personal discomfort as a natural accompaniment of achievement. We must control our environment rather than be controlled by it. We must create change and thrive on it rather than expend our efforts resisting it. We must be sure that *all* our faculties are alive and active every waking moment.

We must live with risk.  Our security, however, lies in our developed ability to think creatively and constructively and, most importantly, to resolve a complex mixture of opinion, ideas, emotions, and facts into a clear judgment and course of action.

In conclusion, we must realize that what we have discussed is the foundation of the Value Engineering Job Plan, and upon this foundation we must build the remainder of our structure.  We must remember and use these techniques every day, in every contact with other individuals.  Just as the "Ten Steps toward Better Value" guide us toward cost improvement, so the following will guide us toward better working relationships:

TEN STEPS TOWARD BETTER RELATIONS

1. Be a good listener.
2. Determine the other fellow's incentives.
3. Put yourself in his position.
4. Discuss everything with an open mind.
5. Explain your objectives.
6. Base all decisions on facts.  Are the solutions all live options?
7. Don't act as the infallible judge.
8. Learn from the experiences of others.
9. Work on a give-and-take basis.
10. Stress the greater rewards available through teamwork.

# Chapter Six

# Information Phase

## General

*It isn't what you know that counts—it's what
you do.*

The Value Engineering Systematic Approach's Job Plan, on which we are
now embarked, is a live program, a program which has been designed and
developed to provide you with updated knowledge or the means of securing
that knowledge. This Job Plan, and its techniques and tools which we
are discussing and will put to use, is applicable to both managerial tasks
and cost control assignments.

In order to master the techniques so that they can be properly applied
to cost improvement and cost prevention alike, it is essential that step-by-
step procedures be followed. To aid you in this part of the task, various
worksheets will be introduced and explained.

These worksheets are to be used primarily as training aids during your
learning and familiarization periods. As you become more proficient in
the use of the Job Plan and its techniques, your use of some of these worksheets will diminish. In the future, when working on the solution to more

difficult problems, you will find these worksheets excellent thought guides. They will also be found to be a simple yet effective means of tabulating the results of your activities and efforts.

## Information Phase

*It's what you learn after you know it all that
really counts!*

This, the first in-depth working phase of the Job Plan, will take you beyond your present knowledge to a fuller understanding of the complete problem being analyzed. This phase encompasses three techniques: securing the facts, determining the costs, and fixing costs on specifications and requirements. Although these techniques may seem simple at first glance, you will find from our discussion that their application is both difficult and tedious. At times, your efforts in relation to them may seem overexacting and unrewarding. However, these efforts will, as you progress through the Job Plan, prove their worth.

It must be noted that although these techniques are shown as three separate items, they do in reality overlap and interlock.

This fact, figure, and data phase is the backbone of the rest of the Job Plan. A thorough understanding of this information is essential. *Remember that facts, not fiction, are the keys to the doors of knowledge.*

## Secure the Facts

*Behold the keeper of the keys—you!*

You hold the keys that unlock the doors to information and facts. If teamwork is the ultimate password to success, then the six one-word questions of constructive discontent are the keys which will unlock the intervening doors. Each key unlocks a succeeding door to knowledge and knowledge leads to success in any endeavor.

These keys have simple names. They are *why, what, when, where, how,* and *who.* Although simply names, their use is difficult and lengthy, yet of the greatest importance. For if ultimate success is to be gained, each door must be opened in its turn.

In opening each door, the key is easily inserted into the lock. It is the turning of it that requires a diligent effort. The turning requires the unflagging exertion of good human relations, the application of tact, and an ability to weigh the information presented.

As each door is opened and information is received, it must be carefully evaluated, sifted, and stored. The evaluation and sifting before storage is necessary to separate fact from fiction, specific information from general hearsay. This is due, in part, to the fact that as individuals none of us likes to be found lacking in knowledge; therefore, we will give an answer. This must be recognized as a normal reaction of our human nature.

When each door has been opened and factual information has been gained, many things become apparent. First, the original problem which seemed both confused and immense is now clearly defined and reduced to its simplest terms. Second, facts which seemed veiled, hidden, or unattainable are in reality quite open and accessible. Last and equally important, it is ofttimes found that the major portion of the solution is already in plain view.

Throughout the opening of each door and the inspection of what is behind it, you will be dealing with individuals—busy individuals. So before you approach each door, be sure that you are prepared, that you know exactly what information you need and what specific questions you want answered. You must also be sure that you record both the information and the source from which or from whom it was secured so that none of it is later overlooked. This will also prevent the interjection of your personal opinions and enable you to give credit where it is due.

To assist us in the first area, the information worksheet (Figure 6-1) and related questions have been developed.

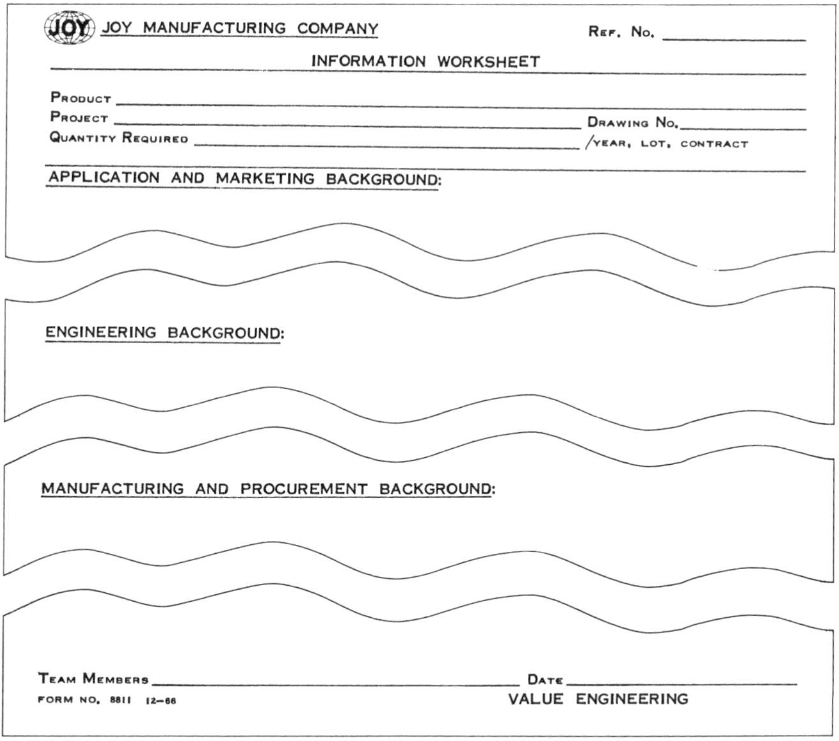
JOY MANUFACTURING COMPANY
REF. NO. ______

INFORMATION WORKSHEET

PRODUCT ______
PROJECT ______ DRAWING NO. ______
QUANTITY REQUIRED ______ /YEAR, LOT, CONTRACT

APPLICATION AND MARKETING BACKGROUND:

ENGINEERING BACKGROUND:

MANUFACTURING AND PROCUREMENT BACKGROUND:

TEAM MEMBERS ______ DATE ______
FORM NO. 8811 12–66 VALUE ENGINEERING

Figure 6-1

## Worksheets — General

Each of the worksheets to be used throughout the Job Plan requires a certain amount of basic information in the heading. This information (i.e., reference number, product, project, drawing number, and quantity) must be supplied each time to identify the project and all the worksheets of that project.

**Project Number**   Each project should be given its own distinctive number so that its progress can be easily followed from inception to implementation. Many project numbering systems are available and in use. Two simple yet effective numbering systems are described below.

1. The simplest is the use of plain sequential numbers. This type of system simply makes sure that each project has an identifying number and can be traced.

2. The second, which is a little more complex, is the grouped numbering system, wherein each number or group of numbers represents specific information. In project number 9-5-68, for example, the 9 indicates the month the project was started (September), the 5 indicates that this was the fifth project started in that month, and 68 indicates the year in which the project was started.

**Product**   This should delineate the overall product, process, or procedure with which the project under study is connected.

**Project**   This delineates the specific assembly, subassembly, part, or process being studied. If applicable, a drawing or sketch number should be shown in the provided space.

**Quantity Required**   This indicates the total number of the parts or items used or manufactured within a given period of time. The quantity should include all spares and replacements.

## Information Worksheet

The major headings in the body of this worksheet indicate those areas, depending on the problem or item being studied, from which information must be secured. In each of these areas (Application and Marketing, Engineering, and Manufacturing and Procurement) certain basic background information is required.

The entire project will become clearer when this information is acquired. That is, the analyst will now be able to achieve a clear and complete understanding of the background of the problem because this is probably the first time that all the information has been put down in one place at one time.

**Application and Marketing Background**   Through consultations with one or more individuals from these sections and additional searching, you must determine, at least, the following information:

A. What are the detailed specifications and requirements established by the users and producers? These should include descriptions of:
   1. The environmental conditions before, during, and possibly after use.
   2. The physical space limitations.
   3. Desired and/or required reliability, serviceability, maintainability, and operability.
   4. The desired and/or required operating life.
   5. Special features desired or required.
B. What has been the actual operating experience with this item or items of similar type? This information should be secured from service reports, field service or repair personnel, and present users, and it should include:
   1. The actual history of replacement parts and spares usage.
   2. The reason or reasons for the replacement part and spares usage.
   3. Actual operating life of project item and components.
C. What are the anticipated total market requirements for the project per year, and what percentage of that total market, as the producer, can you expect to serve?
D. What is the total anticipated market life of the project in years? What effect will proposed improvements have on this anticipated market life?
E. Who are your competitors, how many are there, where are they located, and what are the competitors' prices?
F. Where in the project should investigations, changes, or improvements be considered to make it work or sell better?

In the case of specific problems or projects being analyzed, additional points of basic or specific information may be desired from the Applications and Marketing areas. It may also be found that as background information from other areas is collected, additional questions will arise in this area. Further questioning, for clarification or additional information, is desirable and ofttimes necessary. However, you must be sure that you do not repeat questions that have already been answered; this is a waste of everyone's time.

**Engineering Background**  Through personal consultation and search with individuals from Engineering, you must secure the following information (it should be noted that, in this case, the term *engineer* is used to denote the individual who developed and designed the item being analyzed, whether it is a physical product, a process, or a procedure):

A. What is the broad technical history of the overall product and project? This should include the original need to be satisfied, date of original conception and design, various solutions considered, development problems encountered, and changes in original specifications and requirements.

B. What patents or copyrights should be considered in the analysis of the project? To whom are these patents or copyrights assigned?

C. What physical, performance, and workmanship requirements are necessary or desired in the project? These, where applicable, should include:

1. Materials.
2. Weight.
3. Dimensions, including tolerances.
4. Shock and vibration.
5. Environment.
6. Life.
7. Performance.
8. Appearance.

D. Is this project used in other products? If so, where and in what quantity?

E. What new developments and/or changes are being considered and when are they expected to be finalized?

F. Where should investigations, changes, or improvements be considered in the project to make it work or sell better? How can the project be modified to reduce its cost? Which specifications or requirements involve the greatest difficulties and costs?

The answers that you receive in response to these questions will, in most cases, generate the desire and need for additional information. Don't be afraid to seek it out.

**Manufacturing and Procurement**    Individuals in both the Manufacturing and Purchasing areas should be consulted to secure the information necessary in this area. The fundamental information collected should cover the following:

A. In the producer's facility (either your own or the supplier's), what are (is):

1. The process specifications.
2. The sequence of operations.
3. The quantities produced per run, month, year.
4. The equipment used, special or standard.
5. The specific methods applied.
6. The standard or special tools, dies, molds, or fixtures used, including age, expected life, cost, and to whom they belong.

B. If special equipment is used, what is the nature, type, and cost of such equipment?

C. What are the details of material utilization, including raw material and amount of material removed (scrap or waste) to produce the finished item?

D. What are the figures regarding number of parts, subassemblies, or assemblies scrapped, rejected, and reworked? This information is to include reasons for scrapping, rejection, or reworking (i.e., manufacturing problems, tolerances, poor raw material, etc.).

E. If item is purchased, the following should be established:
1. Who is the present supplier?
2. Where has the item been purchased before?
3. What other sources of supply are available?
4. How are the items purchased (i.e., by yearly contract or in lot quantities)?
5. What is the normal quantity ordered, and what is the minimum quantity order?
6. Who orders the items?
7. How, when, and from where are the items ordered?
8. What is the delivery history on the item?
9. What is the cost of the item, the cost of transportation, and what extras are paid (if any)?

F. The areas in which investigations, changes, and improvements should be considered in order to reduce manufacturing or purchasing problems should be outlined.

This free and open consultation with the individuals who make or buy the item being analyzed will, if handled correctly, provide a good insight into potential areas for improvement.

Once the basic information for this first major area has been secured and recorded, the second can be considered. The second area is cost, which has a direct relation to the facts already collected.

## Consultation Summary

The use of this form is not mandatory, but it is strongly recommended.

As you accumulate the answers to your questions and as your facts are gathered, it has been found advisable to record the source of your information as well as the information received. This is done in order that, if it is found necessary at a later time to recheck or secure additional information, it can be done with relative ease.

Further, this worksheet allows you to make notations regarding the information received and secured. Such notations provide an excellent record, for later project use, of the people from whom and the places from which you were able to secure accurate and meaningful information.

A sample of this consultation summary worksheet is shown in Figure 6-2.

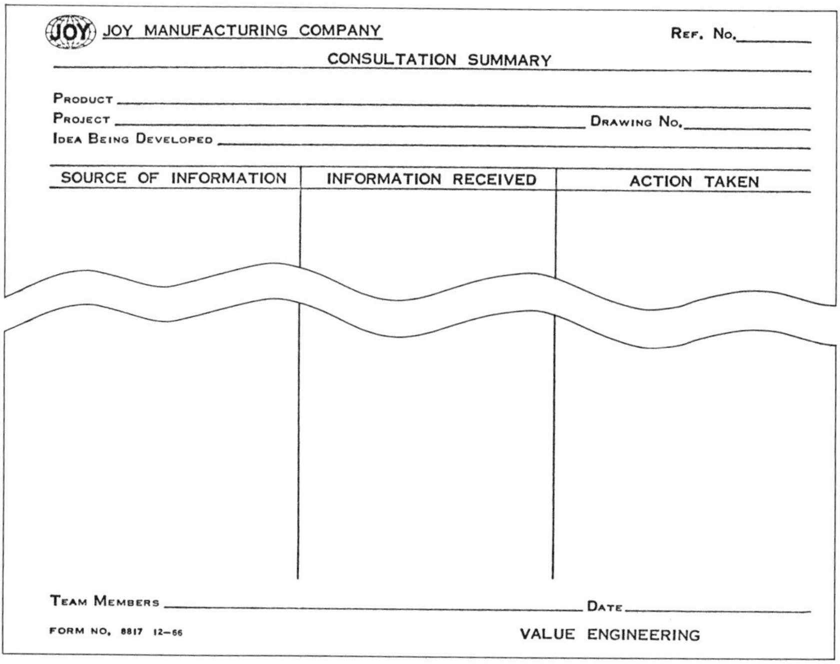

JOY MANUFACTURING COMPANY — REF. NO.________

CONSULTATION SUMMARY

PRODUCT ________

PROJECT ________ DRAWING NO.________

IDEA BEING DEVELOPED ________

| SOURCE OF INFORMATION | INFORMATION RECEIVED | ACTION TAKEN |
| --- | --- | --- |
| | | |

TEAM MEMBERS ________ DATE ________

FORM NO. 8817 12-66 — VALUE ENGINEERING

Figure 6-2

## Determine the Costs

It is necessary that good, accurate costs be obtained. These are just as important to your future work in the Job Plan as detailed facts. In general, they provide two basic tools. First, good costs provide a tool for measuring the facts that you have secured. Second, they provide a means of determining the amount of effort that can economically be expended in a given area of your project.

Certain specific costs are necessary to provide these two basic tools plus an understanding of your project's direct and related costs. First, you must secure the prime costs related to your project; i.e., the direct material and direct labor costs. These prime costs must be in two forms: first, they should show a total for the complete project under analysis; and, second, they should be segregated as labor and material for each of the assemblies, subassemblies, and parts of the project. This task can be simplified if the costs are first noted on the engineering drawings where they are applicable. Second, you must secure the applicable overhead costs relating to your project. These should include the costs of any indirect material or labor expended on the project; tooling costs, including the cost of special jigs and fixtures; boxing, packaging, and shipping costs; and any other special costs involved.

These costs, whether estimated or actual, should be recorded and their source should be noted.

## Definition of Costs

*Cost* is a term we shall encounter repeatedly in Value Engineering. Unfortunately, like many common words, it means many things to many people (i.e., cost of living, food cost, cost of household goods, purchase cost, manufacturing cost, cost of goods sold, total cost, etc.). Since this multiplicity of meaning does exist, it is essential to establish a clear picture of costs and to unify our understanding of its meaning in order to eliminate problems in our later discussion.

*Cost* and *price* are *not* synonymous! Cost is the out-of-pocket expense, the transfer of money, labor, time, or other personal items to achieve an objective, be it the provision of a service or the manufacture of a product. Price, on the other hand, is a fixed sum of money or amount of service given or required in exchange for the transfer of ownership of goods or services. Cost may be a part of price or vice versa—depending on whether we select the seller's or buyer's viewpoint.

In the Value Engineering Systematic Approach, most of our efforts are directed toward costs. Therefore we must look at the building blocks that make up product cost and discuss their classification, the factors affecting them, and their interrelationships.

A typical, generalized cost structure (not to scale) is shown below:

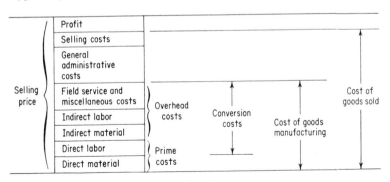

Generalized Cost Structure

**Prime Costs**   These are the direct material and labor costs charged to a specific manufactured product, job order, part order, etc., as they are incurred.

**Overhead Costs**   Also known as *indirect costs* or *burden,* overhead costs are apportioned to a manufactured product, job order, part order, etc. from an indirect cost account into which they have been segregated. These overhead accounts, covering such costs as development, supervision, tooling, maintenance, heat, power, light, buildings, taxes, etc., are distributed to specific orders in proportion to a base such as direct labor cost (most common), direct labor hours, equipment hours, or any number of others depending on the nature of the operation.

**Conversion Costs**   These are the moneys expended in effort and indirect material required to convert the raw material (direct material) into the desired usable item.

Another type of cost classification of interest to us is that of costs shown as recurring and nonrecurring items. Recurring costs are those which we continue to pay as long as we are in production. Nonrecurring costs are one-time costs. A checklist of these costs is shown below.

RECURRING AND NONRECURRING COSTS CHECKLIST

| *Recurring Costs* | *Nonrecurring Costs* |
|---|---|
| LABOR: | LABOR: |
| Manufacturing operations (direct labor) | Engineering |
| Sustaining engineering | Design (layout) |
| Technical support | Drafting and checking |
| Field services | Production planning and |
| Quality control | engineering |
| Administrative support | Procurement |
| Documentation—creation of or input to | Development testing |
| documents related to production volume, as | Qualification testing |
| Inspection records | Field engineering |
| Purchase orders | Training |
| Receiving reports | Administrative support services |
| Shipping documents | Documentation—creation of or |
| Instruction manuals | changes in |
| Parts lists | Drawings |
| End-item certification data | Specifications |
|  | Instruction manuals |
|  | Handbooks |
|  | ECRs or ECPs |
|  | Contracts |
|  | Spare-parts lists |
|  | Parts lists |
|  | Reproduction |
| MATERIAL: | MATERIAL: |
| Raw material | Special tooling and equipment |
| Purchased parts | Prototypes, models, and mockups |
| Subcontracts | Test equipment |
| Intercompany joint effort | Reproduction |
| Reproduction | Packaging changes |

Expendable tooling
Indirect material and supplies
Packaging
OTHER EXPENSES:
Travel
Equipment rental and lease
Contracted services
Computer rental
Freight charges
Spares inventory

Handling equipment
Other

OTHER EXPENSES:
Travel
Equipment rental and lease
Contracted services
Disposition of equipment and/or
  material
Retrofit
Modification of spares

The Value Engineering Systematic Approach is also vitally interested in the *total cost* to the user of the product, a somewhat larger concept, as shown below. The control of this cost structure is of great advantage to the user, the company, and the supplier.

| Total cost | | Maintenance cost |
| --- | --- | --- |
| | | Operating cost |
| | | Shipping, receiving, and, installation |
| | Price First cost | |

Total Cost to User

The control and/or lowering of these costs to the user assures us that he will be satisfied and will request additional products from us. This in turn assures the continuation of our company's business as well as that of our suppliers.

The Value Engineering Systematic Approach can be applied to all the cost areas delineated in both of the above charts. Its application to the various areas may, however, require slight modifications of the approach and specific attention to the time of application. In the areas of "maintenance costs" and "operating costs," it must be applied early in and throughout the development of the product. In the areas of "cost of goods sold" and "cost of goods manufactured," the approach must be applied throughout the product's life cycle. In the area of "prime cost," it has to be applied by all members of the team.

Even so, it is sometimes difficult for you, me, or anyone to determine in which areas of the cost picture we should apply our efforts to gain the greatest and fastest return on our invested time. To aid us in the isolation of the most lucrative areas, certain phenomena of product cost and product design can be used to our advantage. For that matter, these phenomena can be stated as general rules.

## The 20-80 Rules

There are three 20-80 rules which generally exist in all cost structures. If we know, understand, and put these to use effectively, our efforts will be directed toward the areas of greatest return. It will be found that each of these 20-80 rules tends to narrow down the knowledge gained from the preceding one.

### Rule 1: Cost of Goods Manufactured (General Cost Structure)

*Fixed costs = 20 percent of the total*
*Variable costs = 80 percent of the total*

It can be seen from this breakdown that the most lucrative area in which to expend our efforts is the variable-cost area.

### Rule 2: Factory Cost (Modified Cost Structure)

*20 percent of the parts contain 80 percent of the cost*
*80 percent of the parts contain 20 percent of the cost*

Once we have secured the complete factory costs of all the individual components that make up the project being analyzed, we can list them in their descending order of cost (i.e., starting the list with that item which costs the most and ending the list with the lowest-cost item). Normally, when this is done, it is found that the top 20 percent of the parts involves 80 percent of the total cost of the project being analyzed. Therefore, our first efforts should be directed toward this 20 percent.

### Rule 3: Basic and Secondary Function (To Be Explained in Chapter 7)

*Basic function = 20 percent of cost*
*Secondary functions = 80 percent of cost*

From this, we can see that our efforts should be directed to those items or areas providing the secondary functions.

When all of the facts and costs on the project being analyzed have been secured, they can be combined and then segregated into groups. This is done in order to further isolate the costs as they relate to each specification and requirement.

## Fix Costs on Specifications and Requirements

Specifications and requirements are, when carefully studied, some of the primary control factors of the final product, process, or procedure. As such, they are also major contributors to a product's ultimate cost, both in "cost of goods sold" and "total cost." They are therefore a possibly substantial contributing factor to the unnecessary costs that may be included in the price of a product.

Detailed study will show that specifications and requirements are simply statements of the required or desired details to be included in the final product. These details may, however, be distinctly or indistinctly stated in the specifications and requirements. No matter how they are stated, they must be segregated into their individual parts and details. For again it is only by getting down to the specifics that progress can be made.

Once the specific desired or required details have been segregated by total analysis of the facts, the costs can be divided and related to each. The prime costs and the overhead costs can be broken down in terms of each specification or requirement and assigned thereto. Once the costs have been thus allotted to each specification or requirement, we can list them in their descending cost order for further analysis.

This descending-order-of-cost listing, like the second 20-80 rule, provides us with yet another means of studying the information gathered. This study will aid us in the determination of the best areas of study for the purpose of eliminating unnecessary cost. Also it provides a means of analysis of the product's makeup in relation to its cost content.

Such studies and analyses cannot be undertaken or realistically accomplished until we have a thorough understanding of what specifications and requirements comprise. For we will find that the terms *specifications* and *requirements* are truisms which we all understand until asked for concise definitions of them.

## Specifications and Requirements

When we first look at these terms and ask what they mean, the answer seems quite simple. However, the deeper we look the more complex and insoluble becomes the maze, one that seems to have neither beginning nor end. The beginning of the solution to the maze lies in the realization that there is in reality more than one form of specification or requirement. Further, each of these forms has more than one variation.

The first form involves those *specifications* or *requirements imposed by the ultimate user on the producer.* This form is imposed due to specific conditions—such as environment, location, etc.—which the user has found requires it. Such specifications or requirements may also be imposed because of items or conditions which the user wants to have incorporated in the final product.

The second form involves those *specifications* or *requirements imposed by the producer on himself.* This form is imposed on the product due to specific knowledge of conditions which the producer has experienced or learned about during his work on similar products.

The complications come, however, not in relation to these two basic forms of specifications and requirements but in distinguishing the two variations of them; i.e., the real and the imaginary.

The major difficulty comes in separating the imaginary from the real. This is due to the fact that, to the individual imposing an imaginary specification or requirement, it seems real. It seems real because it is based on a lack of information, a lack of ideas, honest wrong beliefs, temporary circumstances, and habits and attitudes. The fact is that such specifications and requirements grow out of all the conditions which inject unnecessary cost into a product.

You will find that most of the stated roadblocks are nothing more than indirect statements of possible imaginary specifications and requirements. Because of this real variation in specifications and requirements, it is necessary to continually and consciously cross-check the given data.

Customers/users and producers almost invariably overestimate their requirements. Overdesign at the start of product development is therefore common. Not surprisingly, many components are heavily overdesigned, with consequent high cost of production. It is also not surprising to find that the habitual carryover of items in a product from year to year can be a costly trap.

The information and knowledge gained in this phase of the Job Plan leads directly into the next phase, the Function Phase. The Function Phase makes use of this information to break down, into specific details, just exactly what the product does or is supposed to do and in what order it is to be done. It is important, therefore, that the Information Phase be completed in every detail before progressing to the next step of the Job Plan.

# Chapter Seven

# Function Phase

## Functional Approach

The Functional Approach is that group of techniques within the Job Plan which sets the Value Engineering Systematic Approach apart from all other cost prevention and cost reduction programs. This Functional Approach comprises three distinct yet interdependent techniques; i.e., defining the function, evaluating function relationships, and developing functional alternatives. These techniques, individually or together, are being successfully applied to everything that affects a business's profit and are helping to improve costs.

Since business or industry profits comprise the results of many items such as products, processes, and procedures, you can see that the knowledge of these techniques, which have a positive effect on profits, becomes vital. These techniques, which are the keystone of the Job Plan, not only aid in clearly defining the problem and its various parts but also establish a relationship between these parts, providing an orderly means of reassembling the partial solutions into a composite solution of the whole problem.

In order that we may come to a clear understanding of the Functional

Approach, it is necessary to have a basic definition of the term *function*. Dictionaries have defined the noun *function* as "normal and characteristic action, special purpose or duty" and the verb as "to fulfill a normal activity, work normally."

Value Engineering defines *function* as "that which makes a product *work* or *sell.*"

As can be seen from a comparison of these definitions, they do not differ in basic concept. In the Value Engineering definition, however, there is a key word. That word is *or*. This word *or* is of great importance because it forces us to separate the "work" functions from the "sell" functions, which is something not normally done in industry.

With this definition firmly in mind, we can proceed to look at the first two techniques of the Functional Approach which make up this phase of the Job Plan. These two techniques, defining the function and evaluating function relationships, are closely related to the Information Phase and ofttimes are considered a continuation of it. This is so because these techniques use the facts that have been accumulated in the Information Phase.

## Define the Function

*In the beginning was the word, and the word*
*was without form.*

This is neither a Biblical nor a famous quotation but a statement that we must closely study. For in its study lies the definition and clarification of numerous problems—personal problems which can block change and cause industrial stagnation, problems which run the gamut from injured personal pride to the individual's inability to see more than one solution. As today's developers of products, systems, processes, and procedures, most times we lose sight of the most important fact about our creations— namely, that in the beginning our creations were but words and that these words were without form. But to these words we added knowledge, thereby giving them form, and this knowledge was (at its best) the newest knowledge and latest technology available at the time.

Yet, when time has passed and a change in our creation is suggested, we fight it. Why?

In our fervor to accomplish the task of creation and as a result of the effort of bringing our ideas into being, we lose sight of the original starting point—words. In order to overcome and remove this resistance to change and the industrial stagnation that may grow out of it, it is necessary to have a means of reestablishing these words which describe the original needs. That is, we require a means of putting the original needs into the simplest workable expressions. Such a means or technique is available and is described under the heading "Define the Function." In this technique, certain basic rules from which we cannot deviate have been established. These rules apply to both the work and the sell functions.

## Rules of Function Definition

Rule 1: The expression of all functions must be accomplished in two words, a verb and a noun.

Rule 2: The expression of work and sell functions uses different categories of verbs and nouns.

    A. Work functions are always expressed in action verbs and measurable nouns which establish quantitative statements.

    B. Sell functions are always expressed in passive verbs and nonmeasurable nouns which establish qualitative statements.

Rule 3: All functions can be divided into two levels of importance, *basic* and *secondary.*

    A. Basic function: The primary purpose for a product or service.

    B. Secondary function: Other purposes not directly accomplishing the primary purpose but supporting it or resulting from a a specific design approach.

We must learn these three rules of functional definition to the point where they become a natural part of our thinking process. In this manner, all problems will be approached in the same way each time. These rules have been established to simplify, standardize, and channel our thinking process. This is done to overcome some of our most detrimental habits and attitudes.

Rule 1 is so stipulated due to a number of conditions and facts. First, if you cannot define a function in two words, you do not have enough information about the problem or you are trying to define too large a segment of that problem. Second, by using only two words, you are forced to break the problem down into its simplest elements. Third, when only two words are used, the possibility of faulty communications and misunderstandings is reduced to a minimum.

Rule 2 does not merely add to the meaning but actually multiplies the effect of rule 1. Applying this rule to separate work and sell functions brings us one step closer to a scientific measurement of any function. In the case of work functions, if the defining verb is not an action verb, the function is useless (i.e., if no action is taking place, nothing is being accomplished). Hence, there is no resultant value. When the noun used is a measurable noun (i.e., weight in pounds, work in foot-pounds, current in amperes), we are one step closer to being able to establish a cost-to-function relationship. It has been said that

*To the seeker of knowledge, the art of using*
*numbers and measures provides greater*
*exactness and truth than all other means.*

The use of measurable nouns provides us with a quantitative means of measuring the work functions. The work functions are those which provide the use value that is a requisite of the item being studied.

In the case of the sell functions, since they are in most cases subjective in nature, their measurement is extremely difficult if not impossible. Hence the use of passive verbs and nonmeasurable nouns. The simple fact, however, that they can be separated from the work functions does help in the assignment of a proportionate amount of the product's cost to them.

Examples of typical verbs and nouns used in the definition of both work and sell functions are shown below. Also shown are some typical *undesirable* nouns sometimes used in the definition of work functions:

WORK FUNCTIONS

|  | *Verbs* | *Nouns,* *Measurable* |  |  |
|---|---|---|---|---|
| Support | Change | Weight | Force | Contamination |
| Transmit | Interrupt | Light | Oxidation | |
| Create | Establish | Heat | Flow | |
| Hold | Shield | Radiation | Current | |
| Enclose | Modulate | Friction | Insulation | |
| Collect | Control | Voltage | Energy | |
| Conduct | Transmit | Force | Density | |
| Insulate | Emit | Damage | Circuit | |
| Protect | Repel | Protection | Repair | |
| Prevent | Filter | Fluid | Liquid | |
| Reduce | Impede | *Undesirable* | | |
| Amplify | Induce | Component | Device | |
| Rectify | Provide | Part | Article | |
| Apply | | Table | Wire | |

SELL FUNCTIONS

| *Verbs* | *Nouns* | |
|---|---|---|
| Increase | Beauty | Symmetry |
| Decrease | Appearance | Effect |
| Improve | Convenience | Exchange |
| | Style | |
| | Prestige | |
| | Features | |
| | Form | |

EXAMPLE

| Items as listed in operation manual | Description as stated in operation manual | Functional definition |
|---|---|---|
| A. Antenna drive sump .. | Used to provide a pressure-tight reservoir for the hydraulic fluid | Contain liquid |
| B. Expansion chamber . . . | Used to accommodate the expansion and contraction of the fluid due to temperature variations and also to provide sump pressure | Contain liquid Provide pressure |
| C. Thermal expansion chamber | Used to accommodate the excess thermal expansion of the fluid (at start-up after filling) due to temperature variations and overfilling | Contain liquid |

Rule 3, through its definition, provides us with the means of establishing the levels of relative importance of the functions expressed. It is normally found that any given item—problem, product, procedure, or process—has only one basic function. Only on the rarest of occasions will there emerge two basic functions. In most cases when there appears to be more than one basic function, the functions involved are simply restatements of each other. In the case of secondary functions, however, it will be found that there are both specific functions and dependent functions. Specific functions are those which require a specific action to be accomplished. Dependent functions are those which cannot be accomplished before a prior action takes place.

As can be seen from the definition of secondary functions, certain functions are contained in a product because of specifications or requirements, and some are contained in it because of the present design or approach.

Starting from this common ground of understanding of the technique of defining the function as it is applied in the Job Plan, use of the applicable worksheet can be undertaken. This technique of the Job Plan involves the use of the training worksheet entitled "Functional Definition," Figure 7-1. The first step in the use of this worksheet is to fill in the reference number, project name, and drawing number (if applicable), as has been done with the previous worksheets.

The input and output of the project are then stated, in their respective places, in as concise a form as possible. Since the input and the output are not "functions," they need not be stipulated in two words. The inputs and outputs are simple statements of the limiting parameters of the project; i.e., the project can be considered a black box which receives given inputs to which it does something and then gives forth certain outputs. It must

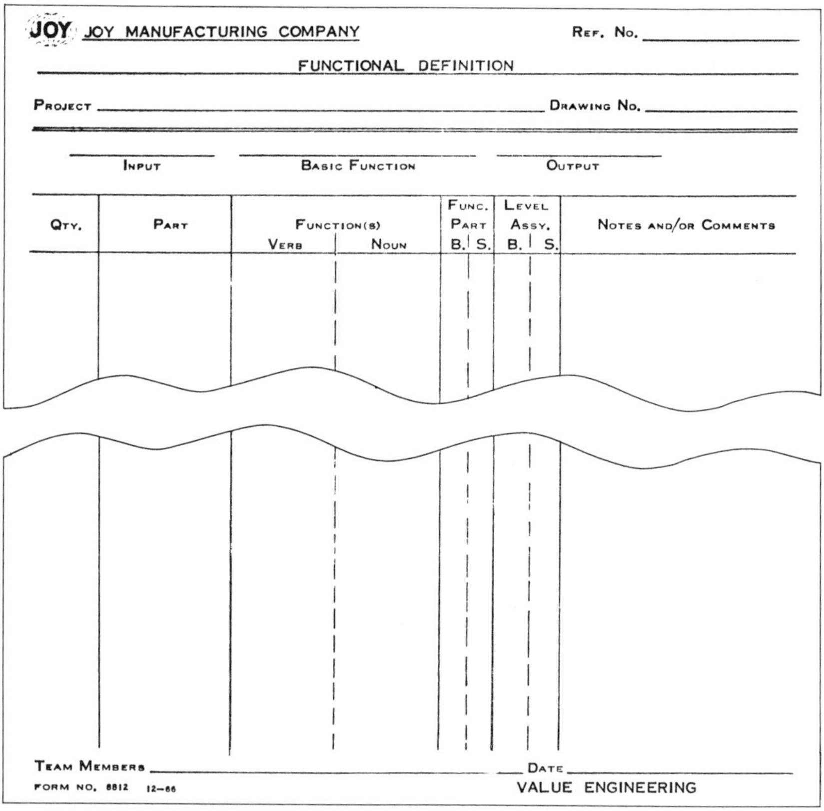

| | | | | | | | |
|---|---|---|---|---|---|---|---|
| **JOY** | JOY MANUFACTURING COMPANY | | | | | REF. No. _____ | |

FUNCTIONAL DEFINITION

PROJECT _____ DRAWING No. _____

| INPUT | BASIC FUNCTION | OUTPUT |
|---|---|---|

| QTY. | PART | FUNCTION(S) | | FUNC. PART B. S. | LEVEL ASSY. B. S. | NOTES AND/OR COMMENTS |
|---|---|---|---|---|---|---|
| | | VERB | NOUN | | | |

TEAM MEMBERS _____ ___ DATE _____

FORM NO. 8812   12-66                              VALUE ENGINEERING

Figure 7-1

be realized that there can be multiple inputs to and outputs from any given project. It is important to note that for anything to have value of any kind, it must have both inputs and outputs.

A few simple examples of common items and their inputs and outputs are shown in the table below.

| *Items* | *Input* | *Output* |
|---|---|---|
| Toaster . . . . | Power (electrical) | Heat |
| | Bread | Dry, discolored bread |
| Vaporizer . . . | Power (electrical) | Heat |
| | Water | Steam |
| | Chemicals | Vaporized and entrained chemicals |
| Forced- | Fuel | Heat |
| air heater | Air | Moving air (in cubic |
| | Power (electrical) | feet per minute) |

The space labeled "Basic function," between the input and output, is not completed at this time, as any attempt to complete it would be based on a mere assumption. The basic function will be determined later in this phase and the space will be filled in at that time.

Moving next to the first two columns at the left of the worksheet, the quantity and name of a part of the project under study are listed in their respective columns. Then, in the third column, every function, no matter how important or unimportant it might seem, is listed using only the verb-noun definition. At this or any future time in the use of this worksheet, any descriptive notes regarding the part or its functions are noted in the far-right-hand column. The second part or group of parts is then treated in the same manner. This procedure is continued until all the items and their functions are listed in the first three columns.

It must be noted that the breakdown of the project into its components varies with the magnitude of the project. When a large or complex project is being studied, it should be divided into its major subassemblies. These then can, on the individual functional definition worksheet, be broken down into their subassemblies. This subdividing process is continued until the project is broken down to its individual parts or items. If necessary, the individual part can be further subdivided into its specific areas, such as surfaces, holes, shoulders, etc. This process can be likened to the building of a functional chart; in essence, it is the construction of the functional family of the project under study.

In most cases, this complete construction of a functional family tree will not be necessary. This is due to the fact that, as the functional family tree is constructed, the second 20-80 rule is applied; i.e., only that 20 percent containing 80 percent of the cost is further developed.

In the case of small projects, the breakdown should be complete by dividing it into its specific and individual parts. With the smaller subassemblies or projects, the 20-80 rule is not required. Through this point, we have been applying the first two rules of functional definition.

At this point in the use of the functional definition worksheet, we bring into use the third rule of functional definition; i.e., the differentiation between basic and secondary functions. We now go back to each part in its turn and study the functions we have listed for the part and determine whether that function is basic or secondary for the part as it is used in the particular project. We then check it accordingly in the appropriate sub-column of column four of the worksheet. When making this determination of the functional levels, we must be careful to consider only how the function could be accomplished. This is due to the fact that we are, at this time, breaking down and expressing in functional statements the present way the problem has been solved or approached.

At this point in the analysis, we must guard against the trap of premature redesign or redevelopment. This has been found, from experience, to be a real trap into which we can fall at this stage of the Job Plan. It must be remembered that we are in the process of analyzing information.

As a part of this stage of information analysis, we can ascertain many things from our functional definitions. First, we can see a number of redundant (duplicate) functions within our breakdown. This is important in that every function has a certain cost associated with its accomplishment; therefore, redundant function means possibly unnecessary cost. Second, we may find similar functions being accomplished in different ways. Again this may also be a guide to unnecessary cost. Third, we start to determine and break out the basic function of the total item under study—our assumption is now becoming more crystallized, but it is still not a positive fact.

An example of this functional definition worksheet, completed to this point on a subassembly (a roof exhaust fan wheel), is shown in Figure 7-2. The above point of analysis can be seen in this example.

We now leave this worksheet and the technique of defining the function and move into the second technique of the Function Phase, i.e., evaluating function relationships. This technique will provide the necessary data to complete the functional definition worksheet and provide us with extremely important quantitative and qualitative data.

## Evaluate Functional Relationships

*Facts by themselves mean very little! It is the relationship of each fact with all others that is important.*

Precise functional balance is that which makes a product work and sell most effectively at the lowest total cost. This balance is determined only through a comparative process which in its turn leads to a perceptual evaluation.

*It can be said almost without fear of contradiction that, if there is no comparison, then there is no evaluation.* — L. D. MILES

To start toward the attainment of this balance, we must first have an understanding of the relationships between all functions. The purpose of this technique is to determine that relationship.

All parts of a given item can be identified in terms of the function or functions they perform. These functions are expressed in terms of a verb and a noun. Their level as basic or secondary at their own particular part level is established. We can then, by this technique, compare and evaluate

**JOY** JOY MANUFACTURING COMPANY       Ref. No. _M-43_

FUNCTIONAL DEFINITION

Project ___Roof Exhaust Fan Wheel___     Drawing No. _145168656_

___Torque, Air___ Input      Basic Function      ___Air, Force___ Output

| Qty. | Part | Function(s) Verb | Function(s) Noun | Func. Part B. | Func. Part S. | Level Assy. B. | Level Assy. S. | Notes and/or Comments |
|---|---|---|---|---|---|---|---|---|
| 1 | Tapper lock bushing | Provide | Support | ✓ | | | | |
| | | Provide | Adjustment | ✓ | | | | |
| | | Provide | Location | ✓ | | | | |
| | | Transmit | Force | ✓ | | | | |
| | | Provide | Connection | ✓ | | | | |
| 1 | Key | Transmit | Force | ✓ | | | | |
| | | Provide | Location | | ✓ | | | |
| 3 | Cap screws (¼") | Transmit | Force | ✓ | | | | |
| | | Provide | Location | | ✓ | | | |
| | | Allow | Disassembly | | ✓ | | | |
| 1 | Lock washer | Induce | Friction | ✓ | | | | |
| | | Transmit | Force | | ✓ | | | |
| | | Provide | Location | | ✓ | | | |
| 1 | Hub | Transmit | Force | | ✓ | | | |
| | | Provide | Support | ✓ | | | | |
| | | Provide | Location | | ✓ | | | |
| 6 | Cap screws (⅜") | Transmit | Force | | ✓ | | | |
| | | Provide | Location | ✓ | | | | |
| | | Provide | Support | | ✓ | | | |
| 1 | Back plate | Provide | Location | | ✓ | | | |
| | | Provide | Support | ✓ | | | | |
| | | Transmit | Force | | ✓ | | | |
| 1 | Shroud | Provide | Location | | ✓ | | | |
| | | Provide | Support | | ✓ | | | |
| | | Direct | Air | ✓ | | | | |
| | | Provide | Protection | | ✓ | | | |
| 12 | Blades | Provide | Location | | ✓ | | | |
| | | Provide | Support | | ✓ | | | |
| | | Transmit | Force | | ✓ | | | |
| | | Convert | Energy | ✓ | | | | |
| | Weld | Provide | Location | ✓ | | | | |
| | | Provide | Support | | ✓ | | | |
| | | Transmit | Force | | ✓ | | | |

Team Members _____ Date _____

Form No. 8812  12-66      VALUE ENGINEERING

Figure 7-2

these defined functions and determine their interrelationships and the order of their relative importance to the whole. The establishment of this order of importance and these interrelationships, coupled with the derived numerical value for the importance of each function, makes it possible for us to study the results and draw specific conclusions on our problem's complexity. Unnecessary functions, low-importance functions requiring a high cost for achievement, and functions incorporated because of preconceived ideas are clearly identified. This enables us to evaluate our problem or project objectively and with the smallest amount of personal or subjective bias.

The constant nature of this interrelationship between the functions can be appreciated only when there is a complete understanding of the functions. This technique, which provides a numerical evaluation of the functional relationships, is a concise yet simple method of determining the necessary interrelationships among the functions.

This method for the numerical evaluation of functional relationships is capable of determining and/or verifying the basic function of the product being studied as well as determining the descending order of importance of the secondary functions. Equally important, it provides us with a means of separating those functions which are in the product because of specifications and requirements and those that are there because of the present or earlier approach or design.

Starting from this common ground, we can now discuss this technique which provides us with a numerical evaluation of the functional relationships.

**Numerical Evaluation of Functional Relationships**    The numerical evaluation of functional relationships is accomplished only after the functional definition worksheet has been completed to the point described in the first part of this chapter, for it is that information that is used in this technique.

This second technique of the Function Phase is accomplished with the use of the training worksheet entitled "Functional Evaluation" (Figure 7-3). Again, as with previous worksheets, the reference number, project name, and drawing number are noted in their proper places.

From the functional definition worksheet, the basic function of each part of the item being studied, as defined and so checked in columns three and four respectively, is placed in the appropriate space in the worksheet section entitled "Evaluation summary." As you list each of these functions on the functional evaluation worksheet, you will see that each one requires a key letter. This key letter is used throughout the succeeding comparisons and evaluations of the functions.

The comparison and evaluation process requires that you have a thorough understanding of the facts, data, and information secured in the Informa-

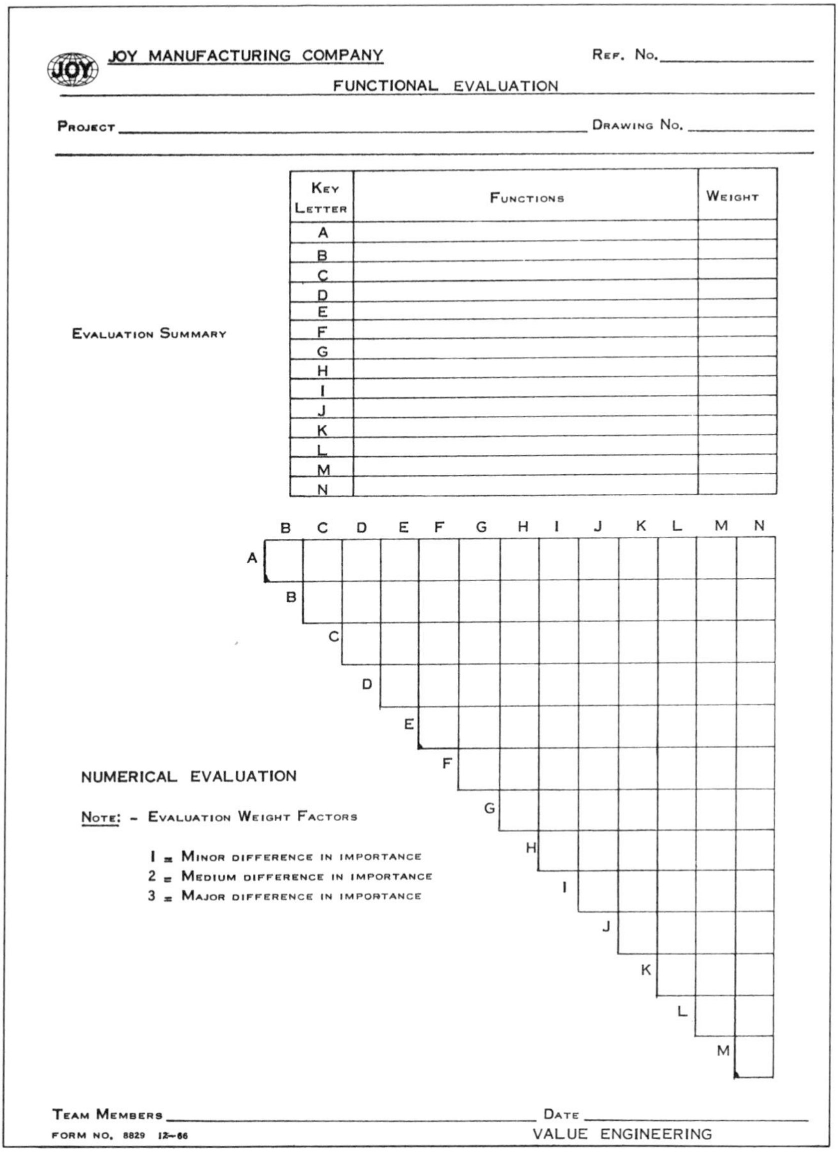
JOY MANUFACTURING COMPANY

REF. NO.

FUNCTIONAL EVALUATION

PROJECT

DRAWING NO.

EVALUATION SUMMARY

| KEY LETTER | FUNCTIONS | WEIGHT |
|---|---|---|
| A | | |
| B | | |
| C | | |
| D | | |
| E | | |
| F | | |
| G | | |
| H | | |
| I | | |
| J | | |
| K | | |
| L | | |
| M | | |
| N | | |



NUMERICAL EVALUATION

NOTE: – EVALUATION WEIGHT FACTORS

1 = MINOR DIFFERENCE IN IMPORTANCE
2 = MEDIUM DIFFERENCE IN IMPORTANCE
3 = MAJOR DIFFERENCE IN IMPORTANCE

TEAM MEMBERS

DATE

FORM NO. 8829 12-66

VALUE ENGINEERING

Figure 7-3

tion Phase. This is necessary because, in the comparison and evaluation of the functions, a bit of subjectivity based on this information must be applied.

The comparison part of this technique is started by relating function *A* to function *B* and determining which is more important. The key letter of the function deemed more important is placed in the upper-left-hand block (the *AB* block) of the numerical evaluation section of the worksheet. Since there is always a difference in the importance of any two functions, this difference, even though it may be small, is also noted in the same block as the key letter.

The difference in the importance of the functions is signified by weight factors, 1, 2, or 3 — where 1 indicates a minor difference in importance, 2 a medium difference of importance, and 3 shows a major difference of importance. These weight factors are used because they are simple yet quantitative. These weight factors for the functions may be arrived at in a simple yet effective way by considering the time required to decide which function is the more important. If the decision is made instantaneously or quite rapidly, there is a major difference of importance and a weight factor of 3 is placed in the numerical evaluation block. If a short period of time is required to make the decision, there is a medium difference of importance between the functions and a weight factor of 2 is placed in the numerical evaluation block. If, however, considerable thought and evaluation is required to decide which of the functions is more important, there is only a minor difference between them and a weight factor of 1 is used in the block with the key letter.

When function *A* has been compared and evaluated with function *B* and the key letter of the more important function has been noted, with its weight factor, in the numerical evaluation, the procedure is repeated, one function at a time, with the remaining functions listed in the evaluation summary. The results of these comparisons and evaluations are noted in the respective blocks across the top of the numerical evaluation. The comparison and evaluation process is then continued by relating function *B* to each of the functions below it in the evaluation summary and placing the results in the respective blocks of the second row of the numerical evaluation. This comparison and evaluation process is continued until every function has been individually compared and evaluated with every other function in the evaluation summary.

When a weighted comparison and evaluation has been made for each function relative to every other function, a summation of these can be compiled. This summation requires a wizardry of simple mathematics. This summation is accomplished by adding the weight factors, both horizontally and vertically, for each function (key letter) in the numerical evaluation chart and placing the total in the evaluation summary weight column on the same line as the key letter.

From a comparison of the totalized figures in the weight column, the basic function of the project being studied is readily determined or verified.

This will be the function which has the highest total weight factor. The basic function thus being determined, it can be filled in on the function definition worksheet. The secondary functions and their descending order of importance are also determined by comparison of each function's weight factors. The descending order of importance is established by the descending value of the functions' weight factor totals.

With these quantitative data on the relationship of each function to every other function, we can now list the functions in their descending order of importance, retaining with them their weight factor totals. This descending-order listing of the functions with their weight factors provides us with additional and significant information for analysis.

From an analysis of this list, we see that there are two distinct drops in the weight factor totals. The first such drop will always appear between the basic and secondary functions, thereby separating for us the two levels of functions. The second of these two drops in the totalized weight factors will appear within the descending order of the secondary functions. This second drop is significant in that, upon analysis, we find that all the functions listed below it are contained because of the present design or approach. It should be noted that this second drop in total weight factor is always quite large.

This descending order of importance and related drops in the weight factor totals can also be shown by plotting the weight factors in graph form on the back of the functional evaluation worksheet. A typical graph form is shown in Figure 7-4.

It is important to note that when this technique is applied to functional evaluation, the graph form will always be in this configuration. The number of functions on either side of the lines may vary, but the basic configuration will remain constant.

We are now able, with the information obtained from this technique, to go back and complete the functional definition worksheet, not only to the point of placing check marks as to whether a function is basic or secondary in the subcolumns of column five but also noting the rank of the function in

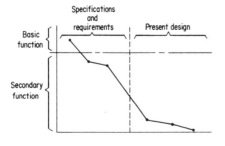

Figure 7-4

JOY MANUFACTURING COMPANY — REF. NO. M-43

FUNCTIONAL EVALUATION

PROJECT Roof Exhaust Fan Wheel — DRAWING NO. 145168656

EVALUATION SUMMARY

| KEY LETTER | FUNCTIONS | WEIGHT |
|---|---|---|
| A | Provide connection | 10 |
| B | Transmit force | 9 |
| C | Induce friction | 3 |
| D | Provide support | 2 |
| E | Provide location | 0 |
| F | Direct air | 11 |
| G | Convert energy | 15 |
| H | | |
| I | | |
| J | | |
| K | | |
| L | | |
| M | | |
| N | | |

| | B | C | D | E | F | G | H | I | J | K | L | M | N |
|---|---|---|---|---|---|---|---|---|---|---|---|---|---|
| A | A-2 | A-2 | A-3 | A-3 | F-2 | G-3 | | | | | | | |
| B | | B-2 | B-3 | B-2 | B-2 | G-3 | | | | | | | |
| C | | | C-1 | C-2 | F-3 | G-2 | | | | | | | |
| D | | | | D-2 | F-3 | G-2 | | | | | | | |
| E | | | | | F-3 | G-3 | | | | | | | |
| F | | | | | | G-2 | | | | | | | |
| G | | | | | | | | | | | | | |
| H | | | | | | | | | | | | | |
| I | | | | | | | | | | | | | |
| J | | | | | | | | | | | | | |
| K | | | | | | | | | | | | | |
| L | | | | | | | | | | | | | |
| M | | | | | | | | | | | | | |

NUMERICAL EVALUATION

NOTE: – EVALUATION WEIGHT FACTORS

1 = MINOR DIFFERENCE IN IMPORTANCE
2 = MEDIUM DIFFERENCE IN IMPORTANCE
3 = MAJOR DIFFERENCE IN IMPORTANCE

TEAM MEMBERS ______ DATE ______

FORM NO. 8829 12–66 — VALUE ENGINEERING

Figure 7-5

the descending-order list of functions and noting the basic function at the top of the worksheet.

After the details of the two worksheets have been completed, it is possible for you to study the results and determine many things about your project. With this knowledge, you can objectively analyze the product

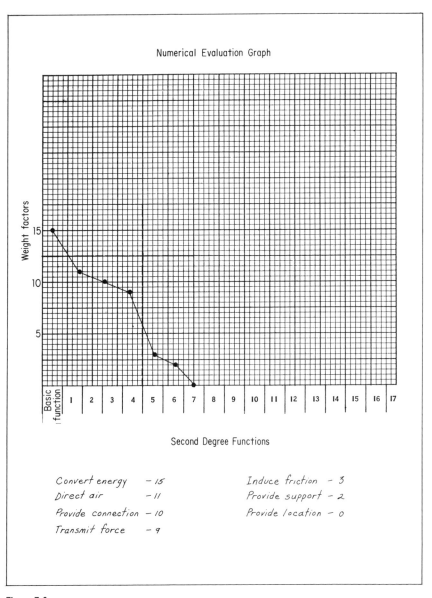

Figure 7-6

with confidence, knowing that you have secured and related all the facts, data, and information about it.

Figures 7-5 and 7-6 show the application of numerical evaluation of the functional relationships to the roof exhaust fan wheel used in the earlier discussion on defining the function.

You can now approach and undertake the techniques of the Creation Phase with confidence, knowing that, basically, you need be creative only on those functions which are incorporated in the project because of specifications or requirements.

*If something makes sense functionally, chances are it will make sense to people.*

— HOWARD K. SPULICK

# Chapter Eight

# Creation Phase

*Each of us has been endowed by our Creator
with infinite creativity and judicial abilities.*

These creative and judicial abilities are ones which we must forge and carefully finish on the anvil of time. In many instances, we must reforge and reshape them over the years. The ingredients required to make these into useful abilities are the fire of ambition, the urge for accomplishment, enthusiasm, the desire for factual evaluation, devotion to truth, and willingness to work.

These abilities, like the muscles of our body, must be exercised and developed over a period of time; and once developed, they must be kept in constant use. We cannot expect to develop these or any other useful abilities without hard work and the application of deliberate effort.

Each of these abilities has equal importance to us and must be so developed. Creativity, however, is too often allowed to wither and die within us from lack of usage—a lack of usage that is most often caused by insufficient stimulation or ridicule. These abilities and the human mind as a whole, like so many other things we've discussed, cannot be captured in one all-encompassing thought or definition.  Rather, they must be seen as comprising many intricate, interrelated, and interdependent parts.

Our minds, when examined, are found to be more complex and to have vastly more capabilities than any computer yet devised.  Yet we find in truthful examination that, because of our individually developed habits and attitudes, they are mainly used as emergency units.  In essence, our active minds take over only when our ingrained habits and attitudes cannot readily cope with a particular problem or situation.

This mind of yours, because of its vast complexities, must be divided into its major parts and so studied.  In this phase of the Job Plan, we are going to deal with only two of these parts: the judicial and creative.  Further, our discussions will be limited to the way these parts affect and are used by and within the Value Engineering Systematic Approach.  We cannot, in this one chapter, expect to cover the whole area of creative and judicial thinking because of its vast scope.  (For the reader who desires to study these subjects in greater depth, a bibliography is provided at the conclusion of the chapter.)

The ultimate actions of the judicial and creative parts of the mind can best be depicted by the use of symbols such as those used in various cartoons and comic strips, Figure 8-1.

These symbols, however, depict only the end result of the long development of these parts of the mind; they do not show the development itself.  Further, they do not show how or when these parts should be applied or the reason for applying them.

Before we discuss the application within the Job Plan of these two parts of the mind, it is important that we first understand the general history of their development.  The chart, Figure 8-2, graphically depicts the development of both our creative and judicial abilities.

JUDICIAL THINKING                    CREATIVE THINKING

Figure 8-1

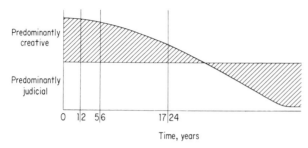

Predominantly creative

Predominantly judicial

0   1 2   5 6          17 24

Time, years

**Figure 8-2**

It can readily be seen from this chart that when we are infants our creative ability develops at a very rapid rate to a point at which we are predominantly creative.  This development continues until we are about two years old.  At this point in our lives, we encounter the first inhibition to our creative development: the home environment.  The influences of this home environment come basically from our parents, our other relatives, and our physical surroundings.  What happens at age two is that what has been considered "cute" in an infant is now becoming inappropriate.  At this age, we must start to learn to conform.  These lessons in conformity are taught us from infancy to early adulthood.  This environment, however, is not the only inhibitor of our predominantly creative mind.

Overlapping this home environment is the environment of our formal education and training.  Such education and training, as most of us encounter it, becomes the second major inhibitor to our creative abilities.  This is caused by the insistence, common in the education and training environment, on doing everything exactly "by the book."  This dogmatic approach to education and training tends to stifle the creative drives of most individuals and forces them closer and closer to a predominantly judicial thinking pattern.  Further, it rapidly develops within us a negative attitude toward those who do not follow the specific rules.  We can therefore see that the overlapping effects of our home and educational environments reverse the pattern of our minds from one that is predominantly creative toward one that is strongly judicial.  These two influences are not the only detractors to our predominantly creative thinking; there is yet a third.  This is the pressure to which we may be subjected by our associates and our peers.

The influence of this third group is actually one that we feel from infancy to death, one that is constantly developing and constantly changing.  From the first time our mother says, "No, that's not right" we are engulfed in this mass of inhibitions to our creative ability.  This environment or source of influence is made up of our parents, our friends, our educators, our business associates, and everyone with whom we have contact.  All these, as individuals or groups, have their effect in changing our thinking from patterns that are predominantly creative to others that are predominantly judicial; i.e., moving us from subjective to objective thinking. Their efforts are to make us conform, not to change the status quo which is caused by the tendency of human nature to resist and fear change. Our varying environments develop within each of us varying degrees of this fear and resistance. These fears and resistances can be separated into three distinct groups: cultural, emotional, and perceptual. Within each of these groups, we can isolate specific fears and resistances.

*In the cultural group there are:*

1. Desire to conform or adapt to the pattern
2. Too much faith in statistics
3. All-or-nothing attitude
4. Too much emphasis on competition or on cooperation
5. Overdependence on generalizations
6. Fear of being considered impolite because of inquisitiveness or constant doubt
7. Belief that indulgence in fantasy is a waste of time
8. Lack of confidence due to too much or too little knowledge about the field you are working in

*In the emotional group there are:*

1. Fear of making a mistake or making fools of ourselves
2. Difficulty in rejecting or setting aside a workable solution and searching for a better one
3. An overriding desire to succeed quickly
4. Lack of confidence in oneself, distrust of associates, and fear of authority
5. Lack of desire to carry a problem through to completion
6. Inability to relax and let "incubation" take place
7. Inability to accept change of direction to attain the ultimate goal
8. Desire for security

*In the perceptual group there are:*

1. Inability to define terms
2. Fear of using all the senses
3. Difficulty in isolating the problem
4. Inability to distinguish between cause and effect
5. Resistance to investigating the obvious
6. Difficulty caused by working with false data

All these fears and resistances are real and are caused by the environment to which each of us is subjected. In order to avoid or counteract their effects, we must constantly work to develop our creative abilities.  In order that we may use the creative and judicial parts of our minds to the best advantage, we must realize three important facts: first, relative to creativity, judgment is negative; second, where judgment is left unchecked, creativity disappears; and third, uninhibited creativity must precede judgment.

From these three facts we can see that the techniques of the Creation Phase entitled "Establish Positive Thinking" and "Develop Creative Ideas" deal with the predominantly creative mind and set aside judgment. In the next two phases of the Job Plan, we will discuss the application of creative judgment.

With this background, we can now discuss the specific techniques of the Creation Phase.

## Establish Positive Thinking

*The mind is like a parachute—it works*
*only when it's open!*

This statement may seem trite, even comical at first glance, but it is neither. On close, thoughtful examination, we shall find that it is both dynamically true and quite descriptive of the condition that must exist if we are to develop a state of mind in which we can think positively, for open-mindedness and positive thinking go together like hand and glove.  They are also the direct opposite of the judicial thinking arising from poor habits and negative attitudes.  In any progressive endeavor, the closed or overly judicial mind is about as useful to us as a parachute that opens on the second bounce.

We cannot condemn these attitudes and say they must not be tolerated or we would be falling into the same trap that we are trying to avoid.  We can say, however, that these attitudes must be modified as well as deferred to a later time for application in the Job Plan.

In investigating the closed or overly judicial mind, the first major cause we encounter is human nature.  Our human nature in these instances is brought into play by our ingrained fear of change, fear of the unknown, and fear of censorship.  These are the fears which have been developed by our environments.  These environments have another telling effect; i.e., they restrict our ability of recall.  This effect is such that we remember only what we are not afraid of, which amounts to about:

10 percent of what we hear
20 percent of what we see
50 percent of what we read
90 percent of what we do

Therefore, it is evident what we must do: actively put into practice as much as possible those techniques that will counteract the effects of our environment. For it has been said that "There is nothing new; there are only things which have been forgotten." Therefore if we cannot remember, we cannot develop; if we cannot develop and rearrange, we cannot be creative.

Again, as with the opening statement of the discussion of this technique, you may partially or completely disbelieve these statements. As a simple example of their telling effect, look at and solve the three simple problems shown below (there are no tricks involved):

### Problem 1

```
•   •   •

•   •   •

•   •   •
```

Connect all nine dots with four straight lines without lifting the pencil from the paper, crossing only one line and never retracing any line or portion of a line.

### Problem 2

9    8    7    6    5    4    3    2    1
18   46   94
Complete the lower group of figures with six positive numbers.

### Problem 3

O, T, T, F, F, S, S, E, —, —
Fill in the last two letters to complete the above sequence to a total of ten letters.

If you have solved all three of these problems in less than five minutes each or have indeed solved all three problems, you have already established an open mind and are ready for the development of creative thinking. However, most of us would not be quite so fortunate, for we have developed numerous mental roadblocks. The solutions to these problems are given below:

### Solution to Problem 1

This problem is unsolved because we impose on ourselves the restriction that the lines must be contained within the area enclosed by the nine dots. If you will examine the original problem, no such restriction is imposed.

## Solution to Problem 2

| 9 | 8 | 7 | 6 | 5 | 4 | 3 | 2 | 1 |
|---|---|---|---|---|---|---|---|---|
| 18 | 46 | 94 | 63 | 52 | 61 | 9 | 4 | 1 |

This problem is unsolved by most individuals because they try to determine a numerical progression on the lower level similar to the one on the upper level. The actual solution is that each lower number is the reverse of the square of the number directly above it; i.e., $9 \times 9 = 81$, and 81 reversed is 18; $8 \times 8 = 64$, and 64 reversed is 46, etc. Again, a self-imposed restriction based on past experience or education limits us in seeking the solution.

## Solution to Problem 3

One
Two
Three
Four
Five
Six
Seven
Eight
Nine
Ten

As can be seen, this sequence is made up of the first letters of the numbers one through ten. Here the problem was that you were not used to seeing these letters by themselves in a single line.

Now that you have reviewed the solution to each of these problems and have seen how and why you were unable to solve all of them, it is important for us to determine how this roadblock can be overcome or removed. It has been said that "The shrewd man looks ahead, the simple man looks up, the resigned man looks down, the frightened man looks back, and the wise man looks within." Let us therefore copy the shrewd, simple, wise man and look ahead, up, and within to formulate corrective action. We soon discover that the corrective action is to do everything possible to open our minds, freeing them from regimentation and overly judicial thought patterns. This positive *doing* action will once again open the gold mine between our ears and develop a thought pattern described in the old song entitled "Accentuate the Positive, Eliminate the Negative."

Positive thinking, as a state of mind, opens the door, for each of us, to the development of creative ideas.

## Develop Creative Ideas

*We are today where yesterday's thoughts have brought us, and shall be tomorrow where today's thoughts carry us.* — ELMER G. LETTERMAN

Ever since man first became man, individuals with a developed talent for creative thought have played major roles in advancing human progress. Few abilities play a greater role in progress than the creative thinking and skilled ingenuity which underlie both inventiveness and resourceful leadership.

Creativity and ingenuity grow by exercise. Contrary to common belief, they become more powerful in the mature mind. As creative thinkers, we must have ambition; for a strong and powerful need to accomplish something of meaning is essential to all creative endeavor. When we meet with the problems that arise in the course of our work, we must persist in struggling with them until they are overcome, no matter how long it may take. For this we need both energy great enough to carry us through the most difficult kind of mental labor and also complete confidence in our ability to attain final success.

Since the scope of our creative work depends on our store of knowledge, we must be constantly engaged in its development by study, observation, and experiment. We must, therefore, be capable of self-instruction.

We must maintain our enthusiasm, devotion, and passions. Creative thinking is not purely an intellectual exercise; on the contrary, we as creative thinkers must be dominated by emotion from start to finish. We must therefore develop and possess inquiring minds and creative imaginations.

So that we will be able to actively develop creative ideas, it is necessary that we first determine how the creative thinker brings new things into existence. In other words, we must find out what the tools of the trade are.

It is probably your impression that these tools are of many different kinds, some being used by composers, others by writers, still others by inventors. This, however, is not the case. There is only a single set used by every creative thinker regardless of his problem or line of work. These tools are of two basic kinds: those used in the noncreative mental processes and those which encompass the creative mental processes.

Most important among the tools of the noncreative mental processes are the following:

Remembering—recall of past experiences and previously acquired ideas
Reflection—total review of the content of the mind
Observation—study of surrounding objects and circumstances
Association—comparison of the present problem parts with the solutions to previous problems

These tools deal with our available supply of raw material, enabling us to collect ideas from our store of knowledge and from the results of experience. This is merely a way of saying that the noncreative mental processes form the basis not only of logical thought but also of creative thinking.

As these processes are fully discussed in extensive literature that is available, we need not consider them further here except to point out a very important limitation: i.e., logical thought is incapable of originating that which is entirely new.

There are, however, special tools that the creative thinker may use to bring into existence that which did not exist before. For these tools we must look to the creative mental processes.

Before looking at these, we must examine two points that require explanation. First, it is commonly said that the creative thinker develops new ideas by recombining the old ideas that are already in his mind. Sometimes these combinations consist wholly of ideas that have long been known, and sometimes they form around ideas that have been newly formed. They come to him in groupings and are rearranged by the creative mental process. Second, although the various creative mental processes are quite different in motivation, action, outcome, and controllability, they are seldom separate and distinct in actual practice. There are three mental processes used in creative thinking.

The first of these processes is *imagination,* which enables us to blend ideas into new combinations while we are engaged in deliberate thinking. Imagination usually deals with common and easily remembered ideas. The second is *inspiration,* which is the result of accidental stimulation. Inspiration occurs when new ideas are triggered by some object, circumstance, or comment which suddenly and spontaneously fits together with old ideas. The third is *illumination,* which is stimulated by strong, deliberate thinking on the problem followed, after the thinking process has been stopped, by the formation of new ideas. Illumination is similar to inspiration in that it occurs without effort at the time the ideas develop, but it is preceded by deliberate thought about a given problem, which is thus introduced into the subconscious mind. This process often brings forward many long-forgotten ideas.

We will readily realize that both the noncreative and the creative mental processes must have stimulation to be brought into action. This stimulation can be supplied by the use of idea activators.

**Idea Activators**    Idea activators may conveniently take the form of checklists. These checklists may consist of direct or indirect questions to be asked about the problem under study. Two such checklists are shown at the conclusion of the chapter. They are entitled "Idea Needlers" and "Idea Stimulators."

These idea activators will not work, however, without constant application and practice. This application and practice can be obtained along with creative ability by using the rules of 24, 25, and 26. These rules are sometimes called the *rules of creativity.*

Rule of 24 — This rule simply urges you to be creative on every problem that you encounter in the twenty-four hours of the day. It is suggested that you write down each problem as it is encountered.  Then, at a given time each day, a time at which you will find yourself to be most creative, develop a quantity of ideas for solution to these problems.

The requirement for a quantity of idea solutions leads us right into the second rule:

Rule of 25 — This rule simply states that you should have at least twenty-five ideas for each problem before you start any evaluation.  On the average, however, it has been found that most of us can generate only about seventeen ideas before we encounter a mental block.

This occurrence of a mental block at approximately seventeen ideas leads us to the third and final rule of creativity:

Rule of 26 — This rule suggests that when you encounter a mental block to further creative ideas, use the twenty-six letters of the alphabet (i.e., What word that begins with the letter A will solve the problem?  What word that begins with the letter B will solve the problem? etc.).  Another way of using this rule is to pick up a dictionary and start looking at the words.  The use of the dictionary brings *inspiration* into active use.

In the case of our Value Engineering Job Plan, we have stated the problems on which we must be creative in two words, a verb and a noun; i.e., the defined functions.  At this point in the Job Plan, and only at this point, the two-word definition of a function is considered a complete problem in itself.  Using the creative worksheet, we list one function and then generate ideas to solve this problem.  Such a worksheet is developed for each function which is contained, because of specifications or requirements, in the project being studied.

Creative thinking and developing creative ideas is not something that is easy; it is an activity which we must constantly practice and continually use.  The development of creative ideas is not an end in itself; rather, it is the basis for the application of creative judgment.  Creative judgment is actively applied in the next phase of the Job Plan, the Evaluation Phase.

*We are today where yesterday's thoughts have*
*brought us, and shall be tomorrow where*
*today's thoughts carry us.*

## Idea Needlers

How much of this is the result of custom, tradition, or opinions?
Why does it have this shape?
How would I design it if I had to build it in my home workshop?
What if this were turned inside out?  Reversed?  Upside down?
What if this were larger?  Higher?  Wider?  Thicker?  Lower?  Longer?
What else can it be made to do?
Suppose this were left out?

How can it be done piecemeal?
How can it appeal to the senses?
How about extra value?
Can this be multiplied?
What if this were blown up?
What if this were carried to extremes?
How can this be made more compact?
Would this be better symmetrical or asymmetrical?
In what form could this be—liquid, powder, paste, or solid?   Rod, tube, triangle, cube, or sphere?
Can motion be added to it?
Will it be better standing still?
What other layout might be better?
Can cause and effect be reversed?   Is one possibly the other?
Should it be put on the other end or in the middle?
Should it slide instead of rotate?
Demonstrate or describe it by what it isn't.
Has a search been made of the patent literature?   Trade journals?
Could a vendor supply this for less?
How could this be made easier to use?
Can it be made safer?
How could this be changed for quicker assembly?
What other materials would do this job?
What is similar to this but costs less?   Why?
What if it were made lighter or faster?
What motion or power is wasted?
Could the package be used for something afterwards?
If all specifications could be forgotten, how else could the basic function be accomplished?
Could these be made to meet specifications?
How do competitors solve problems similar to this?

## Idea Stimulators

1. *Can the dimensions be changed?*

| | |
|---|---|
| Larger . . . . . . . . . . . . . . . | Economy-size packages, photo enlargements, puffed cereals |
| Smaller. . . . . . . . . . . . . . | United States paper money, hearing aids, tabloid newspapers, pocket flashlights, microfilm |
| Longer . . . . . . . . . . . . . . | King-size cigarettes, typewriter carriage for bookkeeping |
| Shorter. . . . . . . . . . . . . . | Men's shorts, women's underwear |
| Thicker. . . . . . . . . . . . . . | Rug pads, heavy edge on drinking glasses, glass bricks |
| Thinner . . . . . . . . . . . . . | Nylon hose, seersucker suits, wristwatches |

Deeper . . . . . . . . . . . . . . .   Deeper pockets in work clothes and army uni-
forms, grooved battery plates

More shallow . . . . . . . . . . .   Wading pools, children's drinking fountain,
cookie sheet

Stand vertically . . . . . . . . .   Skyscrapers (to increase floor space on expensive land); upright pianos

Place horizontally . . . . . . .   Ranch-style homes (to eliminate stair climbing)

Make slanted or parallel. . . .   Reading stands, car mirrors, eyeglass frames

Stratify . . . . . . . . . . . . . . .   Plywood, storage pallets, layer cake, leaf spring

Invert (reverse) . . . . . . . . .   Reversible coats, soft shoes to be worn on either
foot, inverted ink and glue stands

Use crosswise . . . . . . . . . .   Bias-cut brassieres and slips, pinking shears

Converge . . . . . . . . . . . . .   Mechanical artificial hands, ice tongs

Encircle . . . . . . . . . . . . . .   Spring cake form, knitted coasters to slip on
bottoms of highball glasses, Life-Savers

Intervene . . . . . . . . . . . . .   Buffers used in drug products to temper harsh,
active ingredients, padding between dishes

Delineate . . . . . . . . . . . . .   Contour lathe, Scotchlite reflective sheeting

Border . . . . . . . . . . . . . . .   Mats for pictures, movable office partitions,
room separators, road edges

## 2. Can the quantity be changed?

More . . . . . . . . . . . . . . . . .   Extra-pants suits, 3 stockings—a pair and a
spare

Less . . . . . . . . . . . . . . . . .   Variety of 1-ounce boxes of cereals, ginger ale
splits, bite-size pieces

Fractionate . . . . . . . . . . . .   Separate packages of crackers inside single
box, 16-mm movie film usable as two 8-mm
films, faucet spray.

Join something . . . . . . . . .   Trailer, hose couplings

Add something . . . . . . . . .   Cigarette filter tip

Combine with something . . .   Amphibious autos, outboard motors, roadable
airplanes

Complete . . . . . . . . . . . . .   Freezer unit added to refrigerator, Bendix
washer and dryer in single unit

## 3. Can the order be changed?

Arrangement. . . . . . . . . . .   Car steering wheels left-handed in the United
States and right-handed in England, Dewey
decimal system of filing

Precedence . . . . . . . . . . . .   Rear-drive automobiles, rear-wheel steering.

Beginning . . . . . . . . . . . . .   Self-starter, red tab to open cigarette package,
red string to open Band-Aids

Assembly or disassembly . . .   Prefabricated articles, knocked-down boat kits

Focus . . . . . . . . . . . . . . . .   Kellogg packages (name placed in left corner
instead of center), Hathaway shirt ads (man
with eye patch)

4. *Can the time element be changed?*

Faster . . . . . . . . . . . . . . . . Quick-drying ink, dictating machine, intercom system

Slower . . . . . . . . . . . . . . . High-tenacity yarns for longer-life tires, 33⅓- rpm long-playing records, shock absorbers

Longer . . . . . . . . . . . . . . . Jiffy insulated bags for ice cream, wood pre- servative

Shorter . . . . . . . . . . . . . . . Pressure cooker, 1-minute x-ray machines

Chronologized . . . . . . . . . . Defrosting devices, clock-radios, clock switches

Perpetuated . . . . . . . . . . . . Photographs, metal plating, permanent mag- nets

Synchronized . . . . . . . . . . . Uniform vacation periods, group travel tours

Anticipated . . . . . . . . . . . . Thermostat, freezer food-buying plan, wear in- dicators, off-peak heating

Renewed . . . . . . . . . . . . . . Self-charging battery, self-winding watches

Recurrence . . . . . . . . . . . . Switch clocks for lights and electrical ap- pliances

Alternated . . . . . . . . . . . . Cam drive, electric current

5. *Can the cause or effect be changed?*

Stimulated . . . . . . . . . . . . Generator, flashing lights

Energized . . . . . . . . . . . . . Magneto, power steering

Strengthened . . . . . . . . . . . AC transformer, Simonize car coating

Louder . . . . . . . . . . . . . . . Volume control

Softer . . . . . . . . . . . . . . . Sound insulator, rubber heels

Altered . . . . . . . . . . . . . . . Antifreeze chemicals, meat tenderizer, plastic wood

Destroyed . . . . . . . . . . . . . Tree sprays, breath and perspiration deodor- ants

Influenced . . . . . . . . . . . . . Legislation to permit sale of colored oleo, wet- ting agent catalyst

Counteracted . . . . . . . . . . Circuit breaker, air conditioning, filters

6. *Can there be a change in character?*

Stronger . . . . . . . . . . . . . . Dirt-resistant paint

Weaker . . . . . . . . . . . . . . . Pepsi-Cola made less sweet, children's aspirin

Altered . . . . . . . . . . . . . . . Aged or blended whisky, transit-mixed cement

Substituted . . . . . . . . . . . . Low-calorie salad dressing (made without oils)

Interchanged . . . . . . . . . . . Interchangeable parts, all-size (stretch) socks

Stabilized . . . . . . . . . . . . . Sperry gyroscope, waterproof plastic bandage

Reversed . . . . . . . . . . . . . . Two-way locomotives

Resilient . . . . . . . . . . . . . . Foam rubber upholstery, cork floors

Uniformity . . . . . . . . . . . . Standards in foods, drugs, fuels, liquor

Cheaper . . . . . . . . . . . . . . Coach air travel, paper cups

More expensive . . . . . . . . . Cigarettes in cardboard or metal boxes, deluxe editions of books

Add color . . . . . . . . . . . . .    Color television, colored plastics
Change color. . . . . . . . . . . .    Variously colored toothbrush handles, automobiles, electric light bulbs

### 7. Can the form be changed?

Regular. . . . . . . . . . . . . . .    Molded telephone poles
Irregular. . . . . . . . . . . . . .    Bottles shaped for easy gripping
Curved. . . . . . . . . . . . . . .    European-style car fronts, molded chairs
Straight . . . . . . . . . . . . . .    Cement building slabs
Harder . . . . . . . . . . . . . . .    Reinforced hitting surfaces for golf clubs
Softer. . . . . . . . . . . . . . . .    Toilet tissue, Daisy hat bags
Symmetrical . . . . . . . . . . . .    Spherical roller bearings
Notched . . . . . . . . . . . . . .    Zipper, drill, gear
Rougher . . . . . . . . . . . . . .    Hilly highway surfaces, shredded wheat, whole
wheat bread
Smoother . . . . . . . . . . . . . .    Facing tile
Damage avoided . . . . . . . .    Nested shipping cases
Delays avoided . . . . . . . . . .    Plant cafeteria service, automatically printed
railroad tickets
Theft avoided . . . . . . . . . . .    Postage meter
Accidents avoided . . . . . . . .    Improved plant lighting, white edge on step
Something added. . . . . . . . .    Water ices on a stick, chocolate-covered ice
cream
Conformation . . . . . . . . . . .    Contour-shaped bedsheets, moldable explosive,
slip covers, modeling clay

### 8. Can the motion be changed?

Animated . . . . . . . . . . . . . .    Moving staircases, package conveyors
Stilled. . . . . . . . . . . . . . . .    Air brakes, stop-motion lighting (stroboscope),
time-lapse photos
Speeded . . . . . . . . . . . . . .    Meat-slicing machine
Slowed . . . . . . . . . . . . . . .    Shock absorbers, gravel driveway
Directed . . . . . . . . . . . . . .    Flow meters, follow arrows
Deviated. . . . . . . . . . . . . .    Traffic islands
Attracted . . . . . . . . . . . . .    Magnetic devices
Repelled. . . . . . . . . . . . . .    Electrically charged fencing
Admitted . . . . . . . . . . . . .    Turnstiles
Barred . . . . . . . . . . . . . . .    Gate, fence
Lifted. . . . . . . . . . . . . . . .    Fork-lift truck
Lowered . . . . . . . . . . . . . .    Ship locks
Rotated. . . . . . . . . . . . . . .    Waring Blender, boring machine
Oscillated . . . . . . . . . . . . .    Electric fan
Agitated . . . . . . . . . . . . . .    Electric scalp stimulator

### 9. Can the state or condition be changed?

Hotter . . . . . . . . . . . . . . .    Electric hot plate, washed coal
Colder . . . . . . . . . . . . . . .    Freezer, Thermos jug, water cooler

| | |
|---|---|
| Harden............... | Bouillon cubes, cream shampoo (instead of liquid) |
| Soften............... | Krilium soil conditioner, water softeners |
| Open or closed ......... | Visible record equipment, electronically operated doors |
| Preformed............. | Prefabricated housing, prepared Tom Collins mixer |
| Disposable ............ | Bottle caps, Chux disposable diapers, Kleenex tissues |
| Incorporated ........... | Counting register on printing press, cash registers |
| Parted ............... | Tractor-trailers, split-level highways |
| Solidified ............. | Bakelite and other plastics, citrus concentrates |
| Liquefied ............. | Chemical plant foods |
| Vaporized............. | Nasal medication vaporizers, power sprays |
| Pulverized............. | Powdered eggs, lawn mower attachment to powder leaves, disposal garbage pulverizer |
| Abraded............... | Snow tire or chains |
| Lubricated ............ | Self-lubricating equipment, solid lubricants |
| Wetter ............... | Hydraulic brakes, wet roofs |
| Drier ................ | De-Moist drier for cellars, tobacco curling |
| Insulated.............. | Fiberglas, Dr. Scholl's foot appliances (insulate feet against pressures) |
| Effervesced............ | Alka-Seltzer |
| Coagulated ............ | Jell-O and Junket desserts |
| Elasticized ............ | Latex girdles, bubble gum, belts |
| Resistant.............. | Rubber footwear |
| Lighter............... | Aluminum luggage, automatic electric blanket |
| Heavier .............. | Can opener with weighted stand |

10. *Can the use be adapted to a new market?*

| | |
|---|---|
| Men................. | Colognes, lotions |
| Women.............. | Colored-tip cigarettes |
| Children............. | Junior-size tools, cowboy clothes |
| The old.............. | Walking-stick chairs |
| The handicapped........ | Chair lifts |
| Foreigners............ | *Reader's Digest* foreign editions |

# BIBLIOGRAPHY

## Creative Thinking

*A Source Book for Creative Thinking,* by Sidney J. Parnes and Dr. Harold F. Harding, Charles Scribner's Sons, New York, 1962, 393 pages. A source book of significant material in one volume for those who want to go further. Material representative of different schools of thought on the subject.

*Applied Imagination,* by Alex Osborn Ph.D., Charles Scribner's Sons, New York, 1953, 317 pages. Principles of creative thinking.

*The Techniques of Creative Thinking,* by Robert P. Crawford, Professor of Journalism, University of Nebraska; published by Hawthorn Books, Inc., New York, 1954, 287 pages. Contains practical suggestions on how to use your ideas to achieve success.

*How to Increase Your Creative Output,* published by Industrial Relations News, Book Department, New York, 1959, 22 pages. Designed to help companies raise the level of creativity among their technical personnel.

*Your Hidden Brainpower,* by Morton M. Hunt, Birk & Co., Inc., New York, 1956, 16 pages. A few rules for greater thought production.

*Creative Thinking,* by Charles S. Whiting, Market Planning Corp., an affiliate of McCann-Erickson, Inc.; published by Reinhold Publishing Co., New York, 1958, 182 pages. An analysis of the subject of creative thinking.

Creative Education Foundation, Buffalo, N.Y. Will send list of booklets upon request.

*Brainstorming,* by Charles Clark, Doubleday & Company, Inc., Garden City, N.Y., 1958, 263 pages. For solving problems in business, science, government, and your own life.

*How to Create New Ideas,* by Jack W. Taylor, Prentice-Hall, Inc., Englewood Cliffs, N.J., 1961, 243 pages. A simple, systematic process for creating new ideas at will, for producing "inspiration" by intent.

*How to Develop Your Thinking Ability,* by Kenneth S. Keyes, Jr., McGraw-Hill Book Company, New York, 1950, 264 pages. Teaches how to think clearly, not only in the problems of business and day-to-day living but also in questions of world significance.

*The Twelve Rules for Straight Thinking,* by William J. Reilly, Harper and Brothers, New York, 1947, 143 pages. Creative thinking applied to business and personal problems.

*How to Be a More Creative Executive,* by Joseph G. Mason, McGraw-Hill Book Company, New York, 1960, 281 pages. A new approach written specifically for the executive.

*Creativity at Work,* by A. L. Simberg, Industrial Education Institute, Boston, 1963, 188 pages. A practical working guide on applied creativity.

Chapter Nine

# Evaluation Phase

*In the search for and selection of*
*alternatives, attention must be constantly*
*focused on function.* — L. D. MILES

Function and the Functional Approach in this phase, as well as in previous phases, is the guiding force which leads us to low-cost alternatives. The Evaluation Phase, which is directed toward the development of preliminary alternatives, can be considered a continuation of the Creation Phase. The major difference, however, lies in the application of careful appraisal and creative judgment to the ideas developed on each specified or required function. These two ingredients produce effective evaluation and go "hand in glove" with the other phases of the Job Plan.

Successful evaluation and development of ideas culminating in the elimination or prevention of unnecessary cost depends on your skillful application of the techniques of this phase, the removal of obstacles, and the establishment of a positive course of action. Such measures will ensure the complete development of value alternatives of merit.

With the introduction of appraisal and judgment, i.e., creative judgment, it is important that we do not fall into a very common trap. This is the trap of *cheapening* (e.g., the reduction of quality, reliability, or maintainability). For if appraisal and judgment are used in a haphazard manner without specific control, we will end up either degrading the product or increasing its total cost. Both of these defeat our basic purpose.

In order to guard against these possibilities, the Evaluation Phase employs four techniques to develop, or combine and develop alternatives that work. The techniques used are discussed under the following headings: "Refine and Combine Ideas," "Establish Cost on All Ideas," "Develop Function Alternatives," and "Evaluate by Comparison." With and through these techniques, we take every idea developed for a function in the Creation Phase and expand it, singly or in combination with other ideas, into potentially workable solutions to the problem of attaining the desired or required functions.

It must be realized that these four techniques are employed almost simultaneously in this development process. However, before going into our study of these combined applications, it may be best to arrive at a working knowledge of each technique individually.

## Refine and Combine Ideas

*Creative ideas in themselves are useless!*

Having generated and developed a quantity of ideas on a function does not, in itself, accomplish a thing if these ideas are not expanded and put to use. Before they can be put to use, however, further creativity, appraisal, refinement, and judgment must be applied.

Here we must be careful of our appraisal of each idea or combination thereof to determine how it can be used to accomplish the desired function, fulfill its governing parameters, and aid in the accomplishment of all other functions. What looks like a usable idea as first stated may have to be modified to meld with the accomplishment of other specified functions. On the other hand, when a single idea appears to be unusable in its present form, a combination with other ideas should be sought to make it usable. It can be stated from past experience that every idea can be developed into a workable solution.

In essence, this refining and combining of ideas is a dynamic continuation of the creative thought process with creative judgment added. By this addition, we can determine how the ideas from many functions can be used and melded together within the total problem solution.

As this technique is applied, you will find that certain ideas or groups of ideas stand out above the others. This is occasioned by the fact that they are usually the new and different solutions to the basic problem. Some of these, however, you will not be able to put to immediate use because of insufficient data or because the requisite knowledge is not readily available. It is important to note that these ideas are not discarded or thrown away, they are set aside for a future time when the proper data or new knowledge will make them usable. This future time may be hours, days, weeks, months, or years in the future.

One specific way of rapidly developing any idea or group of ideas is to list their advantages and disadvantages. In this way the disadvantages, the new and smaller problems, are isolated, weighed against the advantages, and then overcome by additional creative thought. Also, in this manner the good points of many ideas are combined while the disadvantages are eliminated. While at first glance these steps would seem to make the task of refining and combining ideas monumental, actually they should at most require only a moderate amount of time at this stage of the evaluation. On the other hand, if these steps are ignored, good ideas may be overlooked, efforts may be partially or completely misdirected, or a total failure to gain the ultimate in results may ensue.

When a number of potential solutions have been developed for each function or group of functions, the second technique of this phase, establishing cost on all ideas, is brought into play.

## Establish Cost on All Ideas

*Before progressing, think it through. What are*
*the realistic—not optimistic—cost savings you*
*can expect?*

At this point in the Job Plan, we are like the prospector who believes he has found a gold-laden stream. He must take up and use the tools of his trade. By use of pan, water, and knowledge, he must skillfully segregate the common earth from the gold. He must work diligently and with the utmost skill to refine from the conglomerate the rich and precious gold he knows is there.

Likewise, we must develop and refine the functionally created ideas down to the rich, profit-bearing solutions we know are there. One of the tools of this refining process is that of establishing a relative cost on each idea or combination of ideas. After the creation of many ideas or means of accomplishing the function, we need to estimate the value of each idea. This must be done singly or in idea combinations.

In essence, we are developing a means by which we can establish the potential value of each idea. This potential is established in two areas. First, the return in the way of potential savings is weighted against the cost in time and manpower to develop and implement the idea. Second, the overall cost savings to be realized by the complete development of the idea is estimated.

In order to be able to make these preliminary evaluations, we must, through knowledge, experience, and creative judgment, establish a cost on each and every idea. This cost, at this point, need not be refined to the closest penny. Rather, it should reflect the general cost area into which the idea falls. This is necessary so that the ideas can be realistically compared to determine which ones show the greatest promise of increased profit upon completion.

Another major point to keep in mind in this phase of the Job Plan is that we are only developing and considering these ideas from the standpoint of *whether they will work*. Later, in the Investigation Phase, we shall consider and add refinements, if necessary, which *will make them sell*.

After establishing a cost on all ideas for each function, we can readily take the lowest-cost ideas first in the functional development of alternatives. By starting with the lowest-cost ideas and judiciously working up, as required, we assure ourselves of attaining the lowest-cost method or methods of accomplishing the complete functional requirements.

In essence, we are narrowing down the choices through the use of costs. We must skillfully use our creative judgment at this point to make sure that we sustain the momentum of our progress while at the same time keeping it under control.

During this sustained yet controlled progress, many roadblocks will be encountered. These roadblocks will disclose smaller new problems which require a reshaping of particular parts of the assignment. Only through diligent management can we expect to maintain control and produce ultimate success.

This technique leads to and is a part of the functional development of alternatives, which is the focal point for many changes as well as a doorway to the future.

## Develop Function Alternatives

This technique of the Evaluation Phase, the third part of the Functional Approach, is where the previously gathered information and data, the defined and related functions, and the created and refined ideas are melded together into a number of workable solutions. This melding of refined creative ideas and creative judgment starts the process of the elimination of unnecessary costs and the development of value alternatives of merit.

In our search for and ultimate selection of alternatives, our attention must be constantly focused on function and not merely on a material, part, or device as such. For it is at this point that we can so easily be diverted from our functional path.

The technique of developing function alternatives is a method capable of creating new concepts or alternative solutions to a problem far beyond the unaided imagination of the user. It further helps us by letting us side-step fixed habits and attitudes.

This is made possible by the fact that in this technique we start from base zero—that is, from the two-word definition of the basic function—and we build from there to a workable solution of the problem. The fact of a workable solution is stressed here because, at this point, we are not particularly interested in the solution's salability. The development of a salable solution is undertaken in the next phase, the Investigation Phase. In this manner, we literally separate work functions from sell functions.

The functional development of alternatives is accomplished through the use of the data, information, and ideas developed, generated, and recorded in the previously completed Job Plan phases. It employs the use of the worksheet entitled "Functional Development" (Figure 9-1) plus a pad of sketch paper.

The first step in this technique is to set down, in the form of a simple freehand sketch, the physical parameters within which the stated problem is contained. Next, under this sketch, the essential items of the governing specifications and requirements should be written. This is done in order to confine our development to the immediate project under consideration and to prevent our wandering from the parameters which were accepted when the project was undertaken.

When this has been done, the upper portion of the functional development worksheet is completed by filling in the required data, reference num-

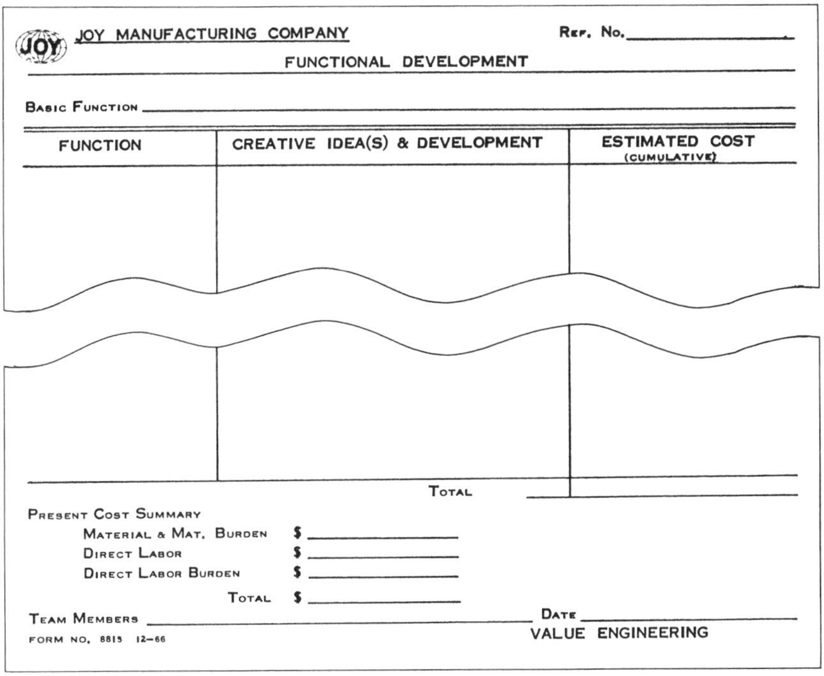
JOY MANUFACTURING COMPANY
REF. NO.
FUNCTIONAL DEVELOPMENT
BASIC FUNCTION
FUNCTION | CREATIVE IDEA(S) & DEVELOPMENT | ESTIMATED COST (CUMULATIVE)
TOTAL
PRESENT COST SUMMARY
MATERIAL & MAT. BURDEN $
DIRECT LABOR $
DIRECT LABOR BURDEN $
TOTAL $
TEAM MEMBERS
DATE
FORM NO. 8815 12-66
VALUE ENGINEERING

Figure 9-1

ber, etc.  Having done this, the preparations for functional development are complete and the developmental work can be undertaken.

From the functional evaluation worksheet, take the basic function—that function having the highest weight factor—and write it in the function column.  Next, from the creative worksheet, for the function just listed, select the idea or combination of ideas which can accomplish the two-word defined function at the lowest cost and write the idea(s) in the column headed "Creative idea(s) and development."  Then, based on your and/or the team's best knowledge, a cost is estimated for the accomplishment of the idea(s) and this cost figure is noted in the column headed "Estimated cost."

As the idea is noted on the worksheet, it is also drawn into the sketch of the physical parameters to pictorially show what is being considered.  The governing specifications and requirements are then reviewed to determine if any of them are pertinent to the particular function under consideration.

When a specification or requirement is found to be pertinent to a particular function, it is noted in the function column directly under that function.  The idea(s) noted for the accomplishment is then reviewed to determine if it meets the specification or requirement or if modifications must be made to the basic idea.  Where modifications are necessary, they are noted in the column headed "Creative idea(s) and development," and the related cost is added to the estimated cost in the cost column.  When all the specifications and requirements related to the function have been noted and met, you can move on to the second function.

The second function, as determined by weight factor, is then taken from the functional evaluation worksheet and placed in the function column.  It is next necessary to consult the creative worksheet on this specific function and ascertain which idea(s) best meld with the previous functional idea at the lowest cost.  This is entered in the column headed "Creative idea(s) and development."  Following through, the cost of accomplishing this idea is added to the previous cost and noted, as a cumulative total, in the estimated cost column.

As with the first function's idea(s) and modifications from specifications and requirements, the means of accomplishing this function are drawn into the sketch of the physical parameters.  Again, as with the first function, the specifications and requirements are reviewed for pertinence to this function.  If pertinent, they are noted and developed as before while constantly keeping the sketch up to date with the latest idea concept.

This procedure of adding each required function in its descending order of importance, with its respective buildup or modification of the basic or preceding ideas and their associated cumulative cost, is continued until all the required functions and their pertinent specifications and requirements have been added to the development.

Finally as a positive cross check, take those functions previously classified as design functions and add them, in their descending order of importance, to the functional development worksheet and determine if anything must be added to the idea concept for each of these functions to make the concept work. This is done to determine if they are indeed required and/or to determine if they have not already been accomplished or if the need for them has been eliminated.

It is important to note that as the above technique of development is being accomplished, additional actions may also be required. These may entail one or more of the following:

1. As any given function, specification, or requirement and its related means of accomplishment is added, a change or major modification in the basic approach may be necessitated. When this is the case, such change should be noted at this point on the functional development worksheet.

2. As any given function causing a major modification and its related means of accomplishment is added, a change in the cumulative estimated cost may also be required. If such is the case, the cost change should be noted at this point on the functional development worksheet.

3. If a pictorial sketch is being used and if any change or major modification affecting this sketch is made, the sketch should be modified or changed to depict the change in the development.

The functional development worksheet is completed by filling in the portions entitled "Present cost summary," "Team members," and "Date" and attaching the pictorial sketch.

The development of a workable solution described above must be recognized first only as a *workable* solution, not necessarily as a salable solution. Second, it must be seen as only *one* possible solution to the project under study.

This same functional development process should be repeated one or more times starting with and using different idea(s) from the various creative worksheets, thereby developing numerous alternative solutions to the project under study.

It is important to note that as this technique is being undertaken to develop a number of alternative workable solutions, it entails a continual cycling of creative, developmental, evaluative, and investigative thinking. Without this complete and continued cyclic type of thinking to overcome the ever-present roadblocks of habits and attitudes, the application of the technique will be of no use.

After the details of developing function alternatives have been completed, we can swiftly move into the last technique of this phase of the Job Plan: evaluation by comparison.

## Evaluate by Comparison

As we progress into this last technique of the Evaluation Phase, it is important to note that the functional alternatives have been developed only to the point where we believe they will work, not necessarily sell. This must constantly be kept in the forefront of our minds as we evaluate these alternatives.

In our process of evaluating each functionally developed alternative by itself or in conjunction with one or more of the others, many factors must be compared.

The first and most important comparison of each alternative is that of the advantages to the disadvantages. This evaluation is accomplished by using the idea evaluation worksheet (Figure 9-2). This is done by writing out, in a short statement, the idea from functional development in the first column. Then, in the second column, list every advantage, no matter how large or small. Next, in the third column, list every disadvantage, no matter how large or small. The advantages and disadvantages can then be compared, their differences evaluated, and a plan of action noted at the bottom of the worksheet. This process is continued until each alternative has been evaluated by itself on a separate sheet and then compared to every other alterna-

JOY MANUFACTURING COMPANY  REF. NO. ________

IDEA EVALUATION

FUNCTION ________

| IDEA FROM FUNCTIONAL DEVELOPMENT | ADVANTAGES | DISADVANTAGES |
|---|---|---|
| | | |

PLANS FOR ACTION ON IDEA(S)

TEAM MEMBERS ________ DATE ________

FORM NO. 8816 12-66  VALUE ENGINEERING

Figure 9-2

tive, at which point the plans for action can be reviewed and work for their accomplishment can be started.

The above description of this important technique might, at this point, seem quite simple and routine—even trite. Such a feeling must be strongly guarded against, for it is a trap into which we can quite easily fall. We become susceptible to this trap because, in some way, we daily make simple evaluations by comparison. However, as with many other things that we do intuitively and think are similar, this technique as used in the Job Plan will be found to be more complex and exacting.

Evaluation by comparison as we will use it in the Job Plan seeks out not only balances but contrasts, not only similarities but differences. Once these have been determined, we must determine their positive and/or negative effect on each other as well as their relationship to the whole.

Throughout our evaluation by comparison, we must constantly maintain a positive attitude and apply good business judgment. Our attitude must be positive so that we do not, through negative judgment, discard an alternative because of one or more disadvantages. It will be found that if we approach any disadvantage with a positive attitude and creative judgment, we will see that it delineates a new but smaller problem to be solved. Most times any disadvantage, when approached in the right way, can be, with little effort, changed into an advantage. Throughout this whole process, we must also be constantly applying good business judgment; we must be comparing the potential time required to fully develop the alternative(s) against the potential return. The return here should be looked at as the potential improvement in cost, quality, maintainability, reliability, or sales advantage—but only to the extent that is required.

The final and equally important evaluation we should be making as we compare our alternatives is whether any of our alternatives are wholly new solutions to the stated problem and, if so, we should note their potential patentability. It is in this phase of creative development and creative judgment that many patentable solutions come to the forefront. These should be noted and followed up as the alternatives are further developed in the next phase of the Job Plan.

Now that the creative ideas have been combined into functional alternatives and evaluated by comparison to determine their order of feasibility, we can start the final step of their development. Through the technique of the Investigation Phase, we will develop these workable alternatives into salable alternatives, for any alternative must both work and sell before it is of any use to us or others.

*I'll be looking for different solutions, because*
*you can't make advances if you only "me-too" it.*
                    —RUSSEL W. HENKE

Chapter Ten

# Investigation Phase

What we achieve in this phase depends on the use we make of the data at our disposal plus the knowledge of new developments, materials, and the economics of competitive techniques. This wealth of data and knowledge need not and cannot be wholly known by us as individuals, but we must know when it can be obtained, seek it out, and put it to use.

By careful, diligent investigation coupled with continued creativity, we will find that what looked like an insurmountable stumbling block has become a stepping-stone to a real developmental breakthrough. It may be that a new atomic engine or computer will be born, perhaps something more modest, like a clever linkage or a new and simpler system.

These achievements also depend, to a great degree, on our perspective. Are we aiming at some minor improvement we are unlikely to miss? Or are we seeking and dynamically searching for a major, evolutionary gain? It has been said that "To shoot at a close target and hit is little success, but to shoot at a distant target and barely miss the bull's-eye is a show of skill."

Imagination, creativity, and the ability to work as a member of a team greatly multiply the probability that our results will be a new conceptual triumph. This work, unlike much other work, is not cut and dried. It does not present textbook problems which have neat, one-and-only correct solutions, that require the simple application of learned formulas, set definitions of problems, and established answers. Rather, it is an approach which simply guides our efforts.

Our results, in this phase, depend on our ability to work in a multidimensional environment of interacting social, economic, scientific, and technological factors. Just as "art ain't all paint," our work here "ain't all action and reaction." Our creative effectiveness demands the use of a broad-based knowledge and technology as well as the application of basic humanities, economics, and sociology.

Above all, we cannot generate a bureaucratic, unimaginative, inflexible administration of the laws of nature or our own wills. True developmental ability is inner-generated and stems from the conviction that we are highly creative and that we can improve that which we have.

All these inner-generated personal demands and requirements are fulfilled or their accomplishment is aided by the techniques of the Investigation Phase. These techniques (using company and industrial standards; consulting vendors and specialists; and using specialty products, processes, and materials) provide the means whereby our partially developed ideas can be brought to fruition.

Although in their actual application they are used simultaneously because they overlap and interlock, we will first discuss them singly. This is done to determine their benefits as well as their potential pitfalls and traps.

## Use Company and Industrial Standards

Throughout the evolution of the industrial age and of this approach, it has been found that the use of standards confers many benefits. Therefore, if there is a possibility of using a standard part or system, it should be pursued with the greatest vigor.

Standard elements of broad usage almost always yield better value because of the following attributes: no developmental costs are required, no tooling costs are entailed, good quality and reliability are ensured, less lead time is required to secure standard elements, their performance characteristics are readily ascertainable, and competition among their suppliers is universal.

The full meaning here is not only the use of applicable standard parts and processes but also the application of individual parts of standard products, concepts, processes, and materials. It also means that we must not use standard elements that do not apply. We must learn to draw out of contrasting and possibly conflicting standards that which is best and most usable. Here, we are interested not in what is wrong with other standards or approaches but in what is right with them.

Changes in approach, material specification, or manufacturing process will enable us to use our own standards or those of other industries. In essence, we want to ask and seek the answer to this question: "Can a standard component or product be found which is usable?"

In searching diligently for standards, we must be just as diligent in avoiding the ever-present traps and pitfalls.

One such, for want of a better name, could be called *the standards hypnosis*. Such a trancelike condition can be caused by any number of situations. The hypnotic powers of a single standard might overtake us when we allow personal bias or prejudice to prevent us from considering other standards. Equally hypnotic is the condition of finding a lower-cost standard which serves part of our problem, tending to make us overlook its effect on the overall cost. In both of these situations, we may use a standard component, even a low-cost standard, but in the long run we may bring about adverse effects on our overall design or total cost because of this component's interaction with others.

Another trap or pitfall into which we can easily be drawn has been expressed in the form of an equation: *standards = fire*. This is so stated due to the fact that to us standards are just like fire. Fire, if we control it, is a servant to us; but if we do not control it, it can cause us untold misery, harm, and even death. In industry, standards, like fire, must be controlled. For when they are controlled, they serve industry and us; but when they are allowed to control industry and us, they will wreak untold misery, harm, and even industrial death (i.e., bankruptcy).

In our use of company and industrial standards, we must be ever alert for the bountiful benefits as well as the disabling traps and pitfalls.

From this technique it is but a short step to consultation with vendors and specialists.

## Consult Vendors and Specialists

As individuals, we know that our most priceless asset, our time, is given meaning by just two things: our ability to think our way through problems and our ability to translate our thoughts into effective action—to produce desired results.

We have also learned that the production of desired results, most times, takes more than personal experience. In fact, experience is not necessarily our best teacher; at times, it may become our greatest obstacle.

Keeping these bits of basic knowledge in mind, we can forcefully apply this technique. We combine our efforts with those of others to best utilize our asset of time. By working with vendors and specialists, we deliberately offset any possible disadvantages of our own experiences.

We must readily employ these individuals in the Investigation Phase because we know that specialized knowledge can prove a useful and reliable source of valuable information to us. Often, because of his accumulated knowledge and experience in a particular field, an outside individual is in a better position to evaluate an idea or suggest ways and means of improving it while reducing its cost.

Here we lay stress on the use of the services of "outsiders," on those outside our normal sphere of knowledge or contact. These outsiders can be individuals within our company or specialists from other companies. From their specialized knowledge and different approaches, we can glean many solutions to a particular part or parts of our problem. More often than not their experience in a particular field makes their advice invaluable in our search for a lower-cost, serviceable approach.

Usually, such experience or advice is offered at little or no cost on the grounds that it will eventually improve our business relationships. Certainly, such help will widen the scope of our knowledge and reduce the time and cost of completing our analysis. This is particularly so if we keep in mind that the vendor may have, or be on the verge of having, developed the very material or part that we are seeking.

To most effectively make use of the potential knowledge that is available to us, we must look to many areas such as:

Specialty manufacturers
Trade associations
Research organizations
Technical societies

All these and others may possess varying amounts of specialized knowledge. We must continually widen and update the scope of our contacts with these groups so that we shall always be in a position to consider today the new materials, processes, techniques, and knowledge that will be used tomorrow.

As before, we must guard against and avoid the various traps and pitfalls associated with this technique. The first and perhaps the most dangerous is what the vendors and specialists from whom we are seeking help classify as *industrial usury*. In this usage the term *usury* is not given its exact dictionary meaning. Rather, it is used as a slang expression to give a name to a poor industrial practice which is deliberately used by a few and unknowingly used by too many. Industrial usury occurs when a vendor or specialist is called in on a problem to which he devotes time, effort, and money and toward the solution of which he provides information, knowledge, or a product—only to have this material deliberately or unintentionally passed on to his competitors. Then these competitors, not having had to spend the corresponding time, effort, and money, can underbid the original vendor or specialist. This we must strongly guard against, as a particular vendor or specialist will allow it to happen only once. When it does occur, we shall have lost, from that time on, the help of that particular individual and his company.

The second pitfall, which is perhaps a part of the first, is the danger that we will find vendors and specialists who, while supposedly providing us with information, are in actuality pumping us for information: information about our company and other competitors' knowledge and prices. Through this second pitfall, we can lose in two ways: by being accused of industrial usury by the individual whose data we have given and by being trapped by the individual who has received the data.

The third pitfall into which we can be snared is that of overenthusiasm. In this condition we become so enraptured with a particular part of a vendor's or specialist's idea or product that we fail to evaluate it completely. In other words, we don't gather all the information and data and ofttimes end up with something that does not work or costs more than the solution we started with. This pitfall is also one of the major pitfalls that we can encounter in the last technique of this phase, that of using specialty products, processes, and materials.

## Use Specialty Products, Processes, and Materials

At first glance it might appear that this technique is in direct opposition to the first one discussed in this phase. This is by no means the case; in actuality, these two techniques complement rather than fight each other.

We have discussed and are now familiar with the various benefits to be derived from standards and standardization. From our viewpoint, however, it is necessary to review continually the use of acceptable "specials" in the light that what is a special today may well become a standard tomorrow. It must also be recognized that what we consider a special, in our scope of endeavor, may well be a standard elsewhere.

With the continued and rapid development of new products, processes, and materials and the improvement of existing ones, materials previously considered ideally suited for a particular function now represent less value than others currently available. For example, a new or improved technology, in one way or another, may provide a lower-cost and/or improved product. Similarly, such a new technology may well replace that which is specified for use in the product.

Naturally, we cannot hope to master all new developments in specialty products, processes, procedures, and materials; but we can and must be aware of all new technologies. At the same time, we must be prepared to call in experts in these fields at the proper time, either during the development of a new product or when analyzing the value of an existing product.

In the use of this technique as well as the other two in this phase, we must constantly consider the total cost of the product, using standards when they provide the lowest total cost and specials when they provide the lowest total cost.

In actuality, since the three techniques of this phase are so closely related and since they overlap so distinctly, we find that the traps and pitfalls of one apply directly or indirectly to the other two.

One trap, however, that is almost completely confined to this technique is that of proceeding in the use of a specialty item before it has been completely developed. Such use can often lead to wasted time, effort, and money if the specialty product, process, or material does not prove out.

As you can see, these techniques, like the rest, do not involve any magic. They entail only hard, intensive work—work that continues even though the first, second, or third solution to a problem may be reasonably workable or unworkable. Work must continue on these until every roadblock has been successfully disposed of and a reliable product has been developed at a lower total cost.

## Final Functional Development of Alternatives

In moving from the Evaluation Phase through the Investigation Phase, we carry our functionally developed alternatives from a semifinished to a finished state. This is to say, we take these alternatives which showed, through comparison, the greatest potential value and carry them to a conclusion whereby they work and sell.

We concluded the Evaluation Phase at a point where we were of the opinion that one or more of our functionally developed alternatives would work but needed additional development to make them sell or be acceptable to the final user. At this stage and condition, we approached the Investigation Phase and its supporting techniques. These techniques, whose workings, traps, and pitfalls have been discussed singly and in detail, can now be applied to finish our functionally developed alternatives.

The use and application to this final development, however, is one of the most difficult to explain. This is caused by two conditions. The first of these is the broad overlapping and interaction of these techniques. Second is the intricacy of our intuitive use of them, which has developed, often unknown to us, over a period of time. As with other techniques used intuitively, we must make a specific effort to apply them knowingly and to best advantage.

These techniques are used to best advantage when applied to the minimizing and elimination of the problems (disadvantages) detailed in our evaluation by comparison. They are also used to further enhance the values and broaden the advantages detailed in our comparison.

Our first step is to closely review company standards to determine if one or more of these incorporate or have incorporated in the past the solution to one or more of the stipulated disadvantages. These should be deliberately studied both in whole and in part for such possible solutions. Most times, when doing this review, company specialists who deal with standards are actively consulted for help and guidance. When such is the case, as in any consultation, the consultation summary (Figure 10-1) worksheet is used to keep a record of the source of information, the information received, and action taken on that information. It is important to note here that this is done so that, when your project is completed, credit can be given where credit is due.

The next step is to consult closely with vendors and specialists outside our immediate area and company to determine how they can help overcome our problems and disadvantages. Here we work both with standards and with specialty products, processes, and materials. In this endeavor, we must keep two things constantly in mind: First, individuals, like ourselves, must have as much information as possible if they are to help us; and second, their and our objective must be *the lowest total cost*.

When working with outside suppliers and vendors, it is best to use the

JOY MANUFACTURING COMPANY                    REF. No._____

CONSULTATION SUMMARY

PRODUCT _____
PROJECT _____                    DRAWING No._____
IDEA BEING DEVELOPED _____

| SOURCE OF INFORMATION | INFORMATION RECEIVED | ACTION TAKEN |
|---|---|---|
| | | |

TEAM MEMBERS _____                    DATE _____

FORM NO. 8817  12—66                    VALUE ENGINEERING

Figure 10-1

```
┌─────────────────────────────────────────────────────────────────────┐
│ (JOY)  JOY  MANUFACTURING  COMPANY              Ref.  No._____  │
│                    VENDOR  QUOTATION  SUMMARY                         │
│                                                                       │
│  PRODUCT_____ │
│  PART NAME _____ DRAWING No._____ │
│  BASIC APPROACH _____ │
│  VENDOR'S NAME & ADDRESS:                                            │
│      I. _____ │
│      2. _____ │
│      3. _____ │
│  ADDITIONAL DATA FOR VENDORS:                                       │
│                                                                       │
│                                                                       │
│         VENDOR  QUOTATION        VENDOR I   VENDOR 2   VENDOR 3      │
│  UNIT PRICE/QUANTITY OF                                              │
│      _____          $  /      $  /      $  /         │
│      _____          $  /      $  /      $  /         │
│      _____          $  /      $  /      $  /         │
│  TOOLING                                                             │
│  DELIVERY                                                            │
│  VENDOR REMARKS:                                                    │
│                                                                       │
│  TEAM MEMBERS _____ DATE _____        │
│  FORM NO. 8818  12-66                   VALUE  ENGINEERING           │
└─────────────────────────────────────────────────────────────────────┘
```

Figure 10-2

vendor quotation summary (Figure 10-2) to evaluate the various quotations and to keep track of specific data supplied by each individual. This can and should be used for comparing different methods and approaches for attaining the same result.

In order to obtain the maximum results from the techniques of this phase, it is essential that we communicate all available data to every individual with whom we have contact. Thus they too will be working from a broad base of knowledge and will therefore be able to provide us with more meaningful data and ideas by which we can overcome our problems and disadvantages. In this manner, we end up with a solution or solutions which are both workable and salable.

The work in this phase is not of a type that can be forced. In actuality, once the problems have been firmly thought out and established in our minds, it is much like hypnosis; for hypnosis is a combination of mental relaxation and imagination. We must work on the mental relaxation by first opening our minds; by breathing deeply of that which others have to offer and by exhaling all our established prejudices, negative thoughts, and mental roadblocks. We must learn to enjoy this experience. As we listen, breathing in and breathing out, our cue word is *relax*. As we exhale, we must let all the tension go out of our minds like sand running through a sieve. By so mentally relaxing, by letting everything go, we empty our minds like sponges wrung dry of water and leave them clear to absorb all new knowledge and data.

Now forget your breathing and turn that job over to your subconscious mind, that part of the mind that handles all your body functions expertly and efficiently. Notice the quietness that comes into your thinking. This is the nature of our subconscious minds. The quietness of the mind affects the quietness of the emotions and the quietness of the body. One interacts on the others to create tranquillity, calm, and poise. Don't try, don't push, don't press. Just listen. Just let your mind absorb.

Use your imagination now. Let a relaxing, successful development experience come into your mind's eye, some accomplishment where you really felt completely relaxed and at ease. Let it come into your mind's eye clearly and vividly as if you had just accomplished it. Now you can relive that pleasant experience. Relax with your problem. The things that formerly disturbed you will no longer bother you, for you realize that in the total scope all disturbing details are insignificant. With your new relaxed attitude, you can put them in their insignificant drawer. You are calm and relaxed inside and meet each problem with a new vision. Each problem is a new opportunity for accomplishment. Make each opportunity the best possible! In so doing, this attitude will become apparent to your associates and anyone who comes in contact with you.

Use your imagination now and see the new relaxed approach to each problem, the new calm and tranquillity, the handling of each problem, the ease of creative expression and development. Notice how quickly you move from one problem to the next. See the control of your emotions and feel the satisfaction in the progress of new developments. You now have constructed a new image of yourself and will match that image in thought and action.

Negative thinking not only saps our energy but, like any habit, can become a pattern. When a negative thought enters your mind you can turn it off instantly and substitute a constructive idea. It isn't a matter of cutting out anything. Since two thoughts cannot occupy the mind at the same time, as soon as you call in the positive thought, the negative thought must go.

With the acceptance of the mental relaxation and imagination by your subconscious mind, your former negative thinking is relinquished and nullified. Your subconscious mind then unleashes a fountain of constructive forces and ideas for your mental and physical development. Your subconscious and conscious minds will then do everything to bring these ideas to fruition.

In this endeavor, we must make up our minds once and for all to withdraw our attention from criticism and defects, our own or anyone else's. We cannot expect perfection from ourselves or anyone else. All we can hope for is progress, and we must help ourselves to attain this progress by self-improvement and change of attitude.

By developing such an attitude while using the techniques of this phase, you will find that your basic ideas are brought to fruition in the final phase of the Job Plan: the Recommendation Phase.

Chapter Eleven

# Recommendation Phase

In undertaking this phase, we are approaching the culmination of all our previous efforts. Therefore, we must be sure that we are *ready, reasonable,* and *right.*

Individuals using the Value Engineering Methodology will readily tell us that they consider the Recommendation Phase the most difficult part of the entire Job Plan. This is not because of the work or effort that is required in this phase. Rather, it is because the fruits of all previous efforts hang on the successful accomplishment of this phase.

The goal that we must attain here is to motivate positive action. Our defense must be to prevent the generation of a negative reaction. Actually, in this phase, we shall be proposing a change. The objective of this proposal, like that of a proposal of marriage, is to receive a positive answer. Therefore, like a proposal of marriage, our proposal for change must be carefully planned, correctly stated, and resolutely carried through to a successful conclusion.

In working through the preceding phases of the Job Plan, you have attempted and accomplished many difficult tasks. You have had to progress from the observation of a need, to the gathering and sorting of facts, to the specific definition and evaluation of the problem and its parts, to creative development, to discovery and responding to intuition, and finally to the development of a workable form. All these tasks have been accomplished through a precise, organized plan. All these have finally brought you to this final phase. Also, all of them point out that this final phase must be accomplished by and with a specific plan. This plan is but a continuation of the overall organized approach.

This final part of the plan, in the last analysis, brings us to the elements of sensible salesmanship; and each one of us is a salesman, for, in truth, we are selling ourselves and our ideas daily. We may be doing it intuitively, but in truth we are constantly selling. Here again we must do it knowingly.

Such knowing salesmanship comprises presenting our ideas, solutions, and changes in terms of benefits to the user. These benefits must be shown and proved by the use of complete facts, accurate information, detailed costs, and a positive conviction. A weakness or shortage in any one of these vital areas can produce an unwanted negative reaction in others, which, in turn, could possibly stymie our own desire to pursue the problem further.

Throughout our planning, we must constantly remember that it is not a part of human nature to accept change readily. We must also bear in mind that in the realm of accepting change, each individual tends to be different. Some individuals resist any change, while others see the need for it very quickly. Some individuals require infinite detail, while others are better equipped to take a raw idea and personally refine it into a workable form. Individuals also differ in the degree of their tenacity and in their ability to absorb factual data. All these things must be considered and dealt with in our final plan.

A major part of our task, then, is in knowing the makeup of the individual with whom we are dealing, finding and understanding how best to approach and deal with him, and determining what we must do to have him accept and put to use our idea, solution, or change.

Such knowledge requires deliberate study of the individual to whom we plan to present our ideas and makes real planning possible. Based on this knowledge of the individual, we must plan the program of our recommendation approach and carry out a reasoned execution of that plan. Such planning and execution must incorporate not only the recommending but the total implementation of our idea or ideas. Without the specific knowledge of the individual and a detailed plan, we are quite likely to contract the common malady sometimes referred to as "foot-in-mouth disease." On the other hand, if we are properly prepared, we shall have the ability to let the other fellow have *our* way.

In order to be certain that we are ready, reasonable, and right, we must prepare our facts so that we can look at the complete problem and each of its parts as if we were looking through the other fellow's eyes. When we have reached this point, we can proceed with our recommendation through the presentation of facts and costs.

The recommendation worksheet presents both facts and costs; both must be presented with extreme care and in the proper manner. Because of the vital importance of their presentation, they will be discussed separately.

## Present Facts

*A little tact and wise management may often evade resistance, and carry a point, where direct force might be in vain.*

Truth, like beauty, varies in its fashions and is best recommended by different means to different minds. Therefore, before you recommend, think it through. In your presentation of facts, you must use the plain facts, presenting them one at a time. In this manner, you build one fact upon another, overlapping and interlocking them, as you would build a strong wall. Facts and truth, so presented, ward off the possible use of generalities both for and against your idea.

In dealing with the presentation of your facts in this phase of the Job Plan, you must be just as careful and deliberate as you were in the securing of facts in the Information Phase. When you gathered your facts at the beginning, you had to be sure that they were not hearsay, half-truths, or opinions. In the presentation of facts, the shoe is on the other foot, for you must be equally careful that, in your zeal to have your idea accepted, you do not shade the truth or present a partial picture.

Facts and truth come slowly and are accepted gradually. You must be constantly measuring the ground you are treading, reviewing with a curious eye to see that everything is right while also surveying and choosing your onward path. In choosing this onward path, you must try to envision all the possible roadblocks ahead. This is best accomplished by viewing the problem, idea, and facts through the other person's eyes. By so doing, you can overcome, beforehand, these objections and roadblocks by the judicious use of factual examples and apt comparisons.

As in the presentation of facts, in the Recommendation Phase you must deal with both parts of the problem: the before and after. You must, as a matter of reference and review, present the facts dealing with the problem as you undertook it. You must, as a motivator for action, present the facts dealing with the problem as you recommend it should be solved and outline the action necessary to bring this solution into being. In both cases, these facts must be presented concisely yet completely. It should be remembered that it is always more effective, even if more difficult, to present a point with a few words than with many.

In presenting the facts about the problem as you undertook it, you should first stipulate the overall conditions wherein the specific problem was detected. Next, it is advisable to outline the points which led you to seek a solution to the particular problem. These points are better established by two or three specific facts than by a thousand arguments, for truth and certainty are obtained only from facts.

In presenting the facts about your solution or solutions to the problem, you should point out your specific findings regarding the various parts of the problem. Then you must show how those findings and resultant solutions have been melded and forged into one integral solution. In this presentation of facts, facts requesting and requiring change, you must move slowly in order that the truth contained in the facts may be digested. For facts and truth, like food, must be taken in small palatable pieces, chewed, swallowed, and digested. A recommendation for change, like an enjoyable meal, is composed of many small and acceptable parts.

In both the presentation of the problem and its solution, a pictorial description, where applicable, will greatly help you to present the situation concisely and completely. This is so because a picture is worth ten thousand words and also because a picture provides a general background for any details you plan to give later for a particular application.

All the technical facts, truths, and drawings, no matter how precise, would be of little use if they were not supported by an equally precise presentation of costs. Therefore, of equal concern in this phase is the presentation of costs.

## Present Costs

*Before you recommend, think it through. What*
*are the realistic, not optimistic, cost savings to*
*be realized?*

Costs, as you present them in this phase, are another group of facets on your jewel of facts. In the presentation of costs, as with all facts, you must be sure that they are realistic, not optimistic.

Meaningful, realistic costs are the vital facets which can make your jewel of facts desirable or undesirable. The presentation of these facts must be carefully planned so that your jewel of facts is well balanced. When balanced in this way, the beauty of this gem becomes awesome. It is strange how deeply its colors and hues seem to penetrate one like a scent from a fragrant flower.

These costs must include many facets which are cut with precision and polished with exactness. These facets include those of present cost, recommended cost, implementation costs, and, most important, expected cost savings.

The first is rather straightforward and is simply a presentation or restatement of that which is already known. The latter three, however, are, to a degree, unknown. At best, they are extrapolations of small quantity development runs; at worst, they are intelligent estimates. Therefore, in actuality, it is to your long-term advantage to be highly critical of what you present. In dealing with these then, it is best to overstate the amounts of the first two (recommended cost and implementation cost) and to understate the last (expected cost savings).

The latter is of the greatest importance. Overstated savings are always uncovered, and from that point on all future savings will be considered exaggerated by at least 50 percent. This has been found to be a common characteristic of human nature. Similarly, if the savings are understated, the same trait of human nature exerts itself and all future savings are likewise considered understated.

Therefore you must present accurate costs, costs which have meaning both to you and to those to whom they are presented. One way of accomplishing this is to approach and discuss them as if you were discussing your own money. In this way, you will not just be talking about cold, hard numbers but about something that has meaning. In essence, you get these costs to become living, meaningful things in everyone's mind.

Since this jewel of facts and costs is a many-faceted gem, it must be presented in the best light and in the most advantageous manner. For us, as with a gem, ofttimes the decision to accept or reject is made almost at the first glance. In order to present these facts and costs in their best light and in the most advantageous manner, the team recommendation is used.

## Team Recommendation

The team recommendation worksheet (Figure 11-1) is one of the most important worksheets you will complete in the total Job Plan. It is a one-page statement of the total facts about the whole problem with which you have been dealing. These facts must be presented in a simple, clear, and precise manner. They should, where possible, be accompanied by a simple sketch of both the present approach and the proposed change.

Your team recommendation must of necessity be kept short, so that the decision maker will both have and take the necessary time to read it completely. Each sketch, as the old maxim says, is equal to ten thousand words. In addition, the longer and more complex your presentation of the facts and your recommendation, the less probability there is that it will be read. Likewise, the less probability there is that it will be accepted.

When writing your recommendation, it is always best to try to envision all the possible roadblocks as well as to view your proposal from the other person's point of view. By doing this, you can overcome most of the basic

```
JOY  MANUFACTURING  COMPANY     COST/ IMPROVEMENT  RECOMMENDATION
                                PRIORITY_____
DATE _____                              REF.  NO. _____
PRODUCT_____  ASSY.  OR  PART_____
PART  NO._____  QTY. /PRODUCT _____ QTY. /YEAR _____

          POTENTIAL  IST  YEAR  SAVINGS  $            SALES FORECAST  _
                                                     (NEXT 12 MONTHS)   PRODUCT OR ASSY.

PRESENT                          RECOMMENDED




    CALCULATION  OF  SAVING   MATERIAL  DIRECT LABOR  FRINGE BENEFIT    TOTAL
  PRESENT                      $          $            $               $
  PROPOSED                     $          $            $               $
  DIFFERENCE PER PIECE OR ASSY. $         $            $               $
  IMPLEMENTATION COST -              MFG.  $_____    ENG.  $_____

FINDINGS  &  RECOMMENDATIONS:




APPROVED  BY _____  REJECTED _____   DATE _____
ENGINEERING  CHANGE  ORDER  NO. _____ FOR  FURTHER  INFO._____
TEAM  MEMBERS_____  FORM
```

Figure 11-1

objections by citing examples or comparisons to bring home your point. In some instances, the judicious use of the source of your basic idea (if other than your own) or basic information may create a favorable influence.

The major purpose of the team recommendation is twofold: to transmit the data the decision maker needs to take action and to make that action a positive action.   In addition, the team recommendation serves as a documentation of all the individuals who have participated in the developed solution, no matter how small their contribution.

This latter point is important since it gives each of the individuals a sense of belonging, recognition, and even a feeling of security.   Each of these is important to the acceptance of your present solution and equally important to all future work you will do.

In order that this one-page document should fulfill its basic and secondary requirements, precise planning must go into its completion. Not only are the facts, sketches, and reasoning of the utmost importance, but the intent behind them is important. The intent or construed intent behind the various parts of the team recommendation must come out positive if you are to motivate positive action.

In addition to your measurable facts, you should also state at the end of the team recommendation those benefits which cannot be directly or positively measured. Indirect savings in improved quality, reliability, maintainability, safety, reduced delivery time, etc., sometimes can mean the difference between acceptance and rejection.

The final step of the Recommendation Phase is that of implementation. For if your ideas are accepted but not implemented, your efforts and those of your teammates have been in vain.

A number of completed, factual recommendation sheets are shown in Figures 11-2 to 11-10. These illustrate most of the points discussed above.

## Project Implementation

The art that each of us must learn is to tread the fine and delicate line between stagnation and change. Someone has said of God that "He is always pleased but never satisfied." That states the attitude which we must assume quite nicely. As a matter of fact, this is also the basic attitude that we must generate and develop in others.

The major factor involved in assuring total acceptance and use of your team recommendations is that the decision maker, like the project team members, must feel a sense of contribution, belonging, and security in that which is being implemented. If this is not achieved, your chances of success are drastically reduced.

Therefore it is toward this end that your project implementation efforts must be planned, directed, and carried out. In the development of the final recommendations, you had to study the individuals involved as well as the project. This you did so that your recommendation could be geared to them and their needs. In order to assure complete project implementation, these same basic factors and characteristics must be taken into account and properly dealt with. You must also realize that what was a successful approach or plan with one individual may not be equally successful with the next individual with whom you must work. This is caused by the simple fact of human nature that each of us is indeed an individual and as such acts and reacts in a different way to a common or similar situation. In essence, you must study and understand the broadest and deepest motivations of each of the individuals with whom you are dealing. You must then trans-

JOY MANUFACTURING COMPANY    COST/ IMPROVEMENT RECOMMENDATION

PRIORITY_____

DATE __Sept. 5__    REF. NO. _Greenock 66_

PRODUCT _Mine Conveyor_    ASSY. OR PART _Flight Assembly_

PART NO. _473201 & 473202_    QTY. /PRODUCT _Varies_    QTY. /YEAR _5,116_

POTENTIAL IST YEAR SAVINGS  $ _5371.00_    SALES FORECAST (NEXT 12 MONTHS) _-6,000_PRODUCT OR ASSY.

PRESENT    RECOMMENDED

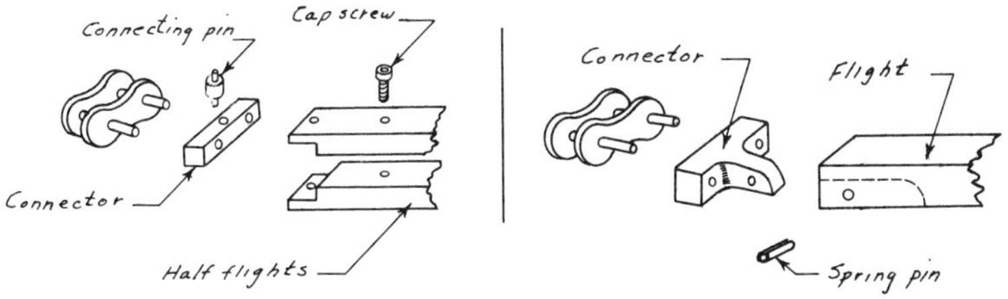

| CALCULATION OF SAVING | MATERIAL | DIRECT LABOR | FRINGE BENEFIT | TOTAL |
|---|---|---|---|---|
| PRESENT | $ 2.40 | $ 2.10 | $ .70 | $ 5.20 |
| PROPOSED | $ 1.75 | $ 1.80 | $ .60 | $ 4.15 |
| DIFFERENCE PER PIECE OR ASSY. | $ .65 | $ .30 | $ .10 | $ 1.05 |
| IMPLEMENTATION COST – | | MFG. $ 480.00 | ENG. $ 720.00 | |

FINDINGS & RECOMMENDATIONS:

On investigation of a customer complaint regarding breakage of the flight assembly, it was found that this assembly was being manufactured from an off- standard material. This caused, in addition to the breakage problem, high material cost and material delivery delivery delays. Stress analysis of the off-standard material in this application brought to light a design weakness.

By using standard material and redesigning with fewer parts, the present weak point can be eliminated. The new concept will be lower in cost while reducing the number of parts to be carried in inventory.

New Numbers  475823 - Connector - 2 required
475824 - Flight    - 1    "
424 x 167 - Spring pin - 1    "

APPROVED BY _H. Ross_    REJECTED _____    DATE _Sept. 5_

ENGINEERING CHANGE ORDER NO. _E.D. 1475_    FOR FURTHER INFO. _A. Laird_

TEAM MEMBERS _J. Bennett, J. Wasson_    FORM

Figure 11-2

JOY MANUFACTURING COMPANY   COST/ IMPROVEMENT RECOMMENDATION

PRIORITY _____

DATE _December 22_                            REF. NO. _Greenock 101_

PRODUCT _Towels_         ASSY. OR PART _—_

PART NO. _—_              QTY. /PRODUCT _—_     QTY. /YEAR _—_

| POTENTIAL IST YEAR SAVINGS $ 300.00 | SALES FORECAST (NEXT 12 MONTHS) _—_ | PRODUCT OR ASSY. |
|---|---|---|

PRESENT                          RECOMMENDED

Paper towels = $40.00/month                   Paper towels = $50.00/month

Laundry of cloth towels = $35.00/month

Total = $75.00/month = $900/year            Total = $50/month = $600/year

| CALCULATION OF SAVING | MATERIAL | DIRECT LABOR | FRINGE BENEFIT | TOTAL |
|---|---|---|---|---|
| PRESENT | $ 900.00 | $ | $ | $ 900.00 |
| PROPOSED | $ 600.00 | $ | $ | $ 600.00 |
| DIFFERENCE PER PIECE OR ASSY. | $ 300.00 | $ | $ | $ 300.00 |
| IMPLEMENTATION COST – | | MFG. $ _—_ | ENG. $ _—_ | |

FINDINGS & RECOMMENDATIONS:

It was found that eight toilets in the plant were using paper towels and that two were using cloth towels. Because of the high cost required to launder the cloth towels for two toilets, it was recommended that paper towels be used throughout the plant.

This change will allow our personnel to service all facilities and eliminate the necessity for outside services.

APPROVED BY _A. EDEN_     REJECTED _____     DATE _12/22_

ENGINEERING CHANGE ORDER NO. _____     FOR FURTHER INFO. _A. Laird_

TEAM MEMBERS _B. Whitson, Nurse Davis_

Figure 11-3

JOY MANUFACTURING COMPANY    COST/ IMPROVEMENT RECOMMENDATION

PRIORITY _____ —

DATE _November 26_

PRODUCT _Compressors_

PART NO. _901313-3_

ASSY. OR PART _Lube System_

REF. NO. _Michigan city 12_

QTY. /PRODUCT _____ 1 _____   QTY. /YEAR _200_

POTENTIAL IST YEAR SAVINGS  $ _652 00_   | SALES FORECAST (NEXT 12 MONTHS) - _200_ PRODUCT OR ASSY.

PRESENT

1-901313-3 Drain cock - $2.52
1-902466-22 Nipple - $.03
                        $2.55
        Assem L & B $1.60
                        $4.15

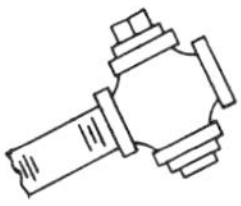

Brass

RECOMMENDED

1-901204 1/2" Pipe plug - $.04
        Assem L & B  -$.80
                        $.84

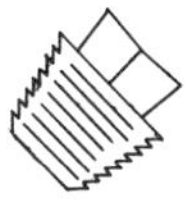

Steel

| CALCULATION OF SAVING | MATERIAL | DIRECT LABOR | FRINGE BENEFIT | TOTAL |
|---|---|---|---|---|
| PRESENT | $ 2.55 | $ 1.20 | $ .40 | $ 4.15 |
| PROPOSED | $ .04 | $ .60 | $ .20 | $ .84 |
| DIFFERENCE PER PIECE OR ASSY. | $ 2.51 | $ .60 | $ .20 | $ 3.31 |

IMPLEMENTATION COST –     MFG. $ ____ —     ENG. $ _10 00_

FINDINGS & RECOMMENDATIONS:

In the course of the value engineering task force efforts to standardize the vertical single cylinder assembly, this sub-assembly was analyzed.

From this analysis, it was determined that the $4.15 solid brass subassembly was too expensive to perform the function required, i.e. "close opening".

It is therefore recommended that a standard steel pipe plug, costing $.84 installed, be used.

This change can be put into effect without waiting for completion of the task force effort.

APPROVED BY _S. Leven_     REJECTED _____     DATE _12/17_

ENGINEERING CHANGE ORDER NO. _E.O 1874_     FOR FURTHER INFO. _E.C Hutton_

TEAM MEMBERS _H. Ponting, A. Simson, D. Ray, F. Wendt_     FORM

Figure 11-4

JOY MANUFACTURING COMPANY    COST/ IMPROVEMENT RECOMMENDATION

PRIORITY_____

DATE __*May 13*__

PRODUCT__*Lamp Socket Carton*__

PART NO._____

REF. NO. *New Philadelphia-3*

ASSY. OR PART ____

QTY. /PRODUCT ___*1*___    QTY. /YEAR _*9,000*_

POTENTIAL IST YEAR SAVINGS $ *63* $\frac{00}{}$

SALES FORECAST (NEXT 12 MONTHS) *-9,000* PRODUCT OR ASSY.

PRESENT             RECOMMENDED

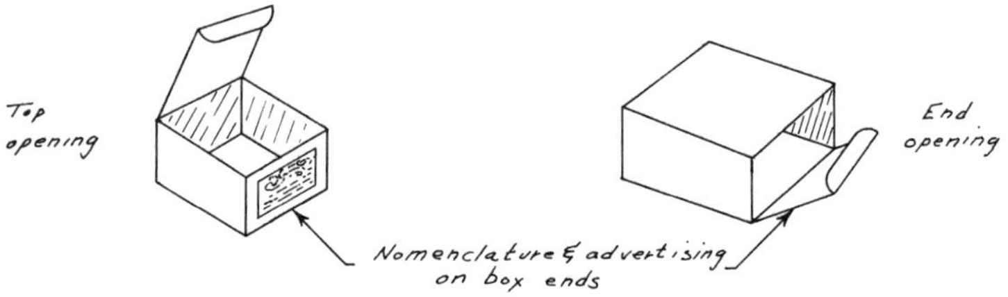

Top opening

End opening

Nomenclature & advertising on box ends

| CALCULATION OF SAVING | MATERIAL | DIRECT LABOR | FRINGE BENEFIT | TOTAL |
|---|---|---|---|---|
| PRESENT | $ .089 | $ | $ | $ .089 |
| PROPOSED | $ .082 | $ | $ | $ .082 |
| DIFFERENCE PER PIECE OR ASSY. | $ .007 | $ | $ | $ .007 |
| IMPLEMENTATION COST – | | MFG. $ ___ — | ENG. $ ___ — | |

FINDINGS & RECOMMENDATIONS:

As a result of the investigation of the total vibration-proof lamp socket product line, the shipping carton was also analyzed.

From this analysis and close cooperation with the carton manufacturer, it has been determined that savings can be realized on this part.

It is recommended that, starting with the next order for these cartons, an end-opening design (as shown above) be ordered in place of the present top-opening type. Base material, nomenclature, and advertising are to remain the same.

This minor modification, requiring no tooling or engineering costs, will provide a 7.9% savings in the cost of the carton.

APPROVED BY _*F. Harrel*_   REJECTED _____   DATE _*5/14*_

ENGINEERING CHANGE ORDER NO._____ FOR FURTHER INFO._____

TEAM MEMBERS _*D. Robinson, C. Schultz, C. Brown, G. Thim*_   FORM

Figure 11-5

JOY MANUFACTURING COMPANY    COST/ IMPROVEMENT RECOMMENDATION

PRIORITY_____

DATE _Sept 9th_____    REF. NO. _Franklin 11___

PRODUCT _Conveyor_____    ASSY. OR PART _Loop____

PART NO. _381789_____    QTY. /PRODUCT _____    QTY. /YEAR _48,000_

POTENTIAL IST YEAR SAVINGS  $ _10,550 00_    SALES FORECAST _____    PRODUCT OR ASSY.
(NEXT 12 MONTHS)

PRESENT                          RECOMMENDED

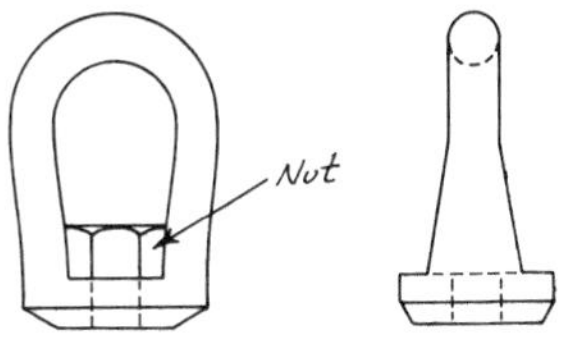

~Nut

*No Longer Required*

| CALCULATION OF SAVING | MATERIAL | DIRECT LABOR | FRINGE BENEFIT | TOTAL |
|---|---|---|---|---|
| PRESENT | $ .22 | $ | $ | $ .22 |
| PROPOSED | $ — | $ | $ | $ — |
| DIFFERENCE PER PIECE OR ASSY. | $ .22 | $ | $ | $ .22 |
| IMPLEMENTATION COST – | | MFG. $ — | ENG. $ 10 00 | |

FINDINGS & RECOMMENDATIONS:

When this piece was designed into the conveyor assembly, it was to allow the maintainence personnel to tighten the contained nut by inserting a pipe or rod into the loop.

Since the time of the original design, the maintainence personnel have changed their basic tools, i.e., they now carry a Crescent wrench in place of a pipe or rod. With this change and with the loop in place, the maintainence personnel have to use the handle of the Crescent wrench for tightening the nut.

It is recommended that this piece be eliminated, thereby reducing our material cost and allowing the customers' maintainence personnel to use their tools properly.

This elimination will also provide secondary savings in reduced purchase orders and inventory costs.

APPROVED BY _F. Delli-Gatti___    REJECTED _____    DATE _____

ENGINEERING CHANGE ORDER NO. _FAS 937_____    FOR FURTHER INFO. _G. C. Dalmaso__

TEAM MEMBERS _J. Davis , T. Shuttstall_____    FORM

Figure 11-6

JOY MANUFACTURING COMPANY    COST/ IMPROVEMENT RECOMMENDATION

PRIORITY_____

DATE _May 13_____                                REF.  NO. _New Philadalphia 31A_
PRODUCT_vibration-proof lamp socket_    ASSY. OR PART _X 8360-2_
PART NO. _X 8360-2_                     QTY. /PRODUCT _____/_____  QTY. /YEAR _9,000_

POTENTIAL IST YEAR SAVINGS  $ _2,286_ _00_    SALES FORECAST
                                              (NEXT 12 MONTHS) _-9000_ PRODUCT OR ASSY.

PRESENT                              RECOMMENDED

| CALCULATION OF SAVING | MATERIAL | DIRECT LABOR | FRINGE BENEFIT | TOTAL |
|---|---|---|---|---|
| PRESENT | $ 1.100 | $ .464 | $ .155 | $ 1.719 |
| PROPOSED | $ .906 | $ .344 | $ .115 | $ 1.465 |
| DIFFERENCE PER PIECE OR ASSY. | $ .094 | $ .120 | $ .040 | $ .254 |
| IMPLEMENTATION COST – | MFG. $ — | | ENG. $ 30 00 | |

FINDINGS & RECOMMENDATIONS:

Through intensive study, it was found that the brass eyelets protected the molded material from being cut by the mounting screws and that fiber washers held the screws in place after assembly. It was further determind that at installation the fiber washers were removed and thown away. The investigation also revealed that considerable hand labor in manufacture was being used to separate and strip the twin conductor wire to two different lengths for assembly to the socket.

It is recommended: That the fiber retaining washers and brass eyelets be eliminated, their functions to be accomplished by molding the support ring in the body of the lamp socket, thus providing the necessary protection; that the thin molded membrane be left in the screw holes to serve as a retainer for the screws; that single conductor wire be used in place of the twin conductor, thus eliminating the hand labor and allowing for machine stripping of the wires plus ease of assembly.

No additional tooling cost will be incurred, as molds are being change at this time, to injection-mold this assembly.

By maintaining the present competitive selling price, this 14% cost improvement will increase the product profit to acceptable possition

APPROVED BY _T. Harrell_    REJECTED _____    DATE _May 13_
ENGINEERING CHANGE ORDER NO. _____  FOR FURTHER INFO. _F. Hubert_
TEAM MEMBERS _D. Robinson, C. Schultz, K. Bueler, G. Thim_         FORM

Figure 11-7

JOY MANUFACTURING COMPANY    COST/ IMPROVEMENT RECOMMENDATION

PRIORITY_____

DATE _Sept. 3_____    REF. NO. _Franklin - 215_

PRODUCT _Conveyor_____    ASSY. OR PART _Bearing Housing_

PART NO. _1554979_____    QTY./PRODUCT  _2_  QTY./YEAR _150,000_

POTENTIAL IST YEAR SAVINGS $ 36,500    SALES FORECAST _-200,000_ PRODUCT OR ASSY.
(NEXT 12 MONTHS)

PRESENT                         RECOMMENDED

Machine form
casting

Deep-drawn and
sized stamping

| CALCULATION OF SAVING | MATERIAL | DIRECT LABOR | FRINGE BENEFIT | TOTAL |
|---|---|---|---|---|
| PRESENT | $ .43 | $ .18 | $ .06 | $ .67 |
| PROPOSED | $ .36 | $ — | $ — | $ .36 |
| DIFFERENCE PER PIECE OR ASSY. | $ .07 | $ .18 | $ .06 | $ .31 |

IMPLEMENTATION COST –    MFG. $ _9,000 00_    ENG. $ _1,000 00_

FINDINGS & RECOMMENDATIONS:

After the evaluation of various methods of manufacture and other
metallic and nonmetallic materials, it is recommended that this part
be a deep-drawn and sized stamping

The present method entails the purchase of a casting at $.43 each
and adding an additional $.24 in labor and fringe to each piece. The
proposed deep-drawn and sized part, at $.36 each, would be recieved
ready for assembly into the conveyor rollers.

In addition to the direct savings, in the following areas, should accrue:
a. Reduction in plant scrap          e. Improved assembly methods
b. Reduced production planning       f. Elimination of special work area
c. Elimination of special machine tools
d. Reduced incoming transportation (present 34 oz, recommended 11 oz)

At the present rate of usage, all implementation costs would amortized
on the first 35,000 parts.

APPROVED BY _F. Delli-Gatti_    REJECTED _____  DATE _Sept. 4_

ENGINEERING CHANGE ORDER NO. _FAS 1025_    FOR FURTHER INFO. _G. Dalmaso_

TEAM MEMBERS _J. Cihon, J. Biery   T. Shuffstall_    FORM

**Figure 11-8**

---

JOY MANUFACTURING COMPANY    COST/ IMPROVEMENT RECOMMENDATION

PRIORITY _____

DATE _December 5_

PRODUCT _Conveyor_    REF. NO. _Frankin 69_

PART NO. _155 4872_    ASSY. OR PART _Anchor stand_

QTY. /PRODUCT ____    QTY. /YEAR _998_

---

POTENTIAL 1ST YEAR SAVINGS  $ _/3/3 °°_ | SALES FORECAST (NEXT 12 MONTHS) _-1500_ PRODUCT OR ASSY.

| PRESENT | RECOMMENDED |
|---|---|

PRESENT:

2 - Drawings (3 pcs)
3 - Production orders
   a. cut sides
   b. cut & form bottom
   c. weld sides to bottom

RECOMMENDED:

1 - Drawing
1 - Production order
   - cut & form 3" channel

| CALCULATION OF SAVING | MATERIAL | DIRECT LABOR | FRINGE BENEFIT | TOTAL |
|---|---|---|---|---|
| PRESENT | $ 1.00 | $ .84 | $ .28 | $ 2.12 |
| PROPOSED | $ .43 | $ .12 | $ .04 | $ .59 |
| DIFFERENCE PER PIECE OR ASSY. | $ .67 | $ .72 | $ .24 | $ 1.53 |
| IMPLEMENTATION COST - | | MFG. $ 113 °° | ENG. $ 100 °° | |

FINDINGS & RECOMMENDATIONS:

In the process of analyzing conveyor products, subassembly came to light as a high-cost component. The performance of the function "support weight" con, in this case, be accomplished for a lower cost than $2.12 each

Our recommendation is that, instead of a weldment, we take advantage of our present equipment and make this subassembly from formed 3" channel.

By using formed channel, we will be able to eliminate parts drawings from the system as well as reduce the number of production orders required to achieve the finished part

APPROVED BY _F Delli - Gatti_    REJECTED _____    DATE _Dec 6_

ENGINEERING CHANGE ORDER NO. _FAS 776_    FOR FURTHER INFO. _G.C. Dalmaso_

TEAM MEMBERS _D. Murphy, C. Delong, J.E. Reagle, G.A. Black_    FORM

---

Figure 11-9

JOY MANUFACTURING COMPANY    COST/ IMPROVEMENT RECOMMENDATION

PRIORITY_____

DATE _Nov. 26_____    REF. NO. _Michigan City -12_

PRODUCT _Compressor_____    ASSY. OR PART _Oil Level Gage_

PART NO. _A 204.356_____    QTY. /PRODUCT _____    QTY. /YEAR _300_

POTENTIAL IST YEAR SAVINGS  $ _494_ 00    | SALES FORECAST (NEXT 12 MONTHS) _-450_ PRODUCT OR ASSY.

| PRESENT | RECOMMENDED |
|---|---|

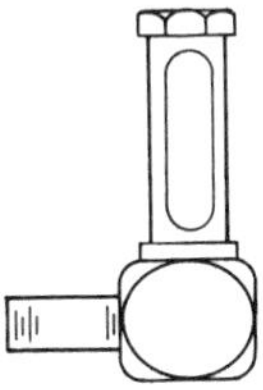

| CALCULATION OF SAVING | MATERIAL | DIRECT LABOR | FRINGE BENEFIT | TOTAL |
|---|---|---|---|---|
| PRESENT | $ 3.02 | $ | $ | $ 3.02 |
| PROPOSED | $ 1.20 | $ | $ | $ 1.20 |
| DIFFERENCE PER PIECE OR ASSY. | $ 1.82 | $ | $ | $ 1.82 |
| IMPLEMENTATION COST – | | MFG. $ 12 00 | ENG. $ 40 00 | |

FINDINGS & RECOMMENDATIONS:

It has been determined that in our present compressor design it is necessary to provide the function "indicate level."

It has been found that this function in now being provided on the compressor by a solid - brass oil level indicating tube assembly at a cost of $3.02 each. It has been further determined that a 2" diameter oil level indicating window is used to perform the same function on another company compressor product line.

We recommend that the means of providing this function be standardized, i.e, that we use the 2" diameter oil level window in all applications. This standardization will provide a direct net savings the first year of $432.00. We will also realize indirect savings as a result of reduced purchase orders, inventory, and scrap.

APPROVED BY _S. Leven_    REJECTED _____    DATE _Dec. 17_
ENGINEERING CHANGE ORDER NO. _MAC 1029_    FOR FURTHER INFO. _E.C. Hutton_
TEAM MEMBERS _H. Ponting, A. Simson, D. Ray, E. Wendt_    FORM

Figure 11-10

late these motivations into a systematized plan and program of positive actions.

Since each situation will be different, no set of rules by which you can be positively assured of project implementation can be established. Imagination, creativity, and the ability to work with others is essential at this point. However, certain guidelines can be stated to help you proceed in the proper direction and help toward total project implementation.

These guidelines provide for two basic steps. The first is the establishment of a plan of action; the second is the development of a timetable for the accomplishment of that plan. These two steps are essential, and without them you cannot and should not proceed.

An action plan should be established before you make your recommendation to the decision maker. By doing this you can, when your recommendations are accepted, put forth a definitive action plan for their implementation. Your original plan may, of necessity, have to be modified, but it is a starting point from which the necessary planning and action decisions can be made for implementation. By having such a starting plan, these action-plan decisions can be made at the same time as the basic acceptance decision.

Your action plan should detail the responsibilities of each individual within the organization who is required to take action to properly and completely implement your recommendations. It must delineate, where necessary, such things as tests to be conducted, materials to be purchased, items to be manufactured, tools to be made or bought, when the change can best be phased into the cycle, and which specialists are to be responsible for these actions.

In conjunction with this action plan, you must have an action timetable which spells out both when each action is to start and when it is to conclude. It must also, where necessary, specify where individual actions overlap or present an interface.

Once the project has been accepted and your action plan and timetable have been finalized, you must follow up to see that the plan is started and pursued to completion. You will find that one of the easiest ways to be sure that your plan is started is to designate yourself as the individual required to take the first action step in the plan. This is so because the most difficult phase of the plan is to get it started. It has been said that "The longest journey starts with but a single step." It is then up to you to make sure that the first step is taken and that the buildup of momentum is started.

When your project implementation has been started and everyone knows the details of the plan, it is relatively easy to keep it moving to the desired conclusion.

Always keep in mind and be prepared for discouragement and setbacks.

By being ready for them, you can readily take positive actions to overcome or completely circumvent them.  If and when these occur, explore every possibility of a new approach, however ridiculous it might seem at the time, for your intuition and subconscious knowledge of the facts may be trying to tell you something of great importance.  Most times these discouragements and setbacks are simply new but much smaller problems which are quite easily solved as long as you don't allow them to become roadblocks to progress.

Project implementation is simply a continuation of the organized approach you have been working with from the General Phase of the Job Plan and have carried through to the Recommendation Phase.  The techniques that you have used in these progressive steps are used similarly in implementing your project as well as on any problem you may encounter in your continuous studies in the "College of Life."

*Over-eagerness to please ruins the effectiveness*
*of more individuals than the lack of zeal; the*
*individual who tries too hard to please usually*
*succeeds only in creating problems where none*
*existed before.*  — L. J. HARRIS

# Chapter Twelve

# Application and Summary

*Application is the price to be paid for mental*
*acquisition.  To have the harvest we must sow*
*the seed.*  — G. BAILY

The application of the mind to a problem through the Value Engineering
Methodology leads to the desired acquisition of facts and a resultant harvest of concrete solutions.

The application of the Value Engineering Systematic Approach is as
broad or as narrow as the individual applying it wants it to be.  There is
always work, and tools with which to do the work, for those who have the
will and the desire.

The story of the application of the Systematic Approach can be compared
with the history of the fiery rocket.  Thousands of years ago the Chinese,
having invented gunpowder, took such explosive powder and confined it
within an elongated cylinder.  When ignited it traveled, due to its configuration, up into the air before exploding.  This was done, it has been
said, to frighten away the demons who lived in the air.  Since that time,
this simple, crude instrument has, with additional knowledge and develop-

ment, been applied by a number of people to a vast array of additional uses.   Throughout history, this airborne explosive, the rocket, has grown from an item which traveled a few feet into the air to scare demons to an instrument of war whose travel was measured in miles, then continents, and now to the point where its travel is measured in millions of miles and is carrying man outside his known environment.   This type of growth in the application of a concept has been limited only by the individual's desire to apply it to a specific use.   For example, the application of this principle has had numerous side developments, one of many being the jet engine. The same type of growth and beneficial side development are possible and in fact usual with the application of the Value Engineering Systematic Approach and its techniques.   A few of these will be explained in Parts 2 and 3 of this book.

The Value Engineering Systematic Approach can also be likened to the waves created by a stone thrown into a pool of water.   At the time the stone first hits the water, there is only a local wave created on the water's surface.   As time progresses, this wave starts to spread in all directions. It spreads in ever-widening circles until the total surface of the pond has finally felt its effects.   This Systematic Approach has and is having the same effect.

When the basic concept was stated by L. D. Miles as Value Analysis, it was applied within one plant of one company—an insignificant ripple in the world pond.   However, as its application progressed, its effect has grown and been felt over vast areas.   From its original penetration within one company, it has spread through the state, the nation, and has finally reached the point at which it is being applied in almost every country of the world.

Each of us, in our application of these principles, is responsible for the successful application and continued development of this Systematic Approach.   However, we cannot look and work toward the broad scope of its application without first having an understanding of the fundamental steps. It is therefore important that we now look at and completely understand the application of this Systematic Approach on a small scale before trying to apply it on a broad scale; for without the detailed knowledge of its application to individual products, assemblies, subassemblies, and individual parts or processes, we cannot hope to successfully apply its principles to an entire industry or company.

Because of conscious or subconscious resistance to change, the value of these new technologies and procedures may be substantially reduced and in some instances they may produce problems that never should have existed in the first place.   Many seem to believe that the acquisition of know-how brings with it a guarantee of economical utilization.   This is far from being the case.  It requires well-planned changes in concepts, methods, and processes in a company's operation, and possibly even structural changes, to assure such benefits.  The proper planning and follow-through of these changes are the critical development phases for the full utilization of the newly acquired know-how.  To be successful, this approach requires both competent management and a willingness on the part of those individuals who are directly affected to accept change.  In most cases, to some degree, this means everyone.

The ability to attract individuals who know how to properly utilize modern technologies and processes and who have the will and ability to think rationally is another vital factor.  The melding together of teams that can be available to management for progressive changes becomes a most important part of the progressive planning program.  What this often boils down to, from a management standpoint, is the foresight to properly train the people necessary to carry through the many changes leading to true progress.

If we look around, we will find that we have many people of latent talent and potential leadership; however, many of these individuals are underchallenged, underutilized, underdeveloped, or underencouraged—at a great loss both to them and to us.  It therefore becomes our responsibility to learn the fine points of the application of this Systematic Approach so that we can in turn pass them on to others.

## Product Application

The Value Engineering Systematic Approach is a relatively simple and proved methodology for reducing and preventing costs without reducing the required standards of reliability and performance.  It is one that can be effectively used by any individual or concern irrespective of size or output.  It represents an important concept in modern management in that, through the Systematic Approach of Value Engineering, management makes a full-time partner of each individual.  This is done by making certain that each action and reaction includes not only the very latest thinking and advances in low-cost techniques but also the thinking of everyone involved in the changes.

In order that you, as an individual and as part of a team, can become an active part of management's overall plan, you must be able to profitably use the Value Engineering Systematic Approach.  This you can accomplish only by having a full understanding of how it is applied to any product at any time in the product's life cycle.  (Product, as used here, is still defined as "anything which is the result of someone's labor.")  The importance of having a full understanding of this is twofold.  It is important, first, for the sake of increasing your own knowledge and, second, to enable you to convey this knowledge to others. These factors are of equal importance to your successful application of this Systematic Approach.

Application of this methodology to improve a product's value can be injected anywhere within a product's life cycle. In fact, when and where possible, it should be applied throughout a product's entire life cycle, from cradle to grave. To secure a graphic view of this broadest type of application, you may look at Figure 12-1.

The usage of the Systematic Approach throughout a product's total life cycle falls basically into four major areas of application: feasibility, application, development, and design configuration. After all the data are collected, strong emphasis is given to the determination of what functions are desired and/or required by the ultimate user and the developer of the product within economically feasible range. From this determination, meaningful specifications and requirements can be spelled out to guide the basic design. At the same time, cost-to-function relationships can be established which in turn aid in the establishment of cost targets to be used in designing the basic product configuration.

In the development application, the basic design configuration and hardware and software development are constantly analyzed to determine if they are meeting and performing the specifications and requirements set forth. This is done with the assistance of all possible members of the team in task force efforts and design reviews. One of the vital areas to be watched at this time is the area of translating words into physical product.

In completing the development, you and your team members must be ready to act and react rapidly to make any and all modifications necessary to bring a faltering product back within the parameters originally set forth.

In the usage application, the area where the Systematic Approach is most often applied, particular pains must be taken to see that no area or step is overlooked. It has often been found that in this area of application, most of us tend to concentrate on the product during its production release and spend little if any effort in the other three parts of the cycle. At no other

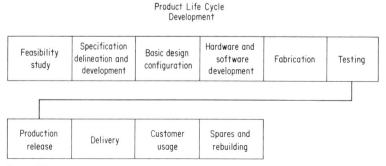

Product Life Cycle
Development

| Feasibility study | Specification delineation and development | Basic design configuration | Hardware and software development | Fabrication | Testing |
| --- | --- | --- | --- | --- | --- |

| Production release | Delivery | Customer usage | Spares and rebuilding |
| --- | --- | --- | --- |

Figure 12-1

time in a product's life cycle is the product so vulnerable to the addition of unnecessary costs. This is caused by "fixes" required to correct minor problems. These are made with little or no thought to the overall product or its specifications and requirements. In many cases, the condition arises whereby you can have fixes being made on fixes. This has been called the "Christmas tree correction plan." When this starts to happen, you must bring it to a rapid halt and, if necessary, go all the way back to the feasibility study and specifications to determine what is really necessary.

Riding herd on these three specific areas in the application of the Systematic Approach is the fourth, the overview application. The overview application is one which encompasses as well as controls the other three areas of application. This control is not to be considered analogous to that of a policeman or dictator but rather to that of a teacher or helper in special cases of need. In order that the ultimate in results may be achieved in the feasibility, development, and usage applications of this Systematic Approach, all the individuals involved must be talking the same basic language. If this is not the case, the results will be like those of the Tower of Babel. By the application of the teaching and helping techniques, all the individuals will be aided in approaching the problem in the same manner. In this way, they will be able to conquer it instead of letting it conquer them.

Where all the individuals involved are talking the same language and thereby approaching the common problem in a common manner, dynamic teamwork is brought into play. Such teamwork is then focused on the specific or major problems when they are encountered anywhere within the product training programs and special task force efforts to solve the problems at hand.

All too often, depending on the management philosophy, the Systematic Approach is applied to only one of the first three areas of a product's life cycle. In most cases, because of habits and attitudes, this application is limited to the usage area alone. The greatest return that you and your team members can achieve, however, is by the full application of the Systematic Approach throughout the complete product life cycle. Such full application is particularly rewarding in that it provides its users with a knowledge of how the approach can be applied to a specific case or problem area.

It has been said that each problem, no matter how complex or simple it may look, is composed of simple parts. Parts of the problem can be separated from the whole, solved individually, and then the partial solutions can be melded once more into a master solution for the whole problem. In actuality, it may also be found that the subproblems must be further divided into their individual parts before they can be solved.

A major part of your application of the Systematic Approach then resides in a knowledge that the problem condition exists and in how to cope with it in a meaningful manner. This mode of application is best visualized in graphic form in Figures 12-2 and 12-3.

A complete understanding of the use of Figure 12-3 will also give you an understanding of Figure 12-2, which is only a small version of Figure 12-3. Problem and function definition are one and the same thing and therefore are treated in the same way. Each problem or part thereof is in reality a function that must be accomplished. As such, they can each be defined in the same manner; that is, as a verb and a noun.

Here, as with the definition of function, it is necessary to know and note the "input" and "output" of the problem as well as the problem itself. The basic problem is written in the block between the input and output arrows (using the verb-noun definition).

Now, going to the second level of indenture (the horizontal row of blocks immediately below the basic problem definition), all the subproblems which make up the basic problem are defined and noted. These are determined from a close evaluation of the basic problem and the specifications and requirements which have a bearing on it. If the problem is of sufficient complexity, each of these subproblems, in turn, is broken down into its respective parts and listed at the third level of indenture.

It must be noted at this point that problems, like functions, fall into two basic categories: basic and secondary. Also the 20-80 rules, presented earlier in the discussion of function, also hold true in relation to problems.

The final step is to connect each basic problem block to the next-higher problem level with a solid line. These problems (blocks which are second degree to the next-higher problem level) are left connected with only the broken line.

When the problem chart has been completed as described above, it is found that a problem "family tree" has been developed. This "family tree" now becomes a valuable working tool, one which can show redundant functions, overlapping problems, subproblems which contribute in different areas to the overall problem, and subproblems which are caused

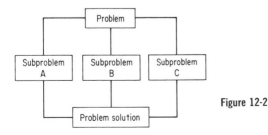

Figure 12-2

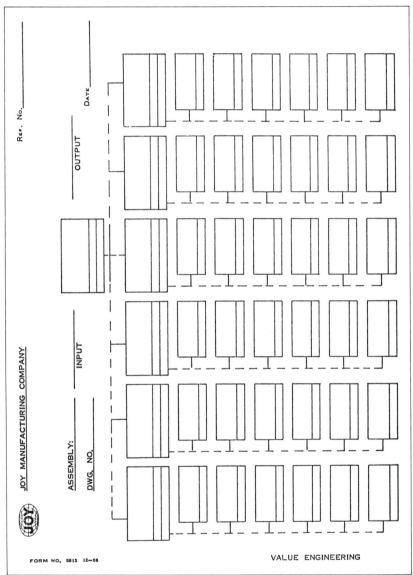

Figure 12-3

JOY MANUFACTURING COMPANY

ASSEMBLY: _____

DWG. NO. _____

INPUT _____

OUTPUT _____

REF. NO. _____

DATE _____

FORM NO. 8813 12-66

VALUE ENGINEERING

134

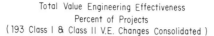

Total Value Engineering Effectiveness
Percent of Projects
( 193 Class I & Class II V.E. Changes Consolidated )

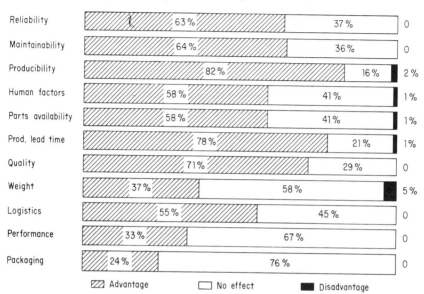

| | Advantage | No effect | Disadvantage |

Source: Report of Technical Subcommittee, American Ordinance Association, August, 1967

**Figure 12-4**

merely by misunderstanding. All these are aids in directing your knowledgeable application of the Systematic Approach toward areas which are most likely to contain high and/or unnecessary costs.

From this knowledge, you and your team can logically apply the Systematic Approach of Value Engineering to those areas most likely to provide the greatest return for your invested time.

Our minds and ingenuity are the only limiting factors to the successful application of any approach.

Many times as you apply this Systematic Approach, particularly to a physical product, you will be questioned as to its detrimental effects on that product. This type of question has been asked before and will be asked again. In an endeavor to answer this question, a technical subcommittee of the American Ordinance Association undertook a study of the Systematic Approach's effects on a product. The results of that study are shown in Figure 12-4, "Total Value Engineering Effectiveness."

As can be seen from this chart, no less than 24 percent of the projects in any category showed improvement and no more than 5 percent showed disadvantage. In most points being measured, the improvement (advantage) was shown in more than 50 percent of the projects.

## Summary

Do you still shudder when you think of all of the crises you had to face and the panic fixing you had to do when your latest problem was encountered? Maybe a more carefully conceived, detailed, painstaking planning process and action plan would have changed your experience into a smoothly running progression! Actually most problems, no matter how simple or complex, can be solved at an early stage through planning, which in turn makes most emergency solutions unnecessary.

Good planning requires many things; for instance, the right selection of alternatives among available resources so that the production process can progress as economically as possible. It requires time for experimentation so that the product is not only functionally satisfactory but also satisfactory from every other point of view. Thoughtful coordination and teamwork are a must if the maximum cost advantages are to be realized with no reduction in reliability.

In this discussion of the fundamentals of the Value Engineering Systematic Approach you would be concerned with feeling even more than with knowledge and thought. For where knowledge is emphasized at the expense of feeling, you merely become a vessel which can be opened, and your knowledge might as well be flushed back into books. The aim here is to put the right words together with the facts so that all of a sudden sparks fly and a new skill—the ability to see—is born. When you have accomplished this, an ability to see a given problem in a different way, you are not the same person that you were yesterday nor will you ever be the same from one day to the next.

Through this change, you have acquired the knowledge that constant questioning is the first key to wisdom and that science does not have absolute answers but is rather a creation of human imagination and intelligence. Therefore you, as well as every individual, can contribute.

You have also ascertained that every bull session is an important aspect of education and that from each of these you can learn something new about the obstacles that arise in your associates' minds. Through these realizations, you conclude that your plan of approach must be revised each time to suit each particular problem. In this manner, you learn not to expect things to be given to you but on the other hand to seize every opportunity that is presented.

Through this Systematic Approach and its step-by-step application, you form a plan of how to think about and approach each problem. Your command of the approach and your enthusiasm for the solution of the problem make you take steps to ensure that you are both informed and intelligent about all its aspects. At the same time, you treat each individual as your peer—as a companion in learning—thus assuring a mutual respect. In addition you find, no matter what the scope of your knowledge of the problem, that you have become the most committed student in the room, for you find that you are learning something new all the time.

As time progresses, you find that the application of the Systematic Approach of Value Engineering is no longer a job but a calling. As this transition takes place, you find that what was at first difficult has become ordinary; what was impossible, possible. In actuality, you find that you have developed a completely new set of habits and attitudes, that you are avoiding honest wrong beliefs and substituting facts. You further find that you are digging for information to create a spectrum of ideas, thus avoiding the consequences of temporary circumstances.

In the final analysis, you find that you, in your development, have studied and mastered the art of communication. And through this communication you find that there is nothing more inspiring than having a mind unfold before you.

Through a mastery of this Systematic Approach of Value Engineering, there opens before you a vast, new, exciting area of challenge, experience, and pleasure. It is all yours just for the asking!

*It ain't what you know that hurts you, it's what
you know for sure that ain't so.* — ABE MARTIN

Part Two

# Value Engineering
# Job Plan Application

## Introduction

*Theory is the guide to practice, and practice the
ratification and life of theory.*

*In reading Part 1, Fundamentals and Theory, you have studied the basis
of the Value Engineering Systematic Approach and gained an insight into
the methodology as well as the inner working of the Job Plan. In addition
you have come to realize that all these embody knowledge of both the
past and the present, wisdom from all walks of life, and philosophies
developed over the ages; for only on this foundation can the Value
Engineering Systematic Approach be the dynamic, forceful, yet practical
approach that it is!*

*At this point you, like all others, are fired up, raring to go, champing at
the bit to go forth and conquer the world. This is good; never lose that
enthusiasm. However, you must remember that you are but an infant in
the use of this methodology and approach. As such, you must take but
small and guarded steps in the practice of its application to real-life
conditions.*

*In order to progress from crawling, to walking, to running, it is best, like
a child, to take the first steps while holding someone's hand. The
discussion of application in Part 2, which follows, will make this possible.
It will discuss, first, how projects are selected; then it will walk you, step
by step, through a simple yet meaningful project.*

*The practice of this methodology and the application of its fundamentals
cannot be undertaken, however, without a properly selected project to*

*which to apply them.  Therefore the first chapter of Part 2 will deal with the important steps of project selection and project preparation.  A sample project will be selected for a step-by-step application of the Systematic Approach.*

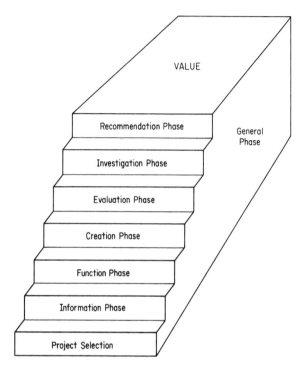

*In this step-by-step application, you will see how a project unfolds from the Information Phase right through the Recommendation Phase.  At the same time, you will be able to observe, throughout the whole process, the vital role played by the techniques of the General Phase and how the various instances of unnecessary cost are steadily and surely overcome.*

# Chapter Thirteen

# Project Selection

The selection of a project should be made from project suggestions you have received. The process of project selection cannot be fully understood until there is a basic understanding of project suggestion. This understanding comes only from a knowledge of the "who" and "why" that is encompassed in the suggestion process. Such knowledge is vital to the final selection of projects on which you and your associates will expend your efforts.

You will find that the "who" of project suggestion may involve a single individual or many individuals. Similarly the "why" of project suggestion may involve few or many different reasons for the suggestion of a project for study.

Although, like many other things discussed, these two points are closely related and interacting, we shall discuss them individually to obtain a better knowledge of them.

## "Who" of Project Suggestion

Projects, you will find, may be suggested and thereby indirectly selected by an individual or group of individuals. These individuals may range from the sweeper to the chairman of the board, from an engineer to a shipping clerk, from yourself to someone unknown to you or anyone in between any of these extremes. Many times a project is not suggested by a single individual but by a group of individuals. The suggesting group of individuals can comprise representatives from one or many departments or functions of the company and can be either a formal or informal group.

Due to this wide variety of potential areas from which projects can be suggested, you must also realize the equally wide variety of possible ways in which a project can be suggested. These ways will run the gamut from the direct suggestion to the indirect or hidden suggestion. You will find, normally, that the further down the ladder of responsibility the suggester is, the more vague and indirect the suggestion will be. Ofttimes in these cases, you will find that the suggestion made is not really directed to solving the actual problem, and only through judicious questioning will the fundamental problem be brought to light. The reasons for this will be discussed later. On the other hand, the further up the ladder of responsibility the suggestor is, the more direct, factual, and to the point will the suggestion be. In these cases, many times, the suggestions are not given as suggestions at all but as edicts telling you what you should work on.

In either case, no matter what the extreme, you must take the same precautions; that is, you must make a preliminary investigation to determine if the potential savings and other benefits are worth the estimated investment of time, effort, and money. In essence, you must determine if there is going to be sufficient return on the capital to be invested. If such return cannot be realized, the project should not be selected for in-depth study.

At this point you may be asking: "How do I tell the chairman of the board that we are not going to work on the project he suggested?" Surprising as it might seem, if you make your preliminary investigation and have your facts in order, it will be easier to convince the chairman of the board than it will be to convince the sweeper why you should not work on the project he suggested. This is caused by the personal involvement of the individual in the suggested idea or problem area. The further the suggester is down the ladder of responsibility, the more personal the suggestion is to him— therefore the less rational he will be about your refusal to work on his suggestion. This is caused by his reason for making the suggestion in the first place.

## "Why" of Project Suggestion

Every suggestion comes as a result of a felt need. Therefore projects may be suggested, and thereby selected, in any number of ways as well as for any number of reasons. The ways may range from the query or indirect suggestion to the edict or direct order, while the reason or reasons may range from personal involvement to that of impersonal detachment or anywhere in between in either set of conditions.  Similarly, a project may be suggested directly or indirectly, in a simple or complex manner.  A further complication of the "why" of project suggestion is that the suggestion may be motivated by a single reason or by a multitude of reasons.

All these points must be considered when you weigh and assess a potential project in your preliminary investigation.  Your investigation must analyze each factor of the "why" of the suggestion.

Most often, the further down the ladder of responsibility the suggester is, the more personal is his feeling toward the suggestion.  This is due to the fact that he has made the suggestion because of a personal problem or gripe.  He therefore wants something done to eliminate this problem or to remove the basis for the gripe.  This accounts for his strong and personal direct involvement.  However, because of his personal involvement the suggester may, unknowingly, not state the exact problem or gripe but skirt around it by presenting indirect suggestions.

On the other hand, the higher up the ladder of responsibility the suggester is, the more impersonal the suggestion is likely to be.  This is because the suggestion, most times, stems from a more impersonal evaluation of the product or problem area.  This impersonal feeling also stems, many times, from the suggester.

As can be seen from the above, the ways and reasons for a project's suggestion can vary quite extensively.  Most times the reason or reasons underlie the way in which a project is suggested.  The reasons, on the other hand, can be either personal or company-motivated, problem- or profit-stimulated, or any combination of these.

Where the reason for the suggestion is of a personal or problem motivation, it is extremely difficult for the suggester to accept any rationalization as to why the suggestion should not be undertaken and worked on to a solution.  It is therefore important, in the beginning, to determine just how personal the suggestion is to the suggester.  This can be accomplished by judicious questioning to determine why the suggestion was made.

From this complex riddle of the "who" and "why" of the project suggestion, you and your associates will learn, at some time, one vital lesson: that at times it is advisable to work on a project even if the preliminary investigation shows that it is not economically practical.  This is done when it is found that the suggestion is of a highly personal nature and when it is deemed necessary to have the suggester's support at a later time on future projects.  Work should proceed on this type of project when the loss of time involved will not be too great.  Most times, when this type of project suggestion is encountered, it is one that is generated by a pet peeve or gripe.  It is also generally found that it can be solved in a relatively short period of time.   Therefore, when it is solved, not only is the personal peeve or gripe eliminated but the suggester will quite willingly provide assistance in future project work.

It should also be noted that this type of highly personal suggestion will be encountered from all departments and functions as well as from all levels of responsibility within them.   Similarly, because of the wide spectrum from which projects can be suggested, it will be found that many different types of projects will be suggested.   The variation in types of projects on which you can work is another subject and will be explained next.

## Types of Projects

The types of projects that you will work on in the application of the Value Engineering Methodology are many.   All of them, however, will fall into one of the two basic groups: hardware or software.   In order that you may have a complete understanding of these two general groups as referred to herein, they are defined below:

**Hardware Projects**   Projects involving any item which is physical in nature — that has weight and/or takes up space.   This "hardware" includes all the material and energy consumed in the manufacture of the product going to the customer.

**Software Projects**   Projects involving items or actions which are not physical in nature and are not directly concerned with or applied to the product going to the customer — that is, projects concerned with intangibles.   This definition includes all items which are intangible and nonconsumable in nature.

These two general groups only start the classification of the types of projects on which you will work, for they, in turn, must be subdivided. These subdivisions not only delineate the various types of projects within the two general groups but tend to provide some guidance as to the minor variations in the approach to them.

In the hardware group there are three subgroups: product, production, and facilities.   Each of these subgroups is defined below and a list of examples of each is given:

*Product:*   Those projects which deal with the physical items that are produced to be sold or distributed to the ultimate customer or user

Examples: Parts, components, subassemblies, assemblies, packaging, forms, materials, etc.

*Production:*   Those projects which deal with the methods and equipment that is used in the manufacture of the product

Examples: Tools, jigs, fixtures, machines, transportation, sequence of operations, time study, etc.

*Facilities:*  Those projects which deal with the environment and re-sources required to manufacture the product

Examples: Buildings, land, heat, light, gas, power, etc.

In the software group there is only one subgroup.  It is defined below with a list of examples.

*System, Process, Procedure:*  Those projects which deal with a series of actions, rather than a physical item, that are necessary to plan, produce, ship, or sell the product

Examples: Product planning, marketing plan, shop loading, distribution program, billing, etc.

As can be seen from the definition of these basic and subgroups, any-thing which is the direct or indirect result of someone's labor can be under-taken as a project.  It should also be remembered that any project sug-gested in any one of these areas is suggested because of a felt need and should be treated as such.

With an understanding of the reasons for project suggestion and the types of projects to be selected, it is next important to understand some of the basic elements necessary to a good project.  Without a majority of these elements, a project is doomed to failure before it is started.

## Elements of a Project

The elements of a project comprise both overall and specific attributes. Each project selected from those suggested should contain one or more attributes from each group.  These two groups of attributes are listed be-low:

A. Overall attributes that a project should possess:

   1. It should have at least three different subassemblies or groups of actions.

   2. It should have between eight and sixteen components or actions.

   3. It should be in current usage or planned usage.

      a. The project should be a "live" project, not something being studied just for the sake of study.

      b. It can be a proposed item or action; i.e., something being re-searched or developed.

   4. No *major* changes in the item should be under study or in process.

   5. It must be something on which changes can be made after recom-mendations have been submitted.

   6. Its purpose or functions should be definable and understandable.

B. Specific attributes that projects should involve:

   1. Components or actions that appear to be difficult to use, perform, or manufacture

2. Components or actions that appear to be larger, more complex, or heavier than necessary
3. Components that include some nonstandard forms, shapes, or sizes
4. Components or actions that appear, in some degree, to be similar to consumer retail items
5. Components or actions that appear to be similar to other company or industry standards
6. Components or actions that, in whole or in part, appear to be similar to frequently used items
7. Excessive work to produce the final item
8. Components that appear to have weaknesses or require excessive maintenance
9. Components made up of critical or expensive raw material
10. Fixtures, tools, or procedures that seem complex and excessive
11. A low profit margin
12. Excessively close tolerances
13. Complete in-house production or purchase as a complete unit
14. A command of only a small share of the potential market
15. Competitive items that appear to be more reliable and/or lower in cost
16. Excessive amounts of equipment or manpower

In addition to the overall and specific attributes, an equally important element of a project is that of timing. For if the timing of project work and resultant recommendations is not right, the work expended is useless. Listed below are a number of factors which should be considered in the timing priority of a project:

1. Personnel safety
2. Effects on a large number of individuals
3. Avoidance of loss
4. Savings and/or improved profit
5. Patent position
6. Customer or company suggestion
7. Availability of material
8. Competitive position
9. Incorporation with other changes
10. Annual volume
11. Anticipated market life

With the exception of the first, these items of timing priority are not listed in any specific order, as they will vary in importance with each project. But personnel safety, at the top of the list, must always be considered

first.   All these factors must be considered and weighed when undertaking
a project.

All elements are very critical when you select your first project.   This
is so because your future use and successful application of the Value Engineering Methodology most often hinges on the success or failure of your
first project.

## Your First Project

The selection of your first project is vital to your future success in the use
of the Systematic Approach of Value Engineering.   This selection delves
into many critical aspects, both personal and impersonal.

One aspect, your attainment of a basic new knowledge, has been finished, and another is about to start.   You are about to take the new tools
and new knowledge you have gained and put them to work.   With their
application, however, you will engage in a major conflict: a conflict of man
against man and of action against inertia.

This conflict, however, will not be one of physical death and destruction
in the true sense of the terms.   In reality, this is to be a conflict of man
against himself.   Literally, it is just that: you in conflict with yourself.   In
this, your first project, it is to be an internal conflict, for it is the conflict
of change.   It is to end in the death and destruction of your resistance to
change.   It will not, however, encourage the development of change merely
for the sake of change, but change for the sake of improvement.

The theory and fundamentals which you have read and absorbed have,
in their way, prepared you for this conflict, this battle against your own
human nature.   For it is a distinct part of everyone's human nature to resist change in almost any form.   Walt Kelly had his comic strip character
Pogo state the problem most ably—"We have met the enemy, and they are
us."

If you are to win this conflict, it is necessary for you to rise above the
common level.   This is something each of us alone must do within himself.
It has been said that every man who rises above the common level receives
two educations: the first from his teachers; the second, more personal and
important, from himself.

The theories have been read, the fundamentals of the art explored.   All
that is left is to engage the enemy: yourself.   In entering upon this or any
conflict, however, it is always best to establish the strategy to be employed.
Where and when possible, the area of battle is judiciously selected, the
site and approach of each engagement are planned, and the type of each
skirmish predetermined.   These factors and conditions must be selected
with the greatest care so that they are as conducive as possible to final
victory.

The total war and initial battle in which you are about to engage will comprise numerous conflicts and skirmishes simply called *projects*—projects of varying magnitude and degree. The selection of your first project, like the first encounter of any battle with an enemy, should be one whereby you can feel out and test the enemy, learn his strengths and weaknesses, and from this knowledge plan and carry out your total campaign.

The selection of your projects, the first as well as all that are to follow, is not an easy task. The selection will not be easy because of the multitude of variables—so many points to be evaluated, so many individuals to be considered. Every one of these must be carefully weighed and balanced, one against the other, always with but one goal in mind—success.

With all these points in mind, your first project should be a simple one, one with which you are fairly familiar. It should also be one in which you are relatively sure recommended changes can and will be voted on. If possible, it should be one with which you can work without too much fear of change. Your familiarity with this project should be such that you can readily progress from one phase of the Job Plan to another without an excess of external assistance. The first project should be relatively simple yet of sufficient complexity to require or permit the application of every phase of the Job Plan to it.

Once you have selected your first project in accordance with the criteria and elements established, it is essential that it be worked to a conclusion and implemented. No matter how simple or complex your first project may be, this is of the utmost importance; for it has been found that what you do and accomplish on your first project establishes the pattern for all succeeding projects.

It is recognized that it is always difficult for anyone to transform theory into practice, words into action. For these reasons, the remaining chapters of Part 2, which follow, will be devoted to the step-by-step application of the theory and fundamentals of the Systematic Approach to a physical example—an example which, at the time of its selection, was a distinct problem.

The finite study of such a step-by-step application will not only help you transform words into action and theory into practice but it will also greatly broaden your understanding. It will also answer many of the questions normally encountered in your future work in the field.

*Nothing succeeds like success.*

# Chapter Fourteen

# Information Phase

## The Project

The project to be used here is one which was selected and worked on by a team consisting of its original designer, a methods man, and a buyer. This project has been selected for this step-by-step explanation because it contains a majority of the points and relationships discussed in the chapter on project selection and is still relatively simple in nature.

The specifics used here and in subsequent chapters are those which the team uncovered and worked with on the project. The only exception is that the facts identifying the specific company involved have been withheld.

The subject of this project, at the time of its selection by the team, was an active part of one of the company's product lines. It was a subassembly required by the Marketing Department, as an essential part of the overall product line.

The assembly, Figure 14-1, is called a *connector*. It is a part of a commercial electrical equipment assembly called a *voltage regulator*. The voltage regulator is used in power-line systems to provide voltage regulation to those lines. The equipment is built by one of the major electrical equipment manufacturers in the United States.

This connector, whose assembly drawing number is 9090547, comprises eleven standard and special parts. Five of these assemblies are used per

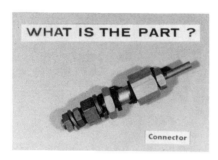

**WHAT IS THE PART ?**

Connector

Figure 14-1

voltage regulator to connect the high- and low-voltage bushings to the core and coil. The annual usage of this particular model of voltage regulator is 175. Each connector is mounted in a ½-inch hole in an insulating panel with the voltage regulator, as shown in Figure 14-2.

These connectors are required by the Marketing Department in order that simple field maintenance can be accomplished. This maintenance encompasses the ability to readily disconnect and replace the porcelain bushings when they are damaged in final manufacture, shipment, or operation. It must be possible to do this when the unit is on the ground as well as when it is mounted on a power pole.

Preliminary investigation discloses that the maximum input through the connector from the cover bushings is 30 amperes of current. This is made possible by connecting the terminal on the bottom end of the cover bushing wire between the two ⅜-inch brass nuts. The connection to the core and coil is accomplished by crimping the core and coil lead into the copper tube at the lower end of the connector, the copper tube being fastened into the assembly by means of a special brass nut. Both of these connections must be readily disconnectable but at the same time be able to withstand normal shipping and operational vibration. The whole assembly is supported by the insulating panel through which it passes.

Due to the way in which the voltage regulator is designed, there is air above the insulating panel and air and transformer oil below the panel. During operation of the voltage regulator, due to the operational heat generated, a pressure of 7 pounds per square inch above atmospheric pressure is generated on the core and coil side of the insulating panel. It is therefore important that the assembly not move and that it seal the opening in the insulating panel through which it passes.

The project and basic information, as stated above, is that which the team had to start with. They, like yourself, were novices in the application of the total Value Engineering Systematic Approach. They therefore deliberately proceeded through each individual step of the Job Plan. They followed and used each phase, technique, and worksheet of the Job Plan to be sure that no step or possibility was overlooked.

Additional preliminary evaluation and discussion of the project disclosed that it had been designed more than 5 years earlier. It had been designed, in a semiemergency situation, when the insulating panel had been put into the voltage regulator for the mounting of other required and newly designed equipment. Further, it was determined that, because of the lack of time, no costs had been established or operational tests conducted. Knowing this to be the case, the designer, with the best knowledge available to him, had incorporated sufficient safety factors to make sure that this assembly would not fail.

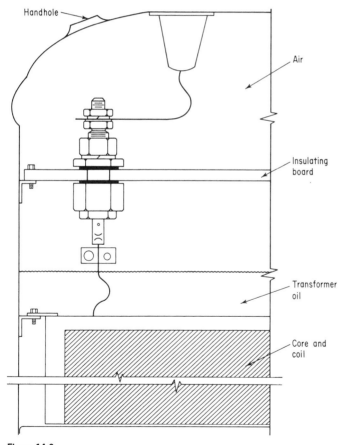

Figure 14-2

Based on this preliminary evaluation and data, the team proceeded into the Information Phase.

## Project Information Phase

Although the team working on the project included the original designer, they decided that because of the length of time since the original design, they would seek complete marketing information. It must be noted that in many similar situations this step is bypassed, thereby ending a project in utter failure.

They therefore proceeded to complete the first part of the information worksheet by seeking the answers to the pertinent application and marketing background questions.

### Secure the Facts

*Application and Marketing Background:*

A. Customer and company specifications and requirements.
  1. The subassembly must fit in the insulation panel.
  2. The subassembly must be such that the connections to it are readily connectable and disconnectable.
  3. No part of the assembly can come within 4 inches of the voltage-regulator tank.
  4. Under normal conditions, no spares are required or expected. Therefore, the expected usage is not to exceed nine hundred assemblies.
B. Field service reports—reliability, serviceability, maintainability, human factors.
  1. In over 5 years of usage no field failures or complaints have been reported by the customers or manufacturing units.
  2. Based on the above fact of not one complaint, it is possible that the subassembly has been highly overdesigned. This, it has been found, is likely to be the case when no field failures occur.
C. Anticipated market life.
  1. Based on steady sales of 160 to 175 units per year plus anticipated growth of power usage, the market life of the model is forecast to be 25 years.
D. Anticipated market requirements.
  1. The market requirements could, based on our and other companies' sales, increase to between 300 and 500 units annually for this model voltage regulator in the next 5 years if the total cost and thereby price were reduced.

E. Application and marketing recommendations for investigation, change, or improvement.
  1. Simplify construction and reduce cost.
  2. Reduce weight.

The team, after securing the pertinent information on application and marketing background, next centered their investigation on securing the necessary engineering background. Due to the fact that the team contained the original designer of the assembly, they realized that they would have to be particularly careful of their facts and be sure that personal fear and prejudice were not interjected at this point in their investigation.

Before seeking the information from the Engineering Department, they secured copies of the assembly, the assembly bill of materials, and the individual parts drawings as well as a sketch of the area in the voltage regulator where the assembly is used (Figures 14-3 and 14-4). With this information in hand, they then proceeded to gather the remainder of the engineering background information.

A. Technical history of product: The original connector design was conceived approximately 5 years ago. It was conceived in order to allow the insulating panel to be put into the voltage regulator for the purpose of mounting new regulating equipment desired by the customer. No changes in the specifications have been made since that time.
B. What is required of this part or assembly in the equipment?
  1. The assembly is required to carry a maximum of 30 amperes of current with minimum losses.
  2. The assembly must withstand shipping and operational vibration. The wires must be readily connected and disconnected.
  3. The workmanship must meet the engineering specifications. It should be such that the individual parts are interchangeable.
C. Quantity requirements for this and other equipments.
  1. This assembly is used only in this model voltage regulator; therefore, the quantity required will be controlled by those needed for new units and for spares.
D. What new developments and/or changes are being considered?
  1. None.
E. Engineering recommendations for investigation, change, or improvement.
  1. "The quantity and price are low. Why bother with it?"

Having secured, from their teammates and others in the Engineering Department the necessary data and engineering background, the team

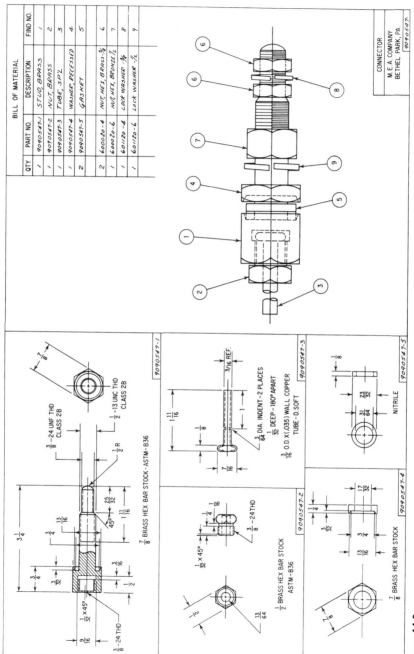

**Figure 14-3**

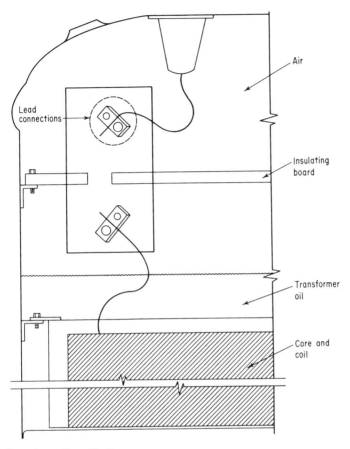

Parameters and specifications
  A. Bushing lead wire input 30 amperes
  B. Bushing and coil lead wires 4¼" apart
  C. Connections to lead wires must be readily disconnectable
  D. Complete unit subject to shipping and operational vibration
  E. Pressure generated in operation 7 P.S.I.
  F. Hole in insulating panel ½" in diameter

**Figure 14-4**

moved on to the Manufacturing Department to secure the necessary data from this area.

*Manufacturing and Procurement Background:*  The team consulted the methods and industrial engineering personnel in the Manufacturing Department for the major portion of the data on how the special parts were manufactured.  They also talked with shop supervision to secure their additional facts and opinions.  From the buyers in the Purchasing Department, they secured the facts regarding those parts of the assembly that were bought from outside suppliers.  The data collected are:

## OPERATION SHEET

| NAME | Stud | | | | | MFG. QTY | 25 PCS |
|---|---|---|---|---|---|---|---|
| MATERIAL | 7/8" Hex Brass – ASTM B 36 x 3 1/2" long | | | | | PART NO. | 909054-1 |
| | | | | SHEETS | SHEET NO. | | |
| | | | | DATE | | DRG. NO. | |

| DEPT. | OPER. SYMBOL | OPERATION DESCRIPTION | CUT | FEED | SPEED | MACH. NO. | TOOLS | STANDARD HOURS SET UP | PER PIECE |
|---|---|---|---|---|---|---|---|---|---|
| | # 1 | Turret lathe | | | | | | | |
| | | Bevel for mill box | | | | | Knee tool | | Std |
| | | Turn 1/2" dia. - 2 1/2" long | | | | | Mill box | | Std |
| | | Turn 3/8" dia. - 25/32" lg w/45° bevel | | | | | Mill box | | Std |
| | | Cut groove under shoulder | | | | | Groove tool | | Std |
| | | Chase 1/2" - 13 thd to 1/16 dim | | | | | Chaser | | Std |
| | | Form 1/4" radius | | | | | Form tool | | Std |
| | | Chase 3/8 - 24 thd - 29/32 lg | | | | | Chaser | | Std |
| | | Cut off - 3 1/4" lg. | | | | | C.O. tool | | Std |
| | # 2 | Remove tip at bench | | | | | Hand file | | Std |
| | | | | | | | Subtotal | .14 hrs | .05 hrs |
| | # 3 | Turret lathe | | | | | | | |
| | | Spot drill | | | | | Spot drill | | Std |
| | | Drill - 5/16" | | | | | Drill | | Std |
| | | Bottom drill | | | | | Bottom Drill | | Std |
| | | Form relief | | | | | Rel. tool | | Std |
| | | Bevel for tap | | | | | 90° Countersink | | Std |
| | | Tap 3/8 - 24 thd | | | | | 3/8 -24 tap | | Std |
| | | Bottom tap | | | | | " Bottom tap | | Std |
| | | | | | | | Subtotal | 1.00 hrs | .03 hrs |
| | # 4 | Burr complete | | | | | Burr bench | | Std |
| | | | | | | | Subtotal | .10 | .04 |
| | | | | | | | Total | 2.50 hrs | .120 hrs |

2.50 s.u. ÷ 25 = .10 hrs s.u./pc.
.120 D.L./pc = .120
.220 hrs/pc.

Form 6426-A-Rev.

**Figure 14-5**

# OPERATION SHEET

NAME __Nut - Brass__

MATERIAL __1/2" Hex Brass - ASTM B36-1" Long__

MFG. QTY. 25  
PART NO. 9090547-2  
DRG. NO.

SHEETS ____ SHEET NO. 1  
DATE

| DEPT. | OPER. SYMBOL | OPERATION DESCRIPTION | CUT | FEED | SPEED | MACH. NO. | TOOLS | STANDARD HOURS SET UP | PER PIECE |
|---|---|---|---|---|---|---|---|---|---|
| | #1 | Turret lathe | | | | | | | Std |
| | | Form bevel, relief, 3/8" dia | | | | | Form tool | | Std |
| | | Spot drill to form bevel | | | | | Drill | | Std |
| | | Drill - 1/4" dia | | | | | 1/4" drill | | Std |
| | | Cut in and bevel head | | | | | Bevel tool | | Std |
| | | Chase 3/8-24 thread | | | | | Short lead chaser | | Std |
| | | Cut to length | | | | | Cutoff tool | | Std |
| | | | | | | | Subtotal | 1.00hr | .06 |
| | #2 | Burr complete | | | | | Burr bench | | Std |
| | | | | | | | Subtotal | .20 | .01 |
| | | | | | | | Total | 1.20 | .07 |

1.20 s.u. ÷ 25 = .048 s.u./pc.

.07/pc. D.L. = .07

.118 hr/pc.

Form 6426-A-Rev.

Figure 14-6

157

# OPERATION SHEET

**NAME** Copper Tube     **MFG. QTY.** 25

**MATERIAL** 3/16" O.D. X .035 Wall Copper Tube – Dead Soft – 2" Long    **PART NO.** 9090547-3

**SHEETS**   **SHEET NO.**   **DATE**    **DRG. NO.**

| DEPT. | OPER. SYMBOL | OPERATION DESCRIPTION | CUT | FEED | SPEED | MACH. NO. | TOOLS | STANDARD HOURS SET UP | PER PIECE |
|---|---|---|---|---|---|---|---|---|---|
| | #1 | Tube saw | | | | | | .30 hrs | .010 hrs |
| | | Cut to length | | | | | | | |
| | #2 | Forming roll | | | | | Forming rolls (#1250) | 1.50 | .030 |
| | | Roll form 9/16" dia. x 1/8" thk | | | | | | | |
| | #3 | Forming roll | | | | | Forming rolls (#1255) | .60 | .005 |
| | | Roll form 2 indents | | | | | | | |
| | #4 | Burr bench | | | | | | .10 | .030 |
| | | Burr complete | | | | | | | |
| | | | | | | | Total | 2.50 | .075 |

2.50 hrs s.u. ÷ 25 = .10 hrs/pc.

.075 hrs/pc. O.L. = .075

$\overline{\phantom{.075 hrs/pc. O.L.}}$ .175 hrs/pc.

Form 6426-A-Rev.

**Figure 14-7**

## OPERATION SHEET

NAME Washer - Recessed

SHEETS SHEET NO. 1

MFG. QTY. 25

PART NO. 9090547-4

MATERIAL 7/8" Hex Brass-ASTM B36 - 1/2" long

DATE

DRG. NO.

| DEPT. | OPER. SYMBOL | OPERATION DESCRIPTION | CUT | FEED | SPEED | MACH. NO. | TOOLS | STANDARD HOURS SET UP | STANDARD HOURS PER PIECE |
|---|---|---|---|---|---|---|---|---|---|
| | #1 | Turret lathe | | | | | | | |
| | | Spot drill | | | | | Spot drill | | Std |
| | | Drill 17/32" dia. hole | | | | | 17/32" drill | | Std |
| | | Form counterbore | | | | | Form tool (#457) | | Std |
| | | Bevel & cut to length - 1/4" lg. | | | | | cutoff tool | | Std |
| | | | | | | | Subtotal | .60 | .04 |
| | #2 | Burr bench | | | | | | | |
| | | Burr complete | | | | | | .10 | .04 |
| | | | | | | | Total | .70 | .08 |
| | | | | | | | .70 s.u. ÷ 25 = .028 hrs s.u./pc. | | |
| | | | | | | | .08 hrs D.L. = .080 hrs | | |
| | | | | | | | .108 hrs/pc. | | |

Form 6426-A-Rev.

Figure 14-8

OPERATION SHEET

NAME: *Gasket* — SHEETS — SHEET NO. *1* — MFG. QTY. *50*

MATERIAL: *Nitrile Tubing – 23/32" O.D. x 31/64" I.D. x 1/8" Long* — DATE — PART NO. *9090547-5*

DRG. NO.

| DEPT. | OPER. SYMBOL | OPERATION DESCRIPTION | CUT | FEED | SPEED | MACH. NO. | TOOLS | STANDARD HOURS SET UP | STANDARD HOURS PER PIECE |
|---|---|---|---|---|---|---|---|---|---|
| | #1 | Lathe | | | | | | | |
| | | Place on mandrel | | | | | 31/64 O.D. Mandrel | | Std |
| | | Cut to length - 1/8" lg | | | | | Tube cutter | | Std |
| | | | | | | | | .50 | .025 |
| | | | | | | | .50 S.U. ÷ 50 = .01 hrs S.U./pc | | |
| | | | | | | | .025 hrs D.L. = .025 | | |
| | | | | | | | .035 hrs/pc. | | |

Form 6426-A-Rev.

Figure 14-9

A. Process specifications, sequence of operations, quantities.
  1. These data are shown on the operation sheets for these parts, Figures 14-5 through 14-9.
  2. Shop Supervision stated that manufacturing problems were being encountered with two parts: the stud (9090547-1) and the copper tube (9090547-3).
     a. On the stud (9090547-1), problems were being experienced when it was rechucked to drill, bottom drill, cut relief, and thread. The rechucking, if done in the $\frac{1}{2}$-13 thread diameter, caused damage to the threads. If the part was chucked on the $\frac{7}{8}$-inch hex, the part tended to be unstable in the chuck.
     b. On the copper tube (9090547-3), unless the tubing used was dead soft and straight, the shop had a high scrap rate due to the material splitting when the head was formed.
  3. It was determined that since these pieces were basically standard in configuration, no special equipment, tools, dies, or fixtures were required in their manufacture.
  4. Shop supervision suggested that, if possible, these parts should be made in lots of 50 to 100 (now in lots of 25), thereby reducing the number of setups required over a year to produce the required parts. One statement made was: "It seems as if we've just finished an order when it's time to set the job up again."
B. Material utilization.
  1. Tolerances. Since standard shop tolerances for fractional dimensions, $\pm \frac{1}{64}$ inch, were used, no basic problems existed in the parts manufacture.
  2. Shop Supervision indicated that once in a great while, if tolerances on the stud (9090547-1) were on the high side, some problems were experienced in assembling the gaskets (9090547-5) onto the stud.
C. Scrap.
  1. As noted above, most scrap is generated mainly on two parts. Fixtures are being looked into to solve the problems on the stud. The outside supplier and Quality Control have been notified regarding the problems with the copper tubing.
  2. The recessed washer (9090547-4) is presently made from $\frac{7}{8}$-inch hex brass; it was suggested by Industrial Engineering that it could be made from a $\frac{1}{2}$-inch brass jam nut.
D. Present suppliers.
  1. Discussion with the buyer disclosed that the $\frac{3}{8}$-inch brass nut (600020-4), $\frac{1}{2}$-inch bronze nut (600020-6), $\frac{3}{8}$-inch lock washer (601120-4), and $\frac{1}{2}$-inch lock washer (601120-6) were standard hardware items used in many places and were therefore bought

| Quantity | Part number | Part name | Material | Labor | Burden | Total |
|----------|-------------|-----------|----------|-------|--------|-------|
| 1 | 9090547 | Connector | | | | |
| 1 | 9090547-1 | Stud, brass | $0.660 | $0.660 | $1.980 | 3.300 |
| 1 | 9090547-2 | Nut, brass | 0.142 | 0.354 | 1.062 | 1.558 |
| 1 | 9090547-3 | Tube, special | 0.228 | 0.525 | 1.575 | 2.328 |
| 1 | 9090547-4 | Washer, recessed | 0.075 | 0.324 | 0.972 | 1.371 |
| 2 | 9090547-5 | Gasket, nitrile | 0.262 | 0.210 | 0.630 | 1.102 |
| 2 | 600020-4 | Nut, hex brass ⅜ in. | 0.148 | . . . . . . | . . . . . . | 0.148 |
| 1 | 600020-6 | Nut, hex bronze ½ in. | 0.129 | . . . . . . | . . . . . . | 0.129 |
| 1 | 601120-4 | Lock washer, ⅜ in. | 0.004 | . . . . . . | . . . . . . | 0.004 |
| 1 | 601120-6 | Lock washer, ½ in. | 0.007 | . . . . . . | . . . . . . | 0.007 |
| Total . . | . . . . . . . . . . . | . . . . . . . . . . . . . . . . | $1.655 | $2.073 | $6.219 | 9.947 |

Figure 14-10

in lots of 1,000 to 10,000 depending on the normal usage of the part.

2. The buyer did question the use of plated washers and of the ½-inch bronze nut. His thought was that since these are not current carrying members and are used in a noncorrosive atmosphere, they would not have to be plated or made of bronze.

**Determine the Costs**    This vital part of the information phase, while listed under the manufacturing data required, is secured from the controller or other source delegated to maintain product cost data. It is important that this data be of the highest reliability, for its analysis will determine whether the project is to be continued. With these thoughts in mind, the team entered into this activity.

A. Product costs for each component and assembly.
1. The costs of the assembly parts are shown in Figure 14-10. These costs, supplied by the Accounting Department, show material, direct labor, and burden.
2. The direct labor content is calculated at $3 per hour.
3. The burden is calculated at 300 percent of direct labor.
B. It should be noted that you should only be interested in the direct material and direct labor costs as these are the only figures on which you can have a direct effect when working on a hardware project. It is recognized that your efforts will have an indirect effect on the burden which should be taken into account by management.

Having thus gathered what at the time appeared to be all the information regarding its project, the team was now ready to relate the costs to the basic specifications and requirements.

**Fix Costs on Specifications and Requirements**    The first specification, the team realized, was the input of 30 amperes to the connector. Looking at their parts and costs, they rationalized that about one-third of the stud's material and labor cost was necessitated to transmit the 30 amperes of current from the input connection to the output connection.

The second specification was that the leads must be attached to the connector and that they must also be readily disconnectable. This, they speculated, was accomplished by the two ⅜-inch brass nuts, by the special brass nut and copper tube, plus about one-third of the cost of the stud (that portion of the cost needed to drill and tap the area for the special nut).

The third specification was that the connector must seal the opening in the insulating panel through which it passed. This, they believed, was accomplished by the two gaskets, the recessed washer, the ½-inch bronze hex nut, and about one-third of the cost of the stud (the ½-inch threaded portion and the recessed area of the stud).

The fourth and last specification or requirement was that the whole assembly should withstand shipping and operational vibrations. This, they determined, was accomplished in the present design by the two lock washers and to a very small degree by the vibration-absorbing qualities of the gaskets.

Using only the material and labor figures, they then related the various costs of the specifications and requirements as shown below:

| Specification or Requirement | Relative Cost |
|---|---|
| 1. 30-ampere input | $0.440 |
| 2. Connection and disconnection | $1.837 |
| 3. Seal opening | $1.404 |
| 4. Resist vibration | $0.011 |
| Total | $3.692 |

With all its information and costs basically interrelated, the team was now prepared to progress to the second phase of the Job Plan: the Function Phase.

*Get all the facts—complete facts lead to more practical recommendations.*

# Chapter Fifteen

# Function Phase

Having secured and documented the basic information and data regarding its project, the connector, the team determined that it was now ready to proceed in its application of the Job Plan. The next step in the Job Plan application to the project was the definition of the functions.

## Define the Function

Since the project was relatively small, the team members decided that the best approach was to define the functions of each part. They then completed the pertinent data part of the functional definition worksheet by filling in the reference number, project name, and project drawing number.

From the information and data, they next determined that the input to their project was 30 amperes of current, also that the output from their project was 30 amperes of current. Realizing that there would be a minor heat effect generated by the conductive resistance of the stud material, they also noted heat as an output.

Next they listed, starting at the physical top of the connector, the various parts of the connector and the quantity of each required (Figure 15-1).

JOY   JOY MANUFACTURING COMPANY                    Ref. No. _MEA-1_

FUNCTIONAL  DEFINITION

Project ___Connector_____ Drawing No. _9090547_

| _30 amps of current_ | | _30 amps of current & heat_ |
| Input | Basic Function | Output |

| Qty. | Part | Function(s) Verb | Function(s) Noun | Func. Part B. | S. | Level Assy. B. | S. | Notes and/or Comments |
|---|---|---|---|---|---|---|---|---|
| 2 | 3/8" Brass nuts 600020-4 | | | | | | | |
| 1 | 3/8" Lock washer 601120-4 | | | | | | | |
| 1 | 1/2" Bronze nut 600020-6 | | | | | | | |
| 1 | 1/2" Lock washer 601120-6 | | | | | | | |
| 1 | Recessed washer 9090547-4 | | | | | | | |
| 2 | Gaskets 9090547-5 | | | | | | | |
| 1 | Stud, brass 9090547-1 | | | | | | | |
| 1 | Nut, brass 9090547-2 | | | | | | | |
| 1 | Tube, special 9090547-3 | | | | | | | |

Team Members _____ Date _____

Form No. 8812   12-66                             VALUE  ENGINEERING

Figure 15-1

While doing this, they made sure that they left sufficient space for more than one function for each part.

They then, with the information and data constantly being reviewed and the assembly in front of them, proceeded to determine the functions of the various parts of the assembly. At the same time the functions for a part were being determined, any pertinent information with regard to the part was entered in the appropriate column of the worksheet.

In order to use as much assistance as possible, they also kept in front of them the list of verbs and nouns of "work" and "sell" functions shown in Part 1, Chapter 7. They did this so that they would not slip into the trap of using the wrong verbs or nouns in their definitions.

With this data in front of them, they were now ready to start at the physical top of the assembly, the two ⅜-inch hex nuts, and define the functions they performed in the assembly and progress from there through the special tube. Their general reasoning and defined functions are detailed below.

**Two 3/8-inch Brass Nuts, 600020-4** In analyzing the functions of these parts, the team first recognized the function of "establish connection" because of the nut's connection of the cover-bushing lead wire to the connector.

Next they determined that in establishing the connection of the lead wire, a "control location" function to the wire was also performed.

Likewise they rationalized that in order for the control of the location to be anywhere near stationary, an "apply pressure" function was being performed.

Finally, they realized that since the bushing lead carried 30 amperes of current and was in contact with at least one of the nuts, the "conduct current" function was being performed.

As each of these functions was determined, they were noted on the functional definition worksheet, in the proper column to the right of the parts. Further analysis showed no other functions for these parts. The team therefore moved on to the analysis of the next part of the connector assembly.

**One 3/8-inch Lock Washer, 601120-4** In the definition of the functions of this simple, everyday part, the team ran into its most heated discussion — a discussion which at times bordered on argument, anger, even physical violence. Such is the case, however, when everyone, in his own mind, is positive of what an item or an object does. (Before reading further, see if you can list the four functions which the team finally determined that the lock washer performed.)

The team, with relative ease, determined that the lock washer did "transmit pressure." That pressure was applied to it by one ⅜-inch nut and it transmitted that pressure to the other ⅜-inch nut.

Lulled into a feeling of confidence by the simplicity of defining functions to this point, the team was not ready for the problem that next confronted it. One team member stated that the lock washer "locked nuts." He was immediately called to a halt by one of his associates who reminded him that the part name "nut" could not be used in the definition of the function. Another team member jumped in with the definition "prevent rotation." This the team pondered over and eventually discarded because it was the result of another action rather than the action of the lock washer. After considerable discussion, table pounding, and vehement pointing of fingers, they consulted the manufacturer's catalog. Upon reading this quite closely, they came to a statement: "The threads of the nut being forced against the threads of the bolt resist both the loosening and tightening of the parts; therefore, proper torquing must be assured." Reading this statement over a number of times gave them the clue they sought, i.e., "The threads of the nut being forced against the threads of the bolt. . . ." From this, they determined, in a quiet and rational manner, that the spring action of the lock washer actually, through its compression, "induced friction," and that it was this friction which prevented rotation.

Having now been through their first confrontation on the definition of function, the team gingerly, even apprehensively, proceeded with their definition of the functions. Looking at the assembly and at the thickness of the compressed lock washer, they realized that it did also "establish location."

Further examination of the assembly as well as the disassembled parts led them to list the function of "resist movement." This function they determined was accomplished by the sharp edges formed by the split in the lock washer. These four functions were those that the team used and put on their functional definition worksheet. From here they were ready, somewhat reluctantly because of the previous disagreements, to analyze the next part to determine what functions it performed in the assembly.

**One 1/2-inch Bronze Nut, 600020-6**  In their examination of this bronze nut, they felt that it, like other nuts, performed the function of "apply pressure"—the applied pressure that was ultimately used to compress the gaskets and seal the opening in the insulating panel.

From the first defined function for this part they moved easily to the second, that being "control location." They rationalized that in applying pressure through the parts below it and ultimately to the insulating panel, it must in some degree control the location of the total assembly.

At this point, they did a considerable amount of thoughtful discussion on what other functions this particular part might perform. The reason for the discussion was that they had only two functions listed for this part while having listed a minimum of four for the previous two. After careful consideration, they found that, as the part was used in the assembly, these were the only two functions it performed.

**One 1/2-inch Lock Washer, 601120-6**    After the heated discussion encountered with the previous lock washer, they examined the use of this one quite carefully. This close examination brought them to one conclusion which was that this lock washer did perform the same functions as the previous one; i.e., "transmit pressure," "induce friction," "establish location," and "resist movement."

Having somewhat breezed through the definition of the functions of this part, the team's confidence started to return. With the return of their confidence came the desire to forge ahead to the next part of the assembly.

**One Recessed Washer, 9090547-4**    This they could readily see "created location" for the gasket by the lip designed around its outside diameter. They also could readily recognize that it did "transmit pressure." That pressure was exerted by the bronze nut down through the lock washer.

The ease with which they were able to define this part's functions further increased their confidence and they hastened to define the functions of the next parts.

**Two Gaskets, 9090547-5**    Now, with the confidence of experts, they determined that the gaskets provide the function "create seal." Likewise they reasoned that these two gaskets, in creating the seal, also, to a degree, did "control location."

Having just gone through the definition of the function of two parts with complete ease, the last one having only two functions, they started to move on to the next part. However, one of the team members brought the others up short by asking if these gaskets didn't also "transmit pressure." On close examination, the other members of the team had to agree that they did indeed transmit the pressure—ultimately to the insulating panel—exerted by the bronze nut.

Being thus brought up short, they took a strong look at the total connector as assembled in the insulating panel and realized that yet another function was performed. This final function was "provide connection." This second, closer look showed them that only the two gaskets and the stud came into contact with the insulating panel, therefore the gaskets had to provide some of the connection of the assembly to the panel.

At this point, all the team members realized that they had become overly confident of their abilities and that they would have to proceed with deliberate care through the rest of the assembly's parts. They also realized that, without too much trouble, this overconfidence could carry over to other projects. They therefore determined that they had been lucky and had learned a vital lesson early in their application of the Job Plan.

Now with assured but guarded confidence, they proceeded to look at the next part to determine what functions it performed within the assembly.

**One Stud, Brass, 9090547-1**    With the gaskets and their last-defined function for them still in mind, they realized that the stud also encompassed the function "provide connection." From the providing of connection, it was easy for them to determine that the stud also did "create location." Their next examination of the assembly as used showed them that the stud did "conduct current" from the bushing to the core and coil lead wires in a direct manner. This they recognized was done through the two nuts at the top and the special tube and nut at the bottom of the assembly.

Again recalling their investigation of the gaskets and the fit of the stud in the hole of the insulating panel, they realized that the stud did "resist movement" of the assembly parallel to the plane of the insulating panel.

Remembering the problems of overconfidence previously encountered, the team took another look at the stud and how it was used. From this close examination, they found yet another function accomplished by the stud, i.e., "transmit pressure." They determined that the pressure applied by the bronze nut was transmitted down the stud, thereby through the hole and up to the lower or second gasket.

Further analysis and examination failed to reveal any further functions accomplished by the stud.

**One Nut, Brass, 9090547-2**    Analysis of this part first showed that it did "create location" for the special tube within the rest of the assembly and that in doing this it did "conduct current." Continued investigation of this part with regard to the assembly showed that it did "establish connection" between the special tube and the stud and that in order to do this, it must "apply pressure" to the tube.

Again close investigation disclosed no additional functions performed by this nut, so the team moved on to the final part of their project assembly.

**One Tube, Special, 9090547-3**    First examination of this part as used disclosed that it did "establish connection" between the core and coil lead crimped into it and the total assembly. The team further realized that in establishing this connection the tube also had to "create location."

Remembering the functions noted for the brass nut above, particularly that of applying pressure, one team member stated that the tube in turn must then "transmit pressure." To this the other team members readily agreed.

Another team member then noted that since the core and coil wire was fastened into the tube by a crimping process, it must "conduct current" also. This function too was listed beside the special tube in the proper column.

The team, not being able to discern any further functions for the special tube, decided to rapidly review all the parts of the assembly once more. This review did not disclose any overlooked functions, but it did make them aware of a number of pertinent facts.

First, in the review of their functional definition worksheet (Figure 15-2) as completed at this point, they realized that there were many redundant functions; i.e., many similar functions performed by different parts. This,

**JOY** JOY MANUFACTURING COMPANY     REF. No. _MEA-1_

FUNCTIONAL DEFINITION

PROJECT _Connector_     DRAWING No. _9090547_

_30 amps of current_     _30 amps of current + heat_
INPUT          BASIC FUNCTION          OUTPUT

| QTY. | PART | FUNCTION(S) | | FUNC. PART | LEVEL ASSY. | NOTES AND/OR COMMENTS |
|---|---|---|---|---|---|---|
| | | VERB | NOUN | B. S. | B. S. | |
| 2 | 3/8" Brass nuts 600020-4 | Establish Control Apply Conduct Resist | Connection Location Pressure Current Pressure | | | Must be readily disconnectable |
| 1 | 3/8" Lock washer 601120-4 | Transmit Induce Establish Resist | Pressure Friction Location Movement | | | Subject to shipping and operational vibration |
| 1 | 1/2" Bronze nut 600020-6 | Apply Control | Pressure Location | | | |
| 1 | 1/2" Lock washer 601120-6 | Transmit Induce Establish Resist | Pressure Friction Location Movement | | | Subject to shipping and operational vibration. |
| 1 | Recessed washer 9090547-4 | Create Transmit | Location Pressure | | | |
| 2 | Gaskets 9090547-5 | Create Control Transmit Provide | Seal Location Pressure Connection | | | Must withstand 7 P.S.I. pressure. |
| 1 | Stud, brass 9090547-1 | Provide Create Conduct Resist Transmit | Connection Location Current Movement Pressure | | | Must fit through 1/2" hole. |
| 1 | Nut, brass 9090547-2 | Create Conduct Establish Apply | Location Current Connection Pressure | | | Must be readily disconnectable. |
| 1 | Tube, special 9090547-3 | Establish Create Transmit Conduct | Connection Location Pressure Current | | | |

TEAM MEMBERS _____     DATE _____
FORM NO. 8812   12-66     VALUE ENGINEERING

Figure 15-2

they realized, could be a strong indication of a duplication of cost and function or the cause of unnecessary cost.

Finally, they noted that the stud contained or played a part in almost every function of the other parts of the assembly. At the time, however, they could not attach any particular significance to the fact.

## Determine Function Levels

In order to accomplish the next step in the functional definition technique, the team had to go back to the two parts of rule 3 of the rules of function definition; i.e., the definitions of basic and secondary functions.

Basic function—The primary purpose for a product or service

Secondary function—Other purposes not directly accomplishing the primary purpose but supporting it or resulting from a specific design approach

Once they had refreshed their memories as to the exact wording of these rules, they were ready to proceed in determining which of the functions for each of the parts were basic and which were secondary. In other words, they had to determine the function levels for each part.

Examining the assembly, and particularly the two ⅜-inch brass nuts and their defined functions, this determined that the "establish connection" function was their reason for being included in the assembly; i.e., their basic function. The team realized that once the connection was established, the location was controlled by the application of pressure by one nut and the resistance of pressure by the other nut. They also saw that since the wire carrying the 30 amperes of current did contact at least one nut, some current was conducted by that nut. The worksheet was therefore checked as shown in Figure 15-3.

After the problems and arguments encountered in the definition of the functions of the lock washer, the team members had little trouble agreeing that this part's basic function was to "induce friction." Similarly they readily agreed that in inducing the friction the lock washer did "transmit pressure," did, because of its compressed thickness "establish location," and because of its shape did "resist movement." Again they marked their decisions on the worksheet.

After a little disagreement, they finally agreed that the bronze nut's basic function, basic reason for being in the assembly, was to "apply pressure." Therefore its secondary function was to "control location."

The determination of the basic function of the ½-inch lock washer, like the defining of its functions, was extremely easy. This is due to the fact that it is just the same as the ⅜-inch lock washer.

As to the recessed washer, the next part in the list, the team determined

**JOY**  JOY MANUFACTURING COMPANY                  Ref. No. _MEA-1_

FUNCTIONAL DEFINITION

Project _Connector_                                    Drawing No. _9090547_

| 30 amps of current | | 30 amps of current + heat | |
|---|---|---|---|
| Input | Basic Function | Output | |

| Qty. | Part | Function(s) Verb | Noun | Func. Part B.\|S. | Level Assy. B.\|S. | Notes and/or Comments |
|---|---|---|---|---|---|---|
| 2 | 3/8 Brass nuts 600020-4 | Establish Control Apply Conduct Resist | Connection Location Pressure Current Pressure | ✓ \| \| ✓ \| ✓ \| ✓ \| ✓ | \| | Must be readily disconnectable |
| 1 | 3/8" Lock washer 601120-4 | Transmit Induce Establish Resist | Pressure Friction Location Movement | \| ✓ ✓ \| \| ✓ \| ✓ | \| | Subject to shipping and operational vibration. |
| 1 | 1/2" Bronze nut 600020-6 | Apply Control | Pressure Location | ✓ \| \| ✓ | \| | |
| 1 | 1/2" Lock washer 601120-6 | Transmit Induce Establish Resist | Pressure Friction Location Movement | \| ✓ ✓ \| \| ✓ \| ✓ | \| | Subject to shipping and operational vibration. |
| 1 | Recessed washer 9090547-4 | Create Transmit | Location Pressure | \| ✓ ✓ \| | \| | |
| 2 | Gaskets 9090547-5 | Create Control Transmit Provide | Seal Location Pressure Connection | ✓ \| \| ✓ \| ✓ \| ✓ | \| | Must withstand 7 p.s.I pressure. |
| 1 | Stud, brass .9090547-1 | Provide Create Conduct Resist Transmit | Connection Location Current Movement Pressure | \| ✓ \| ✓ ✓ \| \| ✓ \| ✓ | \| | Must fit through 1/2" hole |
| 1 | Nut, brass 9090547-2 | Create Conduct Establish Apply | Location Current Connection Pressure | \| ✓ \| ✓ ✓ \| \| ✓ | \| | Must be readily disconnectable |
| 1 | Tube, special 9090547-3 | Establish Create Transmit Conduct | Connection Location Pressure Current | ✓ \| \| ✓ \| ✓ \| ✓ | \| | |

Team Members _____  Date _____

FORM NO. 8812  12—66                          VALUE ENGINEERING

Figure 15-3

its basic function to be "transmit pressure," leaving thereby as secondary the function "create location."

Moving on to the two gaskets, the team members again found their task an easy one. They realized that the only reason that the gaskets were put into the assembly was to "create seal," which had to be the basic function. They also realized that in creating the seal the gaskets did "control location," "transmit pressure," and "provide connection"—these functions all falling into the secondary level.

The team found that some study had to be made of the stud's five defined functions and of the assembly before they could determine its basic function. After discussion and deliberation, they decided that the stud's basic function was to "conduct current," since this was the only part that passed through the insulating panel. The other functions they then checked as being secondary on the worksheet.

Again, after studying the part as used in the assembly followed by some discussion of the part's functions, the team realized that this part's basic purpose was to "establish connection" between the special tube and the stud. They further deduced that in order to assure this connection, the function of "apply pressure" was brought into play which in turn established the function of "create location." In the accomplishment of these functions, they realized that the part did "conduct current." Having determined this, they so marked their worksheet.

Again moving on to the last part of the assembly and having progressed quite well, one team member stated that this part's basic function was "create location." To this a second team member strongly objected because he thought the basic function was "conduct current." Upon this statement, the first and third members of the team disagreed.

At this point, all three team members sat back and laughed because they realized that once again, in their zeal to finish a given step, they had been trapped into making individual snap decisions, decisions which were based on personal feelings rather than facts. With these thoughts in mind, they closely examined the part, its functions, and the assembly, and they simultaneously said that the basic function of the special tube was "establish connection" and that the other functions were accomplished as a result of the connection being established. Having marked their worksheet to this degree, they were ready to move on to the next technique, that of establishing functional relationships, in order to finish this phase of the Job Plan.

It should be noted at this point, however, that the last part of the foregoing technique has accomplished a very significant separation, namely, separation of functional levels. This step has not only separated the basic and secondary functions of the parts but has greatly reduced the number of functions to be considered for the basic function of the assembly. This is due to the fact that if a function is not basic to a part it cannot be basic, or even directly secondary, to the assembly. So in this step, the number of individual functions for consideration has been reduced from twelve to six. At this point, it would be relatively easy to go back to the top of the functional definition worksheet and fill in the basic function of the assembly, although it would still be no more than a strong assumption. This, however, would do little good as there would be no delineation of the descending order of the secondary functions or the establishment of the weighted difference between any of the functions, basic or secondary.

To take all guesswork out of the determination of the assembly's basic function, to determine the secondary function's descending order, and to establish a weighted relationship among all functions, the team moved on to the second technique of the Function Phase.

## Evaluate Functional Relationships

Once the team had secured the full detailed information and data regarding their project and in turn had converted this into defined functions, they were ready to determine the relative importance of these functions, their importance to the assembly, and their importance to each other. To accomplish this, they employed the technique of numerical evaluation of functional relationships.

Taking functional worksheet V.E. 2B, they first filled in the pertinent project data; i.e., reference number, assembly name, and drawing number. This was done, as with all worksheets, so that all the material for their project could be identified and retained for future reference if required.

Then, referring to the functional definition worksheet, they selected the basic function of each part. These they listed in the evaluation summary section of the V.E. 2B worksheet as shown in Figure 15-4. At this point, two facts should be noted. First, although there are nine different parts listed for the assembly, only six functions are listed. This is due to the fact that no function is listed twice in the evaluation summary because it would, during the comparison portion of the technique, have to be compared to itself, which would be useless. Second, that as each function is listed in the evaluation summary, it automatically acquires a *key letter*. This is necessary for use in the comparison step of the technique to reduce the writing that must be done and to hold the record keeping portion to a minimum. Now the team was ready to proceed into the comparison step of the technique.

## Comparison and Weighing of Functions

At this point, the functional definition worksheet is set aside and functional worksheet 2B is fully undertaken. This second step of the technique is car-

JOY MANUFACTURING COMPANY

REF. NO. MEA-1

FUNCTIONAL EVALUATION

PROJECT Connector

DRAWING NO. 9090547

EVALUATION SUMMARY

| KEY LETTER | FUNCTIONS | WEIGHT |
|---|---|---|
| A | Establish connection | |
| B | Induce friction | |
| C | Apply pressure | |
| D | Transmit pressure | |
| E | Create seal | |
| F | Conduct current | |
| G | | |
| H | | |
| I | | |
| J | | |
| K | | |
| L | | |
| M | | |
| N | | |

NUMERICAL EVALUATION

| | B | C | D | E | F | G | H | I | J | K | L | M | N |
|---|---|---|---|---|---|---|---|---|---|---|---|---|---|
| A | | | | | | | | | | | | | |
| B | | | | | | | | | | | | | |
| C | | | | | | | | | | | | | |
| D | | | | | | | | | | | | | |
| E | | | | | | | | | | | | | |
| F | | | | | | | | | | | | | |
| G | | | | | | | | | | | | | |
| H | | | | | | | | | | | | | |
| I | | | | | | | | | | | | | |
| J | | | | | | | | | | | | | |
| K | | | | | | | | | | | | | |
| L | | | | | | | | | | | | | |
| M | | | | | | | | | | | | | |

NOTE: – EVALUATION WEIGHT FACTORS

1 = MINOR DIFFERENCE IN IMPORTANCE
2 = MEDIUM DIFFERENCE IN IMPORTANCE
3 = MAJOR DIFFERENCE IN IMPORTANCE

TEAM MEMBERS ______ DATE ______

FORM NO. 8829 12–66

VALUE ENGINEERING

**Figure 15-4**

ried out using the numerical evaluation portion of the worksheet in conjunction with the evaluation summary portion. This is done by comparing one function to only one other function at a time. While doing this, it is determined which function is of greater importance as well as what the magnitude of the difference in importance is.

Starting with function A, "establish connection," the team compared it to function B, "induce friction." This comparison was made to find out how each function related to the complete assembly, so that the team might determine which one was of the greatest importance. Having compiled and fully understood the pertinent data, a knowledgeable decision was made. When the decision had been reached, the key letter corresponding to the function having the greater importance was placed in the AB block of the numerical evaluation (Figure 15-5). In this case, it was determined that key letter A, "establish connection," was more important than B, "induce friction."

### NUMERICAL EVALUATION

| | B | C | D | E | F | G | H | I | J | K | L | M | N |
|---|---|---|---|---|---|---|---|---|---|---|---|---|---|
| A | A | | | | | | | | | | | | |
| B | | | | | | | | | | | | | |

Figure 15-5

As the above decision was being formulated, the magnitude of the difference in importance was also being rationalized. That is to say, it was being determined whether the difference in importance was of a minor, medium, or major magnitude. When the difference was determined, it also was marked in the AB block (1 indicating a minor difference, 2 for a medium difference, and 3 for major difference). In the above comparison of function A to function B, the team determined that there was a major difference in importance; therefore, a weight factor of 3 was placed in the AB block after the A as shown in Figure 15-6. This, simply stated, was determined by how readily the team arrived at the decision.

### Numerical Evaluation

| | B | C | D | E | F | G | H | I | J | K | L | M | N |
|---|---|---|---|---|---|---|---|---|---|---|---|---|---|
| A | A3 | | | | | | | | | | | | |
| B | | | | | | | | | | | | | |

Figure 15-6

The team then continued their comparison of function A — "establish connection" — with each of the other functions in their turn; i.e., they compared function A to functions C, D, E, and F. As each weighted comparison was made, the key letter and weight factor were marked in the appropriate block of the first line in the numerical evaluation. When they had completed their weighted comparison of function A, the chart was filled in as shown in Figure 15-7.

Function $A$ having been compared to all other functions in the evaluation summary, it can now be forgotten for the time being. The team now moves down to function $B$ — "induce friction" — and compares it to each function below it in the evaluation summary; i.e., they compare it to functions $C$,

Numerical Evaluation

| | B | C | D | E | F | G | H | I | J | K | L | M | N |
|---|---|---|---|---|---|---|---|---|---|---|---|---|---|
| A | A·3 | A·3 | A·3 | E·2 | F·3 | | | | | | | | |
| B | | | | | | | | | | | | | |

Figure 15-7

$D$, $E$, and $F$. Again, as each weighted comparison was made, the key letter and weight factor were determined and marked in the appropriate block of the second line in the numerical evaluation section of the worksheet. When they had completed their weighted comparison of function $B$, the chart was filled in as shown in Figure 15-8.

Continuing with their comparison-weighting evaluation, the team individually compared functions $C$, $D$, $E$, and $F$ to every other function, one at a time, and a weighted comparison was established with each comparison. When this had been accomplished, the numerical evaluation portion of worksheet 2B had been completed as shown in Figure 15-9.

It should be noted that, had the team deemed it necessary to cross-check their individual knowledge of the project information data, each team

| | B | C | D | E | F | G | H | I | J | K | L | M | N |
|---|---|---|---|---|---|---|---|---|---|---|---|---|---|
| A | A·3 | A·3 | A·3 | E·2 | F·3 | | | | | | | | |
| B | B·/ | B·/ | E·3 | F·3 | | | | | | | | | |

Figure 15-8

member could have executed this weighted comparison part of the technique independently of the others and then they could have compared their summary results to determine if there were any misunderstanding or disagreements. This procedure is usually followed on more complex projects to cross-check a team's knowledge of the basic information.

## Preliminary Summation

When the evaluations had been completed and a weighted importance in the comparison of each function to every other function had been determined, the team undertook the preliminary summation. This summation is recorded in the evaluation summary portion of worksheet 2B.

| | B | C | D | E | F | G | H | I | J | K | L | M | N |
|---|---|---|---|---|---|---|---|---|---|---|---|---|---|
| A | A·3 | A·3 | A·3 | E·2 | F·3 | | | | | | | | |
| B | | B·1 | B·1 | E·3 | F·3 | | | | | | | | |
| C | | | C·1 | E·3 | F·3 | | | | | | | | |
| D | | | | F·3 | F·3 | | | | | | | | |
| E | | | | | F·3 | | | | | | | | |

Figure 15-9

Here, the weight factors of each key letter are totaled from the numerical evaluation and placed in the weight column beside the corresponding letter. Care should be used to make sure that all weight factors for a key letter are added to arrive at the total weight; i.e., it is important to add the weight factors in both the horizontal and vertical directions.

The team, referring to the numerical evaluation portion of their worksheet (Figure 15-10), noted that key letter A was placed in the chart three times and had a total weight 9.

Numerical Evaluation

| | B | C | D | E | F |
|---|---|---|---|---|---|
| A | A·③ | A·③ | A·③ | E·2 | F·3 |
| B | | B·1 | B·1 | E·3 | F·3 |

Figure 15-10

They therefore noted in the weight column of the evaluation summary the number nine in the first line opposite to key letter A and the function "establish connection," Figure 15-11. This then indicated that this function, with reference to the total assembly, had a total weight of 9.

In the same manner, for each key letter, the team added the weight factors from their previous independent decisions. The total weight factor for

EVALUATION SUMMARY

| KEY LETTER | FUNCTIONS | WEIGHT |
|---|---|---|
| A | Provide connection | 9 |
| B | Induce friction | |

Figure 15-11

| Key<br>Letter | Functions | Weight |
|---|---|---|
| A | *Provide connection* | *9* |
| B | *Induce friction* | *2* |
| C | *Apply pressure* | *1* |
| D | *Transmit pressure* | *0* |
| E | *Provide seal* | *11* |
| F | *Conduct current* | *15* |
| G | | |

Figure 15-12

each key letter (and function) was noted in its proper line. When this was accomplished, the evaluation summary was as shown in Figure 15-12.

To conclude this preliminary summation, the team on the bottom of worksheet 2B relisted the six functions in their descending order, by totalized weight factor. This list of functions with their weight factors was as follows:

1. Conduct Current . . . . . . 15
2. Create Seal . . . . . . . . . 11
3. Establish Connection . . . 9
4. Induce Friction . . . . . . . 2
5. Apply Pressure . . . . . . . 1
6. Transmit Pressure . . . . . 0
   Assembly Weight . . . . . . 38

## Final Summation

From the descending order list thus established, the team was able to positively state that the Basic Function of the connector was "conduct current;" also that all of the other functions were secondary. This list further showed them, by comparison of the weight factors, the relationship of each function to the assembly plus the magnitude of difference between the individual functions.

The final, and one of the most significant, things shown by this listing is which functions are in the project design because of specifications or requirements and which functions are in the project design because of the present specific approach. All of the above points are perhaps more vividly apparent when the function's weight factors are graphically plotted (Figure 15-13).

This graph form, or function profile, plotted on the back of worksheet 2B, will always have the same basic form when plotted for the weight factors of an object's functions. The points of the graph form to be noted are, first, a single high point; second, a major drop; third, a leveling effect;

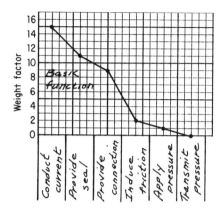

Figure 15-13

fourth, a second major drop; and, last, a final leveling effect ending at or near zero weight. The significance of these facts are as follows:

1. High point: This indicates the basic function of the object studied.
2. First major drop: Isolation of basic and secondary-level functions.
3. First leveling effect: Includes the secondary functions that are in the project to meet specifications and requirements.
4. Second major drop: Separation of the two types of secondary functions.
5. Second leveling effect: Includes the secondary functions that are in the project because of the present approach.

The team completed worksheet 2B by noting their names and the date at the bottom. The completed worksheet 2B is shown in Figure 15-14.

From the knowledge gained from this technique, the team was then able to return to and complete the functional definition worksheet. This they did by first completing the upper portion of the worksheet by filling in the basic function space left blank early in this phase of the Job Plan. Then, in the functional level-assembly subcolumns, they noted beside each part's basic function its position in the descending order of importance; this was done by using numbers rather than check marks in the appropriate subcolumns (Figure 15-15).

## Functional Phase Conclusions

From the knowledge gained through the application of this phase's two techniques, a number of pertinent points can be highlighted:

1. Of the thirty-four individual part functions, only nine are basic to an individual part. Of these nine, three are performed by two or more parts and only one is basic to the whole assembly.
2. It can be seen that there are cases where one part performs multiple

Figure 15-14

functions necessary to the present assembly; i.e., the stud. At the same time, many parts perform the same function.

3. Redundant functions, such as "establish connection" and "create location," can be seen throughout the assembly, and all are suspected of adding unnecessary cost.

4. That there are at least two levels of second-degree functions: those

**JOY**  JOY MANUFACTURING COMPANY          Ref. No. _MEA-1_

FUNCTIONAL  DEFINITION

Project ___Connector___          Drawing No. _9090541_

| _30 amps of current_ INPUT | _Conduct Current_ BASIC FUNCTION | _30 amps of current + heat_ OUTPUT |
|---|---|---|

| Qty. | Part | Function(s) Verb | Noun | Func. Part B. | S. | Level Assy. B. | S. | Notes and/or Comments |
|---|---|---|---|---|---|---|---|---|
| 2 | 3/8"Brass nuts 600020-4 | Establish Control Apply Conduct Resist | Connection Location Pressure Current Pressure | √ | √ √ √ √ | | ③ | Must be readily disconnectable |
| 1 | 3/8"Lock washer 601120-4 | Transmit Induce Establish Resist | Pressure Friction Location Movement | √ | √ √ √ | | ④ | Subject to shipping and operational vibration |
| 1 | 1/2"Bronze nut 600020-4 | Apply Control | Pressure Location | √ | √ | | ⑤ | |
| 1 | 1/2"Lock washer 601120-4 | Transmit Induce Establish Resist | Pressure Friction Location Movement | √ | √ √ √ | | ④ | Subject to shipping and operational vibration |
| 1 | Recessed washer 9090541-4 | Create Transmit | Location Pressure | √ | √ | | ⑥ | |
| 2 | Gaskets 9090541-5 | Create Control Transmit Provide | Seal Location Pressure Connection | √ | √ √ √ | | ② | Must withstand 7 P.S.I. pressure |
| 1 | Stud, brass 9090541-1 | Provide Create Conduct Resist Transmit | Connection Location Current Movement Pressure | √ | √ √ √ √ | ① | | Must fit through 1/2" hole. |
| 1 | Nut, brass 9090541-2 | Create Conduct Establish Apply | Location Current Connection Pressure | √ | √ √ √ | | ③ | Must be readily disconnectable |
| 1 | Tube, special 9090541-3 | Establish Create Transmit Conduct | Connection Location Pressure Current | √ | √ √ √ | | ③ | |

Team Members _John A. Doe, Bill E. Egan, Frank M. Smith_ ___ Date ___9-5-___

FORM NO. 8812  12-66                          VALUE  ENGINEERING

Figure 15-15

required due to specifications and requirements and those due to the present approach.

5. That the only functions which the team must concentrate on throughout the rest of their study are the basic function and the secondary functions needed to fulfill the specifications and requirements.

6. That the function "transmit pressure" is really a dependent secondary function and cannot be accomplished before another work function, above it in the descending order, is accomplished.

When the foregoing was completed and analyzed by the team, it was immediately apparent that changes could be made to reduce the connector's costs. This they believed could be done by accomplishing the necessary functions in a different manner and still retaining the required reliability, quality, and maintainability. In order to start this change process, they moved on to the next phase of the Job Plan, the Creation Phase.

# Chapter Sixteen

# Creation Phase

Leadership, in any degree, is becoming more and more concerned with change. Change has been and is becoming the dominant concern of all individuals, and growth plans are geared to projected changes in technology, habit, taste, power supply, raw material, production methods, wealth, and many other considerations. As these basic factors change, so the individual's activities must change to meet them; and change can only be of two kinds—imitative or creative. Change can be made in the manner and way other people have changed already, or it can be in a new way. The individual can follow or he can lead. The individual can wait until he finds out how others have coped with a problem and follow their lead, or he can think up original ideas that they have not hit on. If he does that, he is being creative in the fullest sense.

Change through creativity is not an on-again, off-again sideline in the business of leadership, it is a specific part of the whole idea. Creativity, change, and leadership are all a part of the same entity; one is not possible without the other two.

To put it in its simplest terms, creativity is the putting together of two unconnected facts or ideas and thus forming a single new idea. This, however, is in itself an art. An art which, without proper preparation, is fundamentally impossible to perform. This preparation is in essence handled by the first technique of the Creation Phase; i.e., establishing positive thinking.

## Establish Positive Thinking

The team members, recognizing that they had been working hard and with considerable concentration, decided to take a break. They decided to unlimber their minds by, for a short time, leaving the immediate work area, forgetting the project, and discussing other things.

In addition, before leaving the work area, they cleared everything referring to the project from sight. They removed from the working area the assembly and all drawings, information, and data. In essence, they removed everything relating to the assembly which could in any way prejudice their minds.

The only thing left to be worked on upon their return to the project was a list of the three two-word functions necessary to the project; i.e., "conduct current," "create seal," and "establish connection." They also left some blank sheets of paper on which to write their creative ideas.

These actions were taken by the team because they knew that if any material relating to the present assembly were in view, their creative thoughts and ideas would be prejudiced by it. They also knew that at this point in the Creation Phase of the Job Plan and particularly in this part of the phase, no thought of the present assembly, in whole or in part, could be considered. Similarly they realized that, in order to be most creative, the only things they could consider were the two words which defined each function.

In this way, they knew that their mental blinders would be to a greater extent removed and that they could develop and produce a multitude of ideas. They also realized that many of these ideas might seem farfetched or ridiculous at the time.

Having taken these actions, the team was ready to progress into the second technique of the phase; i.e., developing creative ideas.

## Develop Creative Ideas

The team decided to approach this technique basically from two directions: unassisted and assisted creativity. Their first approach, unassisted creativity, was nothing more or less than a test of their untrained creative ability. To do this, they decided that each individual would take a single function and list on the creative worksheet as many ideas for that function as he could—first, however, completing the data portion at the top of the worksheet.  Figure 16-1 shows the worksheet started by the team member who was to begin his work on the function "conduct current."

One of the team members, having listed all the ideas he could think of for his assigned function (between six and ten ideas), passed his creative worksheet on to the next man.  The second team member then read the ideas of the first and added his own ideas, including those generated by the first individual.  When this was done, the second man passed the worksheet to the third team member.  Each team member followed the same procedure until each member had acted on every function.  In this manner, they generated for each function a list of between fifteen and twenty-two different ideas.

They then prepared for their second approach: assisted creativity.  Their

---

**JOY**  JOY MANUFACTURING COMPANY                    Ref. No. _MEA-1_

                              CREATION WORKSHEET

Function___ Conduct current_____

| I. |
| 2. |
| 3. |
| 4. |
| 5. |
| 6. |
| 7. |
| 8. |

| 18. |
| 19. |
| 20. |
| 2 I. |
| 22. |
| 23. |
| 24. |
| 25. |

Team Members_____ Date_____

FORM NO.  8814  12—66                              VALUE ENGINEERING

Figure 16-1

preparations for this entailed securing a dictionary and copies of the creativity checklists shown in Part 1, Chapter 8. When they had gathered this material, one team member took the checklists, another the dictionary, and the third the worksheet.

The team member with the worksheets then read all the ideas listed for a function. The other two team members then, using their individual aids, started to single out new ideas to be added to the list. Also during this period of creativity, all the team members would "hitchhike" on each others' ideas. In this way they built on the original idea or added a new idea which had been generated by something said by one of the teammates.

This process was not, and had not been expected to be, a bed of roses. For although they had made a distinct effort to prepare themselves mentally not to be judicial, at times they were. Recognizing in the beginning that this would most likely occur, they had prepared for it. The team as a whole had agreed that, if at any time in their creative session someone thought anyone else was being judicial, he was strongly and loudly to bang the table with his fist.

As you can well imagine, at first the table literally vibrated from the dirge of pounding fists. However, as these vibrations gradually but strongly affected each one's mind, the judicial or negative comments about various ideas stopped. As a matter of fact, as is often the case, the pendulum swung to the opposite extreme for a short period of time. For now each team member, knowingly or unknowingly, put forth crazier and crazier ideas, trying to drive the other two into a negative comment so that he in turn could bang the table (we are all childish at times—no matter what our age).

When both phases of the judicial thinking period had passed, the team members started to rapidly develop their lists of creative ideas on each of the functions. When they would come to a stagnation point, they would exchange material and repeat the process.

When they had finished, they had developed, for each function, a list of from 40 to 100 ideas. Figures 16-2, 16-3, and 16-4 show only a partial list of the team's ideas for each function. The team produced these lists by making a first creative evaluation of the total list for each function and setting aside those ideas, most of which were generated during the second part of the judicial period, which they did not believe were in any way applicable to their project.

In reviewing their list of ideas, as you should do, the team members could readily see how the team effort had assisted them in developing a multitude of ideas for each function. They could readily see where they had, with each function, been able to "hitchhike" on each others' ideas (example: "create seal," ideas 5 through 11). They could also see how the checklists had added ideas (example: "conduct current," ideas 33 through 39).

```
┌──────────────────────────────────────────────────────────────────────┐
│  (JOY)  JOY MANUFACTURING COMPANY              REF. No. _MEA-1____      │
│                         CREATION WORKSHEET                             │
│  ──────────────────────────────────────────────────────────────────   │
│  FUNCTION ___Conduct current_____   │
│  ════════════════════════════════════════════════════════════════════ │
│   1. Wire                          26. Electrolyte                     │
│   2. Bolt                          27. Aluminum                        │
│   3. Welding rod                   28. Ions                           │
│   4. Water                         29. Liquid                          │
│   5. Air                           30. Oil                             │
│   6. Iron                          31. Lead                            │
│   7. Steel                         32. Zinc                            │
│   8. Brass                         33. Tube                            │
│   9. Copper                        34. Pipe                            │
│  10. Paper clip                    35. Wood                            │
│  11. Nail                          36. Fuse                            │
│  12. Laser                         37. Socket                          │
│  13. Magnetic field                38. Plug                            │
│  14. Rod                           39. Washer                          │
│  15. Screw                         40. Transistor                      │
│  16. Nut                           41. Solution                        │
│  17. Clip                          42. Heated glass                    │
│  18. Tape                          43. Foil                            │
│  19. Plastic                                                           │
│  20. Human body                                                        │
│  21. Bar                                                               │
│  22. Carbon                                                            │
│  23. Radiate                                                           │
│  24. Gas                                                               │
│  25. Dirt                                                              │
│                                                                        │
│                                                                        │
│  TEAM MEMBERS _John A. Doe, Bill E. Egan, Frank M. Smith_ DATE _9-5-_  │
│  FORM NO. 8814  12-66                          VALUE ENGINEERING       │
└──────────────────────────────────────────────────────────────────────┘
```

Figure 16-2

JOY MANUFACTURING COMPANY                    Ref. No. _MEA-1_____

CREATION WORKSHEET

Function____Create seal_____

| | |
|---|---|
| 1. Paint | 26. Braze |
| 2. Rubber | 27. Plate |
| 3. Ring | 28. Solder |
| 4. Plug | 29. Glass |
| 5. Dried blood | 30. Vacuum |
| 6. Varnish | 31. Spigot |
| 7. Glue | 32. Labyrinth |
| 8. Plastic | 33. Water |
| 9. Epoxy | 34. Dovetail |
| 10. Wax | 35. Cork |
| 11. Pitch | 36. Flange |
| 12. Chrome | 37. Paper |
| 13. Weld | 38. Rod |
| 14. Rivet | 39. Foam plastic |
| 15. Fit | 40. Stopper |
| 16. Washer | |
| 17. Soap | |
| 18. Gasket | |
| 19. Leather | |
| 20. Grease | |
| 21. Air | |
| 22. Heat | |
| 23. Freeze | |
| 24. Compress | |
| 25. Expand | |

Team Members _John A. Doe, Bill E. Egan, Frank M. Smith__ Date___9-5-_____

FORM NO. 8814   12—66                          VALUE  ENGINEERING

Figure 16-3

JOY MANUFACTURING COMPANY                    Ref. No. _MEA-1_

CREATION WORKSHEET

Function ___Establish connection___

| | |
|---|---|
| 1. String | 26. Heat |
| 2. Rope | 27. Tack |
| 3. Adhesive | 28. Sew |
| 4. Stud | 29. Laminate |
| 5. Bolt | 30. Dovetail |
| 6. Terminal | 31. Wedge |
| 7. Weld | 32. Fuse |
| 8. Clip | 33. Hold |
| 9. Glue | 34. Staple |
| 10. Pressure | 35. Paper clip |
| 11. Screw | 36. Stitch |
| 12. Nail | 37. Vacuum |
| 13. Rivet | 38. Key |
| 14. Tape | 39. Train |
| 15. Tie | 40. Thread |
| 16. Bind | 41. Couple |
| 17. Lash | 42. Button |
| 18. Chain | 43. Magnetic force |
| 19. Join | 44. Weight |
| 20. Fit | 45. Twist |
| 21. Wire | 46. Clamp |
| 22. Solder | |
| 23. Braze | |
| 24. Pinch | |
| 25. Crimp | |

Team Members _John A. Doe, Bill E. Egan, Frank M. Smith_    Date_ 9-5-_

FORM NO. 8814  12—66                              VALUE ENGINEERING

Figure 16-4

The team members could also see from their lists the effects of their individual backgrounds and knowledge, of their fears of being different and their desire to tread the normal path. Besides this, however, they also saw the effects of a gradually opening mind, a moving away from the usual to the unusual, and the advantages of working as a team on creative efforts.

These latter points they knew could, with practice, be developed into useful tools for their everyday work.

Having generated these lists of ideas for each function, they were now ready to put their judicial thinking caps back on and proceed into the next phase of the Job Plan; i.e., the Evaluation Phase.

*The shrewd man looks ahead; the simple man looks up; the resigned man looks down; the frightened man looks behind; only the wise man looks within.* — SYDNEY J. HARRIS

# Chapter Seventeen

# Evaluation Phase

*The key to growth is in increasing value, and
the key to increasing value is essentially one of
good evaluation.*

The team, having completed that portion of the Job Plan which restricted or actually eliminated judicial thinking, now had to mentally shift gears. After having gone through such a deliberate process of eliminating their judicial thinking and then actively guarding against its reappearance, they now had to reverse the process.

This, to say the least, was not easy. This they understood had to be done, but done carefully. It had to be done to be sure that the pendulum, in reverse travel, did not overshoot the desired mark.

The team realized that in this Evaluation Phase they would have to, in essence, walk a straight and narrow path, one on which they had to be judicial toward their creative ideas and at the same time be creative toward any new problems or roadblocks which might occur.

In order to be prepared, in their own minds, for this semitransition, they determined that their best move was to reestablish mental and physical contact with the project. This they did both on paper and in mind.

## Establish the Requirements

In order to thus prepare themselves for their work in the Evaluation Phase the team reassembled, for easy and constant reference, the relevant and related data on their project. Here they once again brought together the information about the connector that they had collected in the Information Phase. They did not, however, bring out the connector or its drawings as they knew this would influence their thinking. They also laid in front of themselves, in separate piles, the worksheets from the Function Phase and the Creation Phase. At this point they had three separate piles of material before them.

Next, in order to graphically or pictorially illustrate the requirements of their project, they sketched all the physical parameters and specifications they could. In addition, at the bottom of this sketch, they noted those parameters and specifications which could not be displayed pictorially. The sketch, Figure 17-1, outlines in pictorial form the major physical parameters within which the project problem exists. In addition, in order to retain their thinking on the basic problem and not let it wander to other possible problems, they boxed in the area which encompassed their specific problem. By so doing, they made sure that all their evaluation and development efforts would be concentrated within this area.

This boxing or limiting process does not, if the occasion should arise, prevent the team from noting for future study problems outside the specific area. It does, however, keep constantly before them the fact that this problem must be solved in its entirety first, before any additional problems are undertaken.

The final step that the team took regarding this description of the problem parameters and specifications was to list those governing factors which could not be shown in pictorial form. In so doing, they established by picture and word the governing parameters and specifications over which they had no control—which they had accepted and therefore could not change.

Having thus collected and prepared the information and data for ready reference and use, they were ready to take the difficult step into judicial-creative development. To make matters worse, the team members realized that in this phase of the Job Plan, unlike the previous phases, all the techniques are applied more or less at the same time. They did recall that the dominating technique, or one to which the others gave assistance, was developing function alternatives.

## Develop Function Alternatives

At this point the team, somewhat reluctantly, undertook the work on the functional development worksheet. Their first step, of course, was to fill in the project reference number and basic function as called for at the top of the worksheet.

This done, they blankly stared at the worksheet literally afraid to take the next step, anticipating all the arguments which they knew were to come and knowing in their respective minds that nothing could be done to avoid them. They forgot, however, the power of teamwork.

Reluctantly, one team member wrote on the functional development worksheet the function "conduct current." This he had selected because it was the basic function of the assembly as determined in the functional

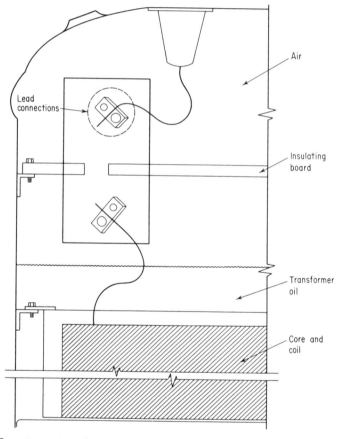

Parameters and specifications

A. Bushing lead wire input 30 amperes
B. Bushing and coil lead wires 4 ¼" apart
C. Connections to lead wires must be readily disconnectable
D. Complete unit subject to shipping and operational vibration
E. Pressure generated in operation 7 P.S.I.
F. Hole in insulating panel ½" in diameter

**Figure 17-1**

| JOY MANUFACTURING COMPANY | | R**ɛ**ᶠ. No.  *M EA- I* |
|---|---|---|
| FUNCTIONAL DEVELOPMENT | | |

B**A**ᵴıᴄ F**U**ɴᴄᴛıᴏɴ ___*Conduct current*___

| FUNCTION | CREATIVE IDEA(S) & DEVELOPMENT | ESTIMATED COST (CUMULATIVE) |
|---|---|---|
| *Conduct current* | *Paper clip* | *$.001* |

**Figure 17-2**

evaluation process. This function had a total weight factor of 15, the highest of all the functions. He, with the other team members' consent, realized that this was the place to start, at base zero. Having noted, in the function column of the functional development worksheet the function "conduct current," the team selected the creative worksheet for this function. Gaining a little confidence at this point, they looked at this worksheet to select that idea or combination of ideas which could possibly perform this function for the lowest cost, making sure that they only considered the two-word function—nothing more. After concentration and thought, with a somewhat flippant attitude, they selected what they believed was the lowest-cost idea they had listed. They selected idea 10—paper clip—which they assured themselves was low in cost, simple, and yet readily accessible. As a matter of fact, it was so accessible that there were a number of paper clips right on the table within arm's reach. How much more accessible could one want anything to be?

This idea, although somewhat frivolous, was added to the worksheet in the creative ideas and development column to the right of the function "conduct current." This brought the team to the last column of the worksheet, also bringing them up short in their thought pattern. They had to assign or determine a cost for the idea they had noted. The team member from Purchasing jumped in at this point, for he knew the cost of the paper clips.

From his experience he knew that, in quantity purchases, boxes of one hundred no. 1 paper clips cost 10 cents per box. Therefore, one paper clip would cost no more than $\frac{1}{10}$ cent. This then was added in the third column, entitled "Estimated cost," of the functional development worksheet. At this time the team members, who until this point, because of numerous apprehensions, had been somewhat frivolous, became quite serious and completed this line of the worksheet as shown in Figure 17-2.

The members also took their sketch of the problem parameters and drew into it a view of the paper clip. In this way, although individually still laughing to themselves, they maintained a pictorial record of their idea development to this point.  The individual members of the team, although reluctant to admit it at this point, were quite intrigued with this idea of conducting current with a paper clip.  As a matter of fact, they thought to themselves "Can't you just see this company of ours putting a paper clip in one of its products?"  They did, however, complete their sketch as shown in Figure 17-3.

Having drawn the paper clip into the sketch, they became intrigued with the parameters and specifications listed below the sketch.  In reviewing these, it became vividly apparent that the stated parameter "*B* bushing and

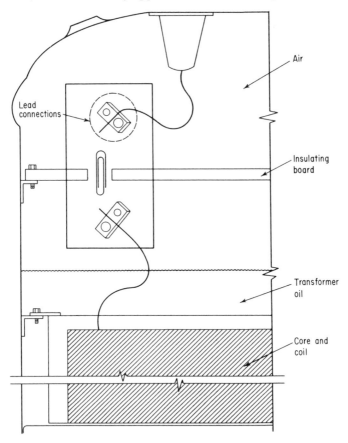

Parameters and specifications
    A. Bushing lead wire input 30 amperes
    B. Bushing and coil lead wires $4\frac{1}{4}$" apart
    C. Connections to lead wires must be readily disconnectable
    D. Complete unit subject to shipping and operational vibration
    E. Pressure generated in operation 7 P.S.I.
    F. Hole in insulating panel $\frac{1}{2}$" in diameter

Figure 17-3

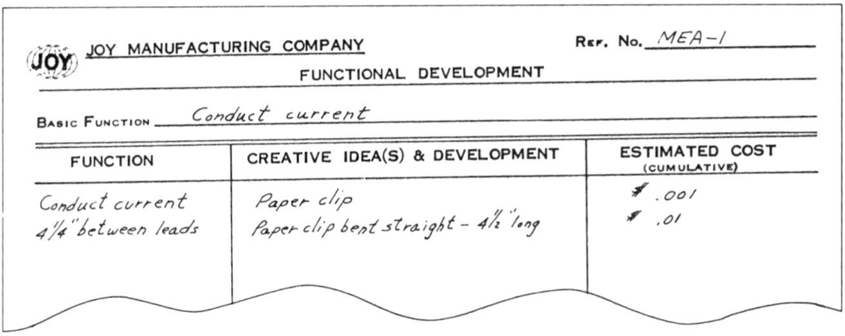

JOY MANUFACTURING COMPANY — REF. No. MEA-1

FUNCTIONAL DEVELOPMENT

BASIC FUNCTION: Conduct current

| FUNCTION | CREATIVE IDEA(S) & DEVELOPMENT | ESTIMATED COST (CUMULATIVE) |
|---|---|---|
| Conduct current | Paper clip | ¢ .001 |
| 4¼" between leads | Paper clip bent straight – 4½" long | ¢ .01 |

Figure 17-4

coil lead wires 4¼ inches apart" was not being met by the paper clip. In recognizing this, they knew that they could not go any further until this parameter and all the others significant to the function "conduct current" were met. They therefore decided that they must meet this parameter before proceeding, in jest or in fact, with their functional devlopment of alternatives.

The first step they took to remedy this deficiency was to again review, in a serious manner, the ideas stipulated in the creative worksheet developed for this function "conduct current." They did this to see if this paper clip idea could be combined with another idea or if it could be further developed to answer this new parameter or specification. Through this effort and search, they determined that when the paper clip was straightened, it would form a piece of wire, similar to idea 1, which would adequately fulfill this parameter because, having done this, they found the paper clip wire to be 4½ inches long. This modification of the original idea, it was estimated, would require approximately 9/10 cent of labor, thus bringing the cumulative total cost to 1 cent. These parameters and specifications plus their associated idea developments were then added to the functional development worksheet under the function "conduct current," Figure 17-4, and to the problem parameter sketch (Figure 17-5). Having therefore satisfied parameter *B*, a preliminary check mark was put beside it, with the number one, so that it would be known that it was taken into consideration with the number-one or basic function.

Now, rapidly losing their frivolity, the team again having changed their idea development reviewed the complete problem parameters and specifications. When they did this, they readily recognized that the now 4½-inch-long wire of paper-clip diameter would not and could not meet parameter and specification *A*—"Bushing lead-wire input 30 amperes."

Although the presently developed idea did not meet this parameter, they reasoned that with thought, it could be easily solved. One team member stated that a slight modification to their functional development idea would solve this newly considered problem.   Using creative yet judicial thinking, this team member delved back in his memory, his knowledge bank, and his previous training to determine that all that was necessary was to increase the wire diameter to 8 gauge if it were copper or to 6 gauge if it were aluminum.

This statement, of course, threw the team into somewhat of a side discussion as to what type of wire they should use.   After a bit of discussion, they decided that they would use copper wire, mainly because there was a copper wire manufacturing facility there in their plant.

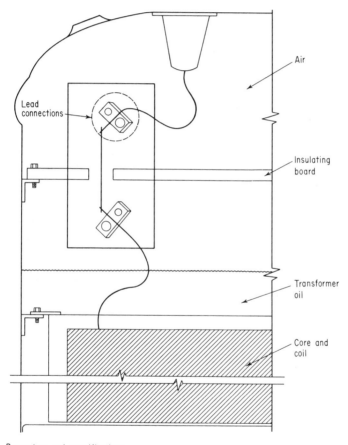

Parameters and specifications
   A. Bushing lead wire input 30 amperes
   B. Bushing and coil lead wires 4¼" apart
   C. Connections to lead wires must be readily disconnectable
   D. Complete unit subject to shipping and operational vibration
   E. Pressure generated in operation 7 P.S.I.
   F. Hole in insulating panel ½" in diameter

**Figure 17-5**

JOY  JOY MANUFACTURING COMPANY                    Rᴇꜰ. No. *MEA-1*
                 FUNCTIONAL DEVELOPMENT

Bᴀsɪᴄ Fᴜɴᴄᴛɪᴏɴ ___ *Conduct Current*

| FUNCTION | CREATIVE IDEA(S) & DEVELOPMENT | ESTIMATED COST (CUMULATIVE) |
|---|---|---|
| *Conduct current* *4¼" between leads* *30 amps of current* | *Paper clip* *Paper clip - bend straight - 4½" long* *Change above to 8 gauge wire* | *$ .001* *$ .01* *$ .02* |

Figure 17-6

Having answered this side problem, it was quite simple at this stage in the idea development to make the size modification in the wire. The governing parameter was noted under the function, the paper-clip wire idea was modified to 8-gauge wire, and the added cost of this modification, approximately 1 cent, was added in the estimated cost column, thus bringing the cumulative total to 2 cents. These latest modifications to the functional development worksheet are shown in Figure 17-6.

Since this latest change would make little if any difference in the problem parameter sketch—simply a thickening of the line shown—it was deemed by the team to be unnecessary to revise the sketch.

The team again reviewed the problem parameters. This time they found that two of the parameters and specifications having a relative significance to the function "conduct current" had been satisfied. Having determined this fact, they now could move in their functional development to the consideration of the second function in the descending order of importance.

For this function, actually the first secondary function, they referred once again to the functional evaluation worksheet. This, of course, they found to be the function "create seal," having a weight factor of 11 and although it was a secondary function it was one which was necessary to realize the original specifications and information. The two-word definition, as with the previous function, was noted in the function column of the functional development worksheet.

In order to continue their development process, the team turned their attention to the creative worksheet developed for the function "create seal." While reviewing this worksheet, they had to keep in mind the idea development they had already accomplished.

From the review of the "create seal" creative worksheet they believed that idea 2, rubber; idea 4, plug; and idea 35, cork could be combined with further creative development to accomplish this function in conjunction with the previous idea. They reasoned that a rubber plug in the shape of a standard bottle-stopper cork could be used if it had a hole in it of such a size that an 8-gauge wire would pass through it as a press fit. After only a brief interval of time, one team member realized that this type of plug or stopper was readily available, as a standard item, in the form of the rubber stoppers used in laboratories for closing test tubes. The team estimated that in the quantities to be used, this type of rubber stopper could be purchased for about 5 cents. The functional development worksheet and problem parameter sketch were then completed to this point of the idea development phase as shown in Figures 17-7 and 17-8.

Looking once more at the bottom of the problem parameter sketch sheet, they saw that the parameter specification $E$ would, during operation, affect their developed idea. As a matter of fact, it only took them a short time to see that this build-up of 7 pounds per square inch pressure during equipment operation would blow their rubber stopper idea right out of the $\frac{1}{2}$-inch hole. Just as rapidly, one of the team members stated that at no additional cost they could reverse the stopper and have the pressure working in their favor. This concept they noted on the functional development worksheet and the problem parameter sketch, Figures 17-9 and 17-10.

Feeling quite good at this point because they had so easily eliminated this last problem, they were again ready to undertake their idea development by selecting the next function in the descending order of importance. While one team member reached for the functional evaluation worksheet, a second member completed the sketch correction.

The team member making the sketch correction suddenly called a pertinent point to his associates' attention. This point was that parameter-specification $D$ would now have a disastrous effect on the idea as developed at this point. As a matter of fact, the shipping vibration would shake the

---

**JOY MANUFACTURING COMPANY**          Ref. No. _MEA-1_

FUNCTIONAL DEVELOPMENT

Basic Function ___Conduct Current___

| FUNCTION | CREATIVE IDEA(S) & DEVELOPMENT | ESTIMATED COST (CUMULATIVE) |
|---|---|---|
| Conduct current 4¼" between leads 30 amps of current | Paper clip Paper clip - bend straight - 4½" long Change above to 8 gauge wire | $.001 $.01 $.02 |
| Create seal | Rubber stopper with hole to accept wire as force fit | $.07 |

Figure 17-7

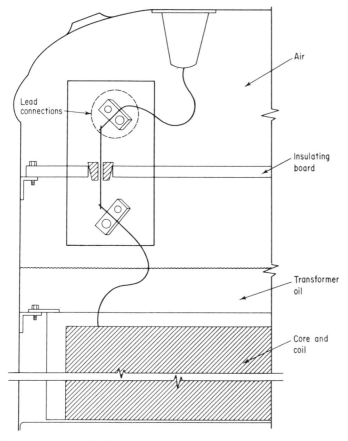

Parameters and specifications
  A. Bushing lead wire input 30 amperes
  B. Bushing and coil lead wires 4 1/4" apart
  C. Connections to lead wires must be readily disconnectable
  D. Complete unit subject to shipping and operational vibration
  E. Pressure generated in operation 7 P.S.I.
  F. Hole in insulating panel 1/2" in diameter

Figure 17-8

rubber stopper out of the 1/2-inch hole long before the equipment was put into operation. At this point, the other team member quickly laid down the functional evaluation worksheet he had by this time picked up.

This new problem situation threw them into somewhat of a quandary; they didn't quite know how to proceed. After some discussion, the team members decided that they would have to scrap their rubber stopper idea and start all over on the solution to the "create seal" function. In order to do this, they went back to the creative worksheet for this function (Figure

JOY MANUFACTURING COMPANY          Ref. No. _MEA-1_

FUNCTIONAL DEVELOPMENT

Basic Function ___ *Conduct current*

| FUNCTION | CREATIVE IDEA(S) & DEVELOPMENT | ESTIMATED COST (CUMULATIVE) |
|---|---|---|
| ① *Conduct current* | *Paper clip* | $¢.001$ |
| *4¼" between leads* | *Paper clip —bend straight— 4½" long* | $¢.01$ |
| *30 amps of current* | *Change above to 8 gauge wire* | $¢.02$ |
| ② *Create seal* | *Rubber stopper with hole to accept wire as force fit* | $¢.07$ |
| *7 P.S.I.* | *Reverse stopper so pressure forces into hole* | $¢.07$ |

Figure 17-9

16-3). After scanning the listed idea a number of times with no thoughts coming to mind, one of the team members' eyes lighted on idea 2, ring. This idea started a thought process which he put into words. Actually he asked, "Couldn't we stay with the rubber stopper idea and snap some sort of a ring onto the small end of it once it was forced through the hole?" He started to sketch this roughly on a separate sheet of paper when this ques-

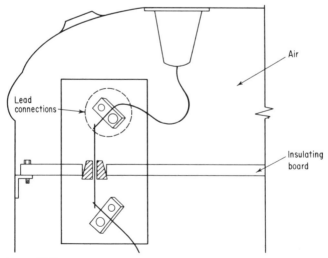

Figure 17-10

tion triggered another idea in the mind of one of his associates, which he in turn expressed.

He asked, "Have either of you seen these molded rubber grommets that have a flange at both the top and bottom?" To which both of his team members answered in the affirmative. All three immediately realized that they didn't have to scrap the rubber stopper idea—just modify it. They quickly modified the functional development worksheet, stating the concept and estimating that the grommet idea would add about 5 cents to the cost. They also changed the parameter sketch to incorporate this latest change (Figures 17-11 and 17-12).

Having run into a parameter-specification oversight, they carefully checked the list at the bottom of the sketch so that it would not happen again. This time they spotted item *F* and listed it on the functional development worksheet for consideration with this function of "create seal." In reviewing their idea development to this point, they said that the grommet they meant to use would be for a ½-inch hole; therefore, no change would be required in the "create seal" solution. This they noted as shown in Figure 17-13.

Seeing no other parameters-specifications having application to this function, they determined that they could now move on to the next function in the descending order. Once again they went to the functional evaluation worksheet, this time to select the number-three function.

The number-three function was the third and last one either specified or

---

**JOY MANUFACTURING COMPANY**        Rᴇꜰ. No. _MEA-1_

FUNCTIONAL DEVELOPMENT

Bᴀꜱɪᴄ Fᴜɴᴄᴛɪᴏɴ ___Conduct current___

| FUNCTION | CREATIVE IDEA(S) & DEVELOPMENT | ESTIMATED COST (CUMULATIVE) |
|---|---|---|
| ① Conduct current 4¼" between leads 30 amps of current | Paper clip Paper clip – bend straight – 4½" long Change above to 8 gauge wire | ⊄.001 ⊄.01 ⊄.02 |
| ② Create seal | Rubber stopper with hole to accept wire as force fit | ⊄.07 |
| 7 P.S.I. | Reverse stopper so pressure forces into hole | ⊄.07 |
| Shipping vibration | Change stopper to double flanged grommet | ⊄.12 |

**Figure 17-11**

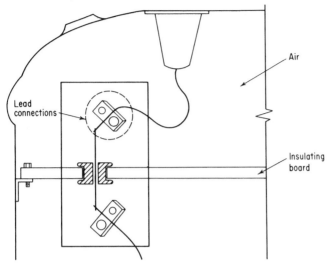

Air

Lead connections

Insulating board

**Figure 17-12**

required, "establish connection." This they noted on the functional development worksheet, and then they selected the creative worksheet that listed the ideas they had created on this function (Figure 16-4).

At first glance, they were ready to use idea 7, weld; 22, solder; 23, bronze; or 45, twist, when they remembered the problem parameters-

---

**JOY MANUFACTURING COMPANY**                    REF. No. *MEA—1*

FUNCTIONAL DEVELOPMENT

BASIC FUNCTION *Conduct current*

| FUNCTION | CREATIVE IDEA(S) & DEVELOPMENT | ESTIMATED COST (CUMULATIVE) |
|---|---|---|
| ① *Conduct current* | *Paper clip* | *$.001* |
| *4¼" between leads* | *Paper clip-bend straight - 4½" long* | *$.01* |
| *30 amps of current* | *Change above to 8 gauge wire* | *$.02* |
| ② *Create seal* | *Rubber stopper with hole to accept wire as force fit* | *$.07* |
| *7 P.S.I.* | *Reverse stopper so pressure forces into hole* | *$.07* |
| *Shipping vibration* | *Change stopper to double flanged grommet* | *$.12* |
| *½" hole* | *Grommet fits hole - no change* | *$.12* |

**Figure 17-13**

specifications—in particular item C—"connections to lead wires must be readily disconnectable." They knew that none of these ideas would work with this parameter, so they again reviewed the list to see what idea or ideas they could use. This second review didn't have to go very far down the list, only to idea 8, clip. Taking this idea, they then had to determine what kind of a clip they could use. After some thought and discussion, they decided on an alligator clip, one that is spring-actuated so that it will be disconnectable and not subject to loosening due to vibration. In this manner, they were able to get a solution to the function and at the same time take into account those parameters-specifications which would affect this function. These points were then noted on the functional development worksheet and the problem parameter sketch, Figures 17-14 and 17-15.

Having thus accomplished the functional development of an alternative encompassing the basic function, the required or specified secondary functions, and their governing parameters-specifications, the team undertook the cross-checking process.

The first step in their cross-check was to be certain that the problem parameters had been met. They found that each had been considered for every function and—where applicable—had been, in some manner, accounted for in the development.

The second step in this cross-check was to review the functional evalua-

| JOY MANUFACTURING COMPANY | | Rᴇꜰ. No. _MEA-1_ |
| FUNCTIONAL DEVELOPMENT | | |

Bᴀsɪᴄ Fᴜɴᴄᴛɪᴏɴ _____ Conduct current

| FUNCTION | CREATIVE IDEA(S) & DEVELOPMENT | ESTIMATED COST (CUMULATIVE) |
|---|---|---|
| ① Conduct current 4¼" between leads 30 amps of current | Paper clip Paper clip -bend straight -4½" long Change above to 8 gauge wire | $.001 $.01 $.02 |
| ② Create seal | Rubber stopper with hole to accept wire force fit | $.07 |
| 7 P.S.I. | Reverse stopper so pressure forces into hole | $.07 |
| Shipping vibration | Change stopper to double flanged grommet | $.12 |
| ½" hole | Grommet fits hole -no change | $.12 |
| ③ Establish connection | Use clip on each end 8 gauge wire (alligator type) | $.20 |
| Disconnectable | No change required | $.20 |
| Shipping vibration | No change required | $.20 |

Figure 17-14

tion worksheet. Here again they found that all the functions spelled out in the specifications and requirements had been met and that those functions incorporated because of the present design had not been considered. To be sure that their evaluation process had not been wrong or led them astray, they now considered each of these functions in the functional development process. These functions, "induce friction," "apply pressure," and "transmit pressure" were considered one at a time to determine if anything would

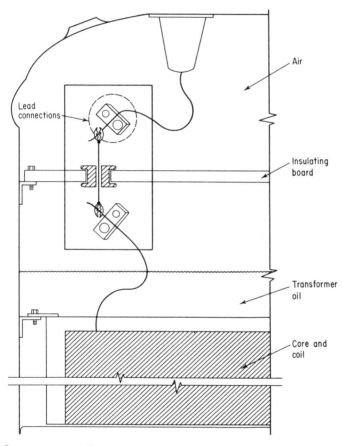

Parameters and specifications
   A. Bushing lead wire input 30 amperes
   B. Bushing and coil lead wires 4¼" apart
   C. Connections to lead wires must be readily disconnectable
   D. Complete unit subject to shipping and operational vibration
   E. Pressure generated in operation 7 P.S.I.
   F. Hole in insulating panel ½" in diameter

**Figure 17-15**

JOY MANUFACTURING COMPANY     Rᴇꜰ. No. _MEA-1_

FUNCTIONAL DEVELOPMENT

Bᴀꜱɪᴄ Fᴜɴᴄᴛɪᴏɴ _____ Conduct current

| FUNCTION | CREATIVE IDEA(S) & DEVELOPMENT | ESTIMATED COST (CUMULATIVE) |
|---|---|---|
| ① Conduct current | Paper clip | $.001 |
| 4¼" between leads | Paper clip - bend straight - 4½" long | $.01 |
| 30 amps of current | Change above to 8 gauge wire | $.02 |
| ② Create seal | Rubber stopper with hole to accept wire as force fit. | $.07 |
| 7 P.S.I. | Reverse stopper so pressure forces into hole | $.07 |
| Shipping vibration | Change stopper to double flanged grommet | $.12 |
| ½" hole | Grommet fits hole - no change | $.12 |
| ③ Establish connection | Use clip on each end 8 gauge wire (alligator type) | $.20 |
| Disconnectable | No change required | $.20 |
| Shipping vibration | No change required | $.20 |
| ④ Induce friction | No modification required | $.20 |
| ⑤ Apply pressure | No modification required | $.20 |
| ⑥ Transmit pressure | No modification required | $.20 |
| | Tᴏᴛᴀʟ | $.20 |

Pʀᴇꜱᴇɴᴛ Cᴏꜱᴛ Sᴜᴍᴍᴀʀʏ
    Mᴀᴛᴇʀɪᴀʟ & Mᴀᴛ. Bᴜʀᴅᴇɴ   $ _____
    Dɪʀᴇᴄᴛ Lᴀʙᴏʀ   $ _____
    Dɪʀᴇᴄᴛ Lᴀʙᴏʀ Bᴜʀᴅᴇɴ   $ _____
        Tᴏᴛᴀʟ   $ _____
Tᴇᴀᴍ Mᴇᴍʙᴇʀꜱ _John A. Doe, Bill E. Egan, Frank M. Smith_ Dᴀᴛᴇ ___ 9-5- ___
FORM NO. 8815  12-66         VALUE ENGINEERING

Figure 17-16

have to be done to the idea thus developed. When this was done, it was found that they either were already being accomplished or were no longer required. Therefore, no additional development is required or cost incurred because of them. This being the case, the functional development worksheet can be completed. After noting these latter three functions, the team filled in the present cost summary, team members, and date as shown in Figure 17-16.

## Summary

At this point in the Job Plan, the team realized that they must make a critical and objective review of the functionally developed solution.

From this review, a number of points became apparent. First, the solution as developed does incorporate all the required functions and governing parameters-specifications. Second, while accomplishing this, the cost generated is only a fraction of the original cost. Third, although this developed idea is quite low in cost, it will *work*. Last, even though the idea will work, they realized that "only by the grace of God and good luck" would it ever sell.

This review also made another fact apparent; i.e., they had completed the Evaluation Phase. They had "refined and combined ideas," "established cost on all ideas," "developed function alternatives" and "evaluated by comparison." They now knew that if there were problems with their developed ideas they would have to pinpoint and eliminate them in the next phase of the Job Plan. In the Investigation Phase, they knew they would have to convert this developed idea from one that was barely workable to one which was completely workable and also salable. They therefore eagerly took the necessary steps to move into the Investigation Phase.

Chapter Eighteen

# Investigation Phase

*Wisdom consists not so much in knowing the right answers as in knowing the right questions to ask.* — SYDNEY J. HARRIS

The wisdom of the investigation phase is in asking the right questions to determine the advantages and disadvantages of an idea. Then, from this knowledge, ways of overcoming the disadvantages and of strengthening the advantages are developed so that an idea that is both workable and salable is generated.

The Investigation Phase, the team members readily understood, had to start with consultation—consultations with specialists and, where necessary, vendors to determine the strong and weak points of their developed idea. From this consultation, they could isolate the disadvantages and weak points of their idea and, through further consultation, apply those standard or specialty items or ideas that would make their idea both work and sell.

## Consult Vendors and Specialists

The team approached this first, critique-type consultation with some foreboding and apprehension. They therefore decided to first contact a specialist with whom they were all familiar, within the company. And since he was a marketing specialist, they reasoned that he would look at their idea from that point of view. They also knew that he had been indoctrinated in the Value Engineering Methodology and therefore would not tear their idea apart just for the sake of tearing it apart. They also figured that, because of his similar training, he would approach their idea in a positive manner and give them constructive criticism.

Because of their apprehensions, they asked this specialist, when they contacted him, if he could come to their project work area. In this way, they knew that they would be more at ease and believed that he would be also.

In preparation for his arrival and critique of their idea, the team laid out on the table their functional development worksheet and problem parameter sketch. In addition they prepared the alternate idea evaluation worksheet by first completing the top portion; i.e., filling in the reference number and function they had started with. Next, in simple but descriptive terminology, they stated the idea that they had functionally developed (Figure 18-1). They were then prepared for their own and the specialist's joint critique of their idea.

The team and the marketing specialist sat down and reviewed the developed idea. Based on their training, all four individuals stated and discussed in some detail the advantages of the idea as shown, each individual speaking for his own specialty; i.e., Marketing, Engineering, Manufacturing, and Purchasing. In this manner, the team and its guest were able to quite rapidly list on the idea evaluation worksheet the major and minor advantages of the developed idea.

While doing this, however, as in the creative phase, they had to be extremely careful to be sure that they discussed and noted only the idea's advantages. This, like the turning off of the judicial mind, is no easy task.

Only after they had listed the advantages did they consider the disadvantages. This, of course, came much easier to the marketing specialist than it did to the team. This was due to the fact that it was not the marketing specialist's idea. However, because of his training, he guarded against outright condemnation of the idea. Rather, he made sure that the disadvantages that he spelled out were indeed specific problem areas. Once the team members saw his approach, they too joined in and openly discussed the potential problem area noted by the specialist plus one or two that they thought of. After an open and productive discussion, they noted the disadvantages on the idea evaluation worksheet (Figure 18-2).

Figure 18-1

At this point in time, the team realized that they had an idea that would most likely work but, of equal importance, most likely would not sell. They therefore knew that they had two courses open to them. First, they could junk their present idea and start all over again or, second, they could critically analyze the disadvantages of their idea to see how they could be overcome.

As they prepared to start on this undertaking, they found that they had acquired another team member. The marketing specialist, having become engrossed in the discussion and thus in the idea, decided that he wanted to help them to overcome the problems that he had put in front of them. As a matter of fact, he practically became the team leader at this point so that he could assist them in overcoming the roadblocks he had established.

| JOY MANUFACTURING COMPANY | REF. No. _MEA-1_ |
| IDEA EVALUATION | |

FUNCTION     _Conduct current_

| IDEA FROM FUNCTIONAL DEVELOPMENT | ADVANTAGES | DISADVANTAGES |
|---|---|---|
| Conduct current through a half inch thick insulating panel with an 8 gauge wire. A rubber grommet having a press fit hole for the wire and being a press fit in the insulating panel will form the required seal. Two alligator clips, fastened to the 8 gauge wire, will be used to connect and disconnect the assembly and the leads. | A. Low cost B. Simple in design C. Parts readily obtainable D. Maximum of two parts drawings required E. Number of assembly parts reduced from 11 to 4 F. Reduction of number of parts to be stocked G. Only grommet may be special and require drawing H. Simple to assemble in plant I. Assembly is interchangable with present design J. Assembly will work and will perform all the necessary functions | 1. Seal may release under pressure. Should be tested 2. Alligator clips will have to be fastened to wire at assembly - might be problem in manufacturing. 3. Wire could slip through grommet, which would require panel disassembly 4. Due to shipping and operational vibrations, 8 gauge wire and connectors may be too small. |

PLANS FOR ACTION ON IDEA(S)

   _Annalyze and overcome disadvantages_

TEAM MEMBERS _J.A. Doe, B.E. Egan, F.M. Smith, S.W. Goodrich_     DATE _9-5-_

FORM NO. 8816   12-66                          VALUE ENGINEERING

Figure 18-2

The team, which now comprised four members, decided to tackle the disadvantages in the same manner in which they had approached the functional development; i.e., to start with the disadvantage that had to do with the basic function and redevelop their idea from there. They therefore took their functional development worksheet and in the estimated cost column drew a line to the right of their present estimated cost and headed this column "sell." This would allow them to show the difference then between the work cost and the sell cost as they redeveloped the idea. They also took a copy of the problem parameter sketch so that they could sketch their redeveloped idea.

## Final Development of Alternatives

Now with the idea evaluation, functional development worksheets, plus the problem parameter sketch in front of them, they were ready to proceed with their idea redevelopment.

Looking at the disadvantages listed on the idea evaluation worksheet, they found that numbers 3 and 4 had something to do with that part of their original idea accomplished by the basic function "conduct current." They realized that number 4 was probably the more critical of the two. This they determined was so because the shipping and operational vibration could work-harden the wire and make it snap, thus making the assembly and the voltage regulator unstable.

This they believed could be overcome by increasing the size of the conductor from 8-gauge wire to ¼-inch-diameter rod. This, of course, would increase the cost for the accomplishment of this function from 2 cents to an estimated 10 cents. In order to overcome disadvantage number 3, they agreed that a circular spring clip would answer the problem at a cost of about 2 cents. This then gave them a total increase in cost of 10 cents for a new estimated cumulative cost of 14 cents. They noted their change of idea on the functional development worksheet and started their new sketch on the problem parameter drawing, Figures 18-3 and 18-4.

Looking again at the idea evaluation worksheet, they saw that the next disadvantage they had to consider was number 1. In looking at their present idea in conjunction with this problem, they realized that they would have to put another circular spring clip on the rod below the insulating panel. By doing this, they would thus locate the one above the panel in such a way as to prevent the grommet from popping out or releasing under pressure. This they easily noted on the functional development worksheet and depicted on the problem parameter sketch. Of course, at the same time they modified the grommet idea, believing that they could secure a grommet similar to their original idea to fit the ¼-inch-diameter rod at the same cost. These modifications are shown in Figures 18-5 and 18-6.

On the basis of his specialty knowledge, the purchasing man on the team suggested the circular spring clips. It was his knowledge of this standard item that answered both of the latter disadvantages.

From here, buoyant from their easy solutions to the first disadvantages, the team was ready to move to the fourth and last disadvantage. As they

Figure 18-3

looked at this disadvantage, they realized they had a problem, but not the one spelled out on the worksheet. The problem was one which they had not considered—that when they converted the conductor from 8-gauge wire to ¼-inch rod, they in essence eliminated the possible use of alligator clips for their connection purpose or function. At this point, they were tempted to discard the whole idea and start all over from the beginning. However, after a short period of dejection, they took another look at the problem and decided to continue. This decision was based on the realization that, up to this point, they had encountered and with some thought had overcome numerous problems; problems which, at the time, had seemed as difficult if not more so.

With this renewed positive attitude, they tackled the problem of "establishing connection" again. Since it was necessary to start completely fresh

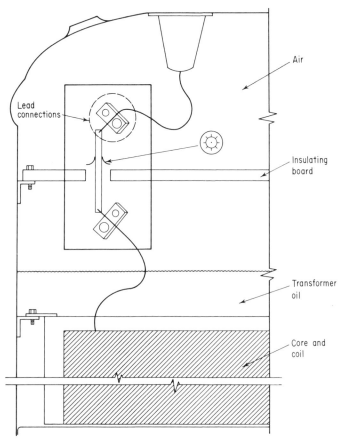

Parameters and specifications
   A. Bushing lead wire input 30 amperes
   B. Bushing and coil lead wires 4¼" apart
   C. Connections to lead wires must be readily disconnectable
   D. Complete unit subject to shipping and operational vibration
   E. Pressure generated in operation 7 P.S.I.
   F. Hole in insulating panel ½" in diameter

**Figure 18-4**

Figure 18-5

on the accomplishment of this function, they went back to the creative worksheet developed for it. In reviewing the ideas on this sheet a few times, their thoughts came to rest on idea 4, stud. Their thinking on this idea brought them to the fact that in the ¼-inch-diameter rod, they had a stud. Further thought reminded them that on most occasions which they could recall, parts were fastened to studs by the use of nuts. As a matter of fact, they asked themselves, isn't this the manner in which the top lead was connected on the original connector? With their idea-development thought patterns again working in high gear, they worked out a relatively simple solution. Their solution was to thread both ends of the rod and put two ¼-inch jam nuts and a lock washer on each end.

The threading of both ends of the rod, they estimated, would cost 10 cents; the jam nuts they believed could be purchased at a cost of 3 cents

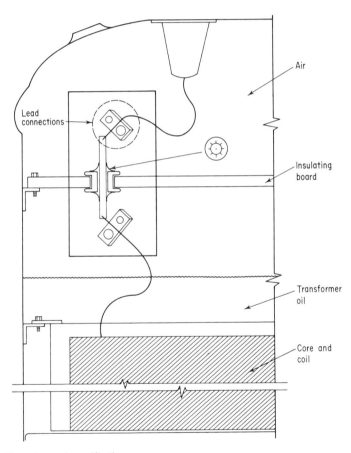

Parameters and specifications
    A. Bushing lead wire input 30 amperes
    B. Bushing and coil lead wires 4¼″ apart
    C. Connections to lead wires must be readily disconnectable
    D. Complete unit subject to shipping and operational vibration
    E  Pressure generated in operation 7 P.S.I.
    F. Hole in insulating panel ½″ in diameter

**Figure 18-6**

each; and the lock washers, because they were a standard stock item, would cost 1 cent each.   This would then bring the total cost of this change of idea to 24 cents.   They then changed their functional development worksheet and problem parameter sketch to bring them up to date (Figures 18-7 and 18-8).

| JOY MANUFACTURING COMPANY | | Ref. No. _M EA-1_ |
| --- | --- | --- |
| | FUNCTIONAL DEVELOPMENT | |
| Basic Function _Conduct current_ | | |

| FUNCTION | CREATIVE IDEA(S) & DEVELOPMENT | ESTIMATED COST (CUMULATIVE) | |
| --- | --- | --- | --- |
| ① Conduct current | Paper clip | $.001 | SELL |
| 4¼" between leads | Paper clip-bend straight- 4½" long | $.01 | |
| 30 amps of current | Change above to 8 gauge wire (¼" diameter rod (brass) with spring clip for location | $.02 | $.14 |
| ② Create seal | Rubber stopper with hole to accept wire as force fit | $.07 | |
| 7 P.S.I | Reverse stopper so pressure forces into hole | $.07 | |
| Shipping vibration | Change stopper to double flanged grommet | $.12 | $.16 |
| ½" hole | Grommet fits hole-no change (Add 1 spring clip to aid in gasket retainment) | $.12 | |
| ③ Establish connection | Use clip on each end 8 gauge wire (alligator type) | $.20 | |
| Disconnectable | No change required | $.20 | $.40 |
| Shipping vibration | No change required | $.20 | |
| ④ Induce friction | No modification required | $.20 | $.40 |
| ⑤ Apply pressure | No modification required | $.20 | $.40 |
| ⑥ Transmit pressure | No modification required | $.20 | $.40 |
| | TOTAL | $.20 | $.40 |

Present Cost Summary
Material & Mat. Burden    $ _____
Direct Labor              $ _____
Direct Labor Burden       $ _____
TOTAL    $ _____
Team Members _____    Date _____
FORM NO. 8815  12—66                    VALUE ENGINEERING

Figure 18-7

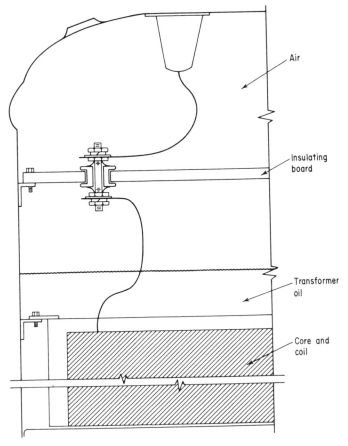

Parameters and specifications
   A. Bushing lead wire input 30 amperes
   B. Bushing and coil lead wires 4¼" apart
   C. Connections to lead wires must be readily disconnectable
   D. Complete unit subject to shipping and operational vibration
   E. Pressure generated in operation 7 P.S.I.
   F. Hole in insulating panel ½" in diameter

**Figure 18-8**

   With this concept, they would use one of the holes in each of the connector tabs on the leads to fit over the stud.  These connector tabs would go between the nuts and lock washer to make the connection.  Their totally developed idea, at this point, had an estimated cost of 40 cents, which was just double the cost of their originally developed idea.  The big question now in their minds was whether this concept would be salable as well as workable.  For the answer to this question, they again turned to the marketing specialist.

The marketing specialist, although a semiofficial member of the team, took a long and objective look at this new concept. As a matter of fact, he tended to be overly critical because of his personal involvement. After considerable thought, however, he could not find any of the previous weaknesses and had to say that this concept was indeed salable as well as workable. The latter observation was, of course, still to be proved by test.

## Use Company and Industry Standards

Having now redeveloped their idea to the point where they firmly believed it was workable and salable, they again, because of their limited knowledge, decided to contact and bring in another specialist. This time they contacted both a purchasing specialist and a manufacturing specialist. The purchasing specialist was called to advise them of any other industry standards or specialty products, processes, and materials they might use to improve and/or further reduce the cost of their new idea. The manufacturing specialist was contacted for basically the same reason, i.e., for his knowledge of company standards or materials or processes which might help them improve and/or further reduce the cost.

They were all agreed, however, that the only improvements they would allow to be made were those which would make the idea sell better or to make it work if it was found that, for some reason, it did not. When these two specialists arrived at the team's project study area, these points were explained before anything was said about the project.

After a short explanation of what they had done and the steps they had taken, they showed the two specialists their latest problem parameter sketch, nothing else. Again fate was on their side, as both of these specialists had had value training so that they understood what was being said without detailed explanations.

The two specialists then, with the team looking over their shoulder, reviewed the team's idea, asking questions when necessary. After a short time, the purchasing specialist said that he had a couple of suggestions. However, before he could make them, the manufacturing specialist said he would like to ask a question that might further simplify the idea as well as reduce its cost. Hearing this, the purchasing specialist said that his ideas would wait.

The manufacturing specialist then asked, "Could a $\frac{1}{2}$-inch-diameter stud be used in place of the $\frac{1}{4}$-inch stud?" To this the team members answered "yes," but in turn they asked, "Why increase the stud diameter and its cost?" The manufacturing specialist told them that there was in standard stock a fully threaded $\frac{1}{2}$-inch stud about $4\frac{1}{2}$ inches long, and that it was used in many of the company's transformers and voltage regulators. Also there were, in standard stock, $\frac{1}{2}$-inch brass jam nuts, lock washers, and lathe-cut gaskets. As a matter of fact, they could use the same gaskets that were used in the original design if the ones in stock were not the right size.

After thinking this over for a short time, the team and the specialists agreed that this would work as well if not better than their present idea and would probably cost less since the parts were stock items. With this decision, they sent one of the team members with the manufacturing specialist to secure one set of parts; i.e., one stud, six nuts, two lock washers, and two gaskets from the stockroom. At the same time, the other team members and the purchasing specialist went to the Accounting and Purchasing Departments to secure the costs on these standard parts.

When they all returned to the project study area, they first assembled the parts on the insulating panel they had and found that this concept would work. Also, the marketing specialist said that it would definitely sell because of its rugged appearance.

Compiling their costs, they listed the following:

```
(1) 600019-119  Brass rod, ½-13 UNC thread, 4½ in. long  ...   $0.20
(6) 600020-6    Nut, jam; brass, ½-13 UNC; @ $0.05 ........    0.30
(2) 601120-6    Lock washer, steel, plated, @ $0.02 ........    0.04
(2) 9090547-5   Gasket, nitrile, @ $0.132 ...............      0.262
    Total .  .........................................        $0.802
```

When they had compiled this list, they were somewhat dismayed by the fact that the total cost was just double their developed idea's cost. Then they realized that even though this was indeed the case, the actual cost of the new concept was far less than that of the connector they had started with in the beginning.

They thanked the specialists for their assistance, sat down, and were about to proceed into the recommendation phase of the job plan when the engineer on the team, the original designer of the connector, asked them to hold on a minute. Somewhat surprised, the other team members asked him what was wrong.

He said that he had just been reviewing the costs that they had listed and realized a rather startling fact: that it was costing them $0.362 (two nuts and two gaskets) to provide the function "create seal" and that this was more than the cost of accomplishing any other function. He also thought that they should examine this fact more closely.

When the team dug into this fact, they found that in order to accomplish this function they had used two nuts and two gaskets, and that the designer was right; it did cost $0.362 to provide it. They were sure they could do something to reduce the cost.

In the discussion that followed, one team member asked why two gaskets were needed; wouldn't one provide the required seal? The designer, in order to answer this question, started to review the problem parameter sketch. He then dug out, from their original material, a print of the total assembly. After looking at this for a short time, he in turn asked a question. With a smile on his face, from ear to ear, he asked, "Why do we need any gasket at all?" Before any of the team members could answer, he pointed to the assembly drawing and the problem parameter sketch. In so doing, he pointed out the fact that there was no gasket, no seal at all between the insulating panel and the tank wall. What he had realized was that because there was no seal between the tank and insulating panel, the 7-pound per-square-inch pressure was equal throughout the inside of the tank, there being equal pressure at both ends of the grommet.

At this point, he started to laugh because he realized that the "create seal" function and the 7-pound per-square-inch parameter had been self-imposed specifications. At this point, the rest of the team laughed with him. At the same time, however, they all took a close look at their assembly of standard parts.

They quickly stripped the assembly of the two gaskets and started to reassemble it, recognizing that they had just removed $0.262 in cost from it, thus giving them a new total cost of 54 cents. While doing this, the team member from manufacturing asked, somewhat as a joke, why the devil did they need three nuts on each side of the insulating panel? The other team members immediately came back with the reason: to locate the stud and to keep the leads 4¼ inches apart. A little miffed by his associates' quick and overly positive answer, he asked the simple question, "Why must the leads be 4½ inches apart?" Their answer was again immediate and simple —"Because."

At this point they stopped, looked at each other, then looked closely at the drawing and the problem parameter sketch. From this examination they realized that they had another self-imposed specification. They had really imposed this specification on themselves because the original connector had held the leads 4¼ inches apart, not because the leads were not long enough to be fastened closer together.

Examining this new twist of circumstances more closely, they found that the only specification they had to really take cognizance of was one stipulated by NEMA (National Electrical Manufacturers Association). This specification was basically that no current-carrying wire could pass through an insulator or insulating panel.

At this point, they realized that they had missed this specification in their information search. However now, because of it, they could remove two nuts, giving them a total cost of 44 cents for the total assembly. The standard parts they now required were:

(1)  600019-119   Brass rod, ½-13 UNC thread, 4½ in. long . . .  $0.20
(4)  600020-6   Nut, jam; brass, ½-13 UNC, @ $0.05 . . . . . . .  0.20
(2)  601120-6   Lock washer, steel, plated, @ $0.02 . . . . . . . .  0.04
Total . . . . . . . . . . . . . . . . . . . . . . . . . . . . . . . . . . . . . . . . . . .  $0.44

They then contacted the manufacturing specialist again to determine if there was a shorter stud in stock. When they explained what they wanted and why, he checked his listing of standards. He told them that there was no standard near the roughly 2-inch length that they wanted. They then asked him what it would cost to manufacture such a stud as a special. After a quick calculation, he informed them that the shorter studs would cost between 19 and 21 cents apiece in the quantities they would require. He also stated that he would prefer not to have to make these as it would add a part to inventory, require small-lot processing, and involve a number of other costly factors. The team then decided to keep the parts they had in the present configuration.

Really feeling elated at this point, knowing that they had worked through most of the Job Plan, knowing that they had developed a lower-cost usable assembly, they were now ready to take the last step. They were ready to tackle the Recommendation Phase.

## Chapter Nineteen
# Recommendation Phase

*Act in haste, regret in leisure.*

The team, in preparing to enter the Recommendation Phase, believed that they could rapidly secure acceptance of their ideas by the decision maker, in this case the product manager. This, however, was not their objective. Their objective was to motivate positive action, which in turn would result in positive change.

The team members, fully understanding their own high enthusiasm, recognized that they could not attain their objective except by the use of cold, hard logic and facts such as costs, etc. And to move too rapidly, at this point, could destroy the effect of all their efforts on the project. They therefore, more to quiet their minds than to gain physical rest, took their first major break in the work on the project.

In order that they might be completely fresh in mind, attitude, and thought, they left the project work area and refrained from active thought on the project for a number of hours. This they did because they knew, from other individuals' experience and comments that, if they approached this part of the project work in a tired condition, a number of detrimental effects might readily occur.

First, because of their personal enthusiasm, they might not consider everyone's point of view regarding the individual parts of their ideas and conclusions.  Second, because of their familiarity with the project, they might not develop or properly explain a concise plan of action by which their recommended ideas could be implemented.  Third, because of their specific involvement and close, continued contact with the project, they could not be sure that they would be mentally ready, reasonable, or right in the manner or words used to convey their thoughts and ideas.

All these points had to be taken into consideration so that they would not jeopardize any of the benefits to be derived by the company from their efforts.  In addition, in the back of their minds was the realization that the wrong words or meaning behind the words could have a detrimental effect on the outcome of their project.

## Motivate Positive Action

The team, on returning to the project work area, determined that in order to motivate positive action they would have to develop two separate plans.  The first was the organization of the presentation of their ideas and supporting facts and the second was the development of the sequential steps to be taken to implement these ideas in the most rapid and economical manner when they were accepted.

Jumping right into this planning operation with gusto, they first reviewed all the material they had developed on the project.  They started with the basic data collected in the Information Phase and progressed through to their developed idea in the Investigation Phase.

Throughout this review, they noted specific items which they would want to use in their idea presentation. As this operation was taking place, they realized that they had not just one solution to present but many—also that these solutions fell into two distinct categories: major and minor changes. They also determined that to do their job properly, they must present both types of recommendations even though their feelings were strongest for the major change.

After considerable discussion on the two types of possible recommendations they decided, because of their personal bias, to present the minor modifications first and the major modifications later.  In both types of recommendations, they would have to make it a point to present accurate facts and costs, detail the advantages and disadvantages, and try to restrict their own personal feelings.  This latter point, they knew, was going to be the most difficult.

Having thought over and talked out their plan, they noted it down for future reference as well as inclusion in their project folder.

PROJECT PREPARATION AND PRESENTATION PLAN

A. Secure facts and data on ideas.
B. Prepare recommendations sheets.
  1. On minor changes.
  2. On major changes.
C. Note both advantages and disadvantages.
D. Present ideas to project manager.
E. Be sure to give credit to proper individuals.
  1. For information.
  2. For ideas.
  3. For assistance.
F. Present action plans for implementation of accepted ideas.

On noting this last point, they realized that they must now make the general plans to cover this item. Here again, since they were somewhat unfamiliar with this part of the approach, a discussion started.

One of the team members brought up the question: "Why should we have to plan the implementation of the idea?" This he immediately followed with the statement: "We developed the idea, let someone else put it into effect." At first, this seemed a reasonable question and answer to the other team members.

After some thought and discussion on these points, they changed their minds. This they did because they realized that the only way positive action was sure to be started was if they started it—also that because of their individual involvement in the project, they would be the most interested in being sure that the first and subsequent action steps were taken. Having settled this point, one which faces everyone working with this approach, they concentrated on developing their implementation action plan outline.

They reasoned that their action plan would have to contain specific steps, but that these steps would have to be broad enough to encompass any type or number of ideas that were accepted. They quickly determined that the first step in the plan would be to have the engineering drawings and/or specifications modified. The second logical step would be to put a hold on the manufacture or purchase of any parts no longer required. The third step would be to have new manufacturing routers prepared for the manufacture and assembly of the new or modified assembly. The fourth step, somewhat of a "waiting game" based on manufacturing lead time, would be to start production of the new parts so that they would be ready to phase into production when the old parts inventory was depleted. The fifth and next to the last step would be to see that the new parts were used and that no problems existed. Finally, they would have to be sure that the new approach was costed out, the overall equipment cost modified to reflect the new cost, and the savings audited and documented. Having developed this general plan, they made the following notes below their project preparation and presentation plan.

IMPLEMENTATION PLAN

A. Have engineering change orders prepared.
B. Issue parts requisition hold notices.
C. Have manufacturing and assembly routers developed.
D. Start manufacture of new assembly parts as required.
E. Phase in new assembly and correct problems if required.
F. Have assembly costed and actual savings determined, audited, and reported.

## Project Preparation

Having made their general plans for the motivation of positive action, they now turned to the critical task of converting these plans into actions. They then returned to their review of the project data and the listing of the changes to be recommended. Working with deliberate care, they carefully screened and rescreened this data in search of possible ideas for change. The type of changes they sought were those consisting of minor modifications.

In this search, they found and noted a number of significant points. The points they listed for consideration are listed below:

A. From the information phase.
  1. Under normal operating conditions, no spares are required—possible reduction of size or elimination of excess reliability.
  2. Simplify construction and reduce weight—ties in with comment 1.
  3. Parts must be interchangeable—substitutions can be made.
  4. Problems being encountered with the stud and copper tube—changes should be considered to eliminate these problems.
  5. Increase lot size to reduce number of setups—since usage is approximately 900 per year, lot size could be increased to at least one month's supply, i.e., 75 pieces.
  6. Reduce stud size to eliminate gasket assembly problem—because of tooling cost, it would be easier and less expensive to reduce stud OD than to increase gasket ID due to tooling cost.
  7. Are plated lock washers and ½-inch bronze nut necessary? Investigate plain steel washers and nut to reduce cost.
B. From project work.
  1. Since no seal is required at the insulating panel, modify design—eliminate gaskets and eliminate recess in stud and recessed washer.

Taking these facts one at a time, they analyzed them for possible recommendations for minor change of the present design. The first three they noted were so general that nothing specific could be derived from them but that these would have to be taken into consideration in making all their recommendations for minor changes.

Coupled with this decision was the determination that, on all recommended changes, minor or major, they would use an annual usage factor of 850. This they decided in order that all their savings figures would be on the conservative side.

When they reached notation 4, they believed that in the second item mentioned in the statement there was a possible recommendation for change. The buyer on the team believed that he could purchase a flat-headed hollow rivet or eyelet that would do this job and thereby eliminate the problems encountered in making the special copper tube. He therefore, by telephone, started a search for such a copper rivet or eyelet. After a number of calls, he located a manufacturer who produced the type of rivet he was looking for to replace the copper tube. This rivet had a flat head $\frac{3}{8}$ inch in diameter, had the right size hole, and was $\frac{3}{4}$ inch long. These rivets would cost, since they were semispecial, $25 per hundred. The team realized that when the rivets were received, they would have to be subjected to an indenting operation which would increase their cost by another $20 per hundred. This, however, would still provide them with a much lower cost than the present copper tube. They therefore made out a recommendation sheet on this minor change (Figure 19-1).

Pursuing these minor changes because of the fair savings on the first, the team moved on to consider notation 5: "Increase lot size." This time, in order to determine the magnitude of the savings, if any, they had to refer back to the routing sheets obtained in the Information Phase. Here, of course, they could only obtain a savings on those pieces manufactured in their plants, these parts being the brass stud, 9090547-1; brass nut, 9090547-2; special tube, 9090547-3; recessed washer, 9090547-4; and gasket, 9090547-5. From the routing sheets, they readily determined that the total number of setup hours was 7.40. They also realized that if the present practice of ordering and manufacture were continued, 34 setups would be required per year. Based on the shop supervisor's recommendation of increasing the number of parts per order to approximately 1 month's usage, only 12 setups would be required per year. This they calculated and made note of on their second minor recommended change (Figure 19-2).

Somewhat elated by the simplicity with which potential savings were being obtained from these minor changes, the team moved rapidly on to their next notation: "Reduce stud size to eliminate gasket assembly problem." As they analyzed this notation, they realized that it would not

JOY MANUFACTURING COMPANY    COST/IMPROVEMENT RECOMMENDATION
PRIORITY _____
DATE __9-5-__    REF. NO. _MEA-1_
PRODUCT _Voltage regulator_ #3116    ASSY. OR PART _Tube -Special_
PART NO. __9090547-3__    QTY./PRODUCT __5__    QTY./YEAR __850__

POTENTIAL 1ST YEAR SAVINGS $ _257.00_    SALES FORECAST (NEXT 12 MONTHS) __-175__ PRODUCT

PRESENT    RECOMMENDED

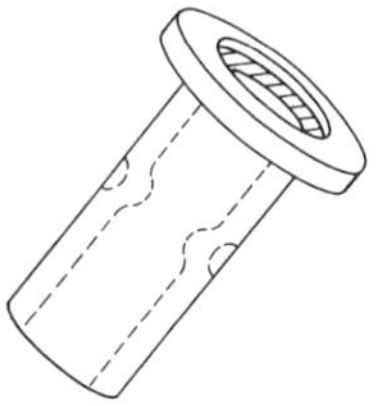

| CALCULATION OF SAVING | Material | Direct Labor | Fringe Benefit | Total |
|---|---|---|---|---|
| Present | $ .228 | $ .525 | $ | $ .753 |
| Proposed | $ .250 | $ .200 | $ | $ .450 |
| Difference per piece or Assy. | $ | $ | $ | $ .303 |
| Implementation Cost - | | MFG. $ ___—___ | ENG. $ _20.00_ | |

FINDINGS & RECOMMENDATIONS: _It has been found that the present copper tube has a high scrap rate in manufacture due to splitting of the material when the head is formed._
_By changing to a purchased hollow rivet as shown above, this problem would be eliminated while realizing a saving. It would, however, require a change in the drawing and bill of material plus the addition of a part to inventory._
_To make this change, two hours of engineering would be required to modify the drawings and bill of material._

APPROVED BY _____    REJECTED _____    DATE _____
ENGINEERING CHANGE ORDER NO. _____    FOR FURTHER INFO. _____
TEAM MEMBERS _J.A. Doe, B.E. Egan, F.M. Smith_

Figure 19-1

directly remove any cost from the product.    However, they determined that a recommendation sheet had to be made up to point out and correct this assembly problem.    In discussing this problem, they came to the conclusion that the stud diameter could be reduced by $\frac{1}{64}$ inch.    This would alleviate the problem and not affect the basic fit of the $\frac{1}{2}$-13 UNC thread. When this conclusion was reached, they made out their third recommendation for a minor change (Figure 19-3).

The team was at this point, to say the least, a little taken aback because

Figure 19-2

they had to make a recommendation which would cost money to implement but would not show any measurable direct savings. This, of course, they were not used to, nor did they ever expect such a condition would arise. Shrugging their shoulders at this state of affairs, they understood that this recommendation would improve manufacturing even if it didn't reduce cost and that it would show the shop supervisors that they had listened to everyone's problems. They were now ready to move to the last notation they had made from the data on the Information Phase.

This notation ("Are plated lock washers and ½-inch bronze nuts necessary?"), they realized, again fell into the buyer's area of influence as well as that of the team member from manufacturing. After considerable discussion between these two team members and contacts with the materials control and stockroom personnel, it was determined that this would not be put in as a recommended change on this project. This action was taken due to two facts. First, these parts are used in a multitude of other assemblies, therefore an elimination of the present parts would require the changing

JOY MANUFACTURING COMPANY — COST/IMPROVEMENT RECOMMENDATION

PRIORITY ______

DATE 9-5- REF. NO. MEA-3

PRODUCT Voltage regulator #3116 ASSY. OR PART Brass stud

PART NO. 9090547-1 QTY./PRODUCT 5 QTY./YEAR 850

POTENTIAL 1ST YEAR SAVINGS $ 0 SALES FORECAST (NEXT 12 MONTHS) -175 PRODUCT

PRESENT RECOMMENDED

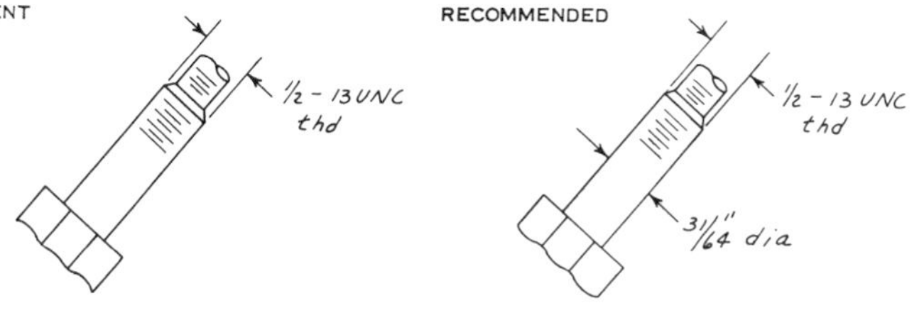


| CALCULATION OF SAVING | MATERIAL | DIRECT LABOR | FRINGE BENEFIT | TOTAL |
|---|---|---|---|---|
| PRESENT | $ — | $ — | $ — | $ — |
| PROPOSED | $ — | $ — | $ — | $ — |
| DIFFERENCE PER PIECE OR ASSY. | $ — | $ — | $ — | $ — |

IMPLEMENTATION COST – MFG. $ 10.00 ENG. $ 10.00

FINDINGS & RECOMMENDATIONS: On a number of occasions, it has been found by manufacturing that when the stud is on the large side of the standard tolerance, trouble is encountered in assembling the gaskets onto the stud.

It is recommended that the basic diameter of this part of the stud be reduced from ½ inch to 31/64 inch. This would eliminate the manufacturing problem.

This change would require one hour of engineering time to change the drawing and one hour of manufacturing engineering time to change the routers.

No direct savings would be realized.

APPROVED BY ______ REJECTED ______ DATE ______

ENGINEERING CHANGE ORDER NO. ______ FOR FURTHER INFO. ______

TEAM MEMBERS J.A. Doe, B.E. Egan, F.M. Smith

**Figure 19-3**

of a multitude of other assemblies and their drawings. Second, if unplated lock washers and steel nuts were purchased just for use in this assembly, the cost of the parts plus the cost to order them plus the inventory cost to stock them as specials would be greater than the cost of the present parts. The team, however, did not throw this idea away. They did make a notation to discuss the overall problem with the Standards Department at a later date. This they believed could be studied by the department as an overall plant and product project.

This, then, completed the work on the notations they had made as a result of their review of the Information Phase data. They now moved on to the notations they had made as a result of their findings throughout the remainder of the project work.

In this category, they had only one notation for a minor modification: "Since no seal is required at the insulating panel, modify design." This they thoroughly discussed and concluded that a change could be recommended. They determined that the gaskets could be eliminated and that the stud and recessed washer could be modified. Once this conclusion had been reached, they proceeded to complete a recommendation sheet on this change (Figure 19-4).

Having completed their list of possible minor modifications, they prepared, for use in their presentation, a summation list of the potential savings from the recommendations in this category. The list was as follows:

MINOR MODIFICATIONS

| Reference no. | Parts | Potential savings |
|---|---|---|
| MEA-1 . . . . . | Tube, special | $ 257.00 |
| MEA-2 . . . . . | Increase lot size | $ 488.40 |
| MEA-3 . . . . . | Brass stud | $  0 |
| MEA-4 . . . . . | Stud, washer, gaskets | $ 782.80 |
| Total  . . . . | . . . . . . . . . . . . . . . . | $1,528.20 |

This total, they realized, would be reduced to some degree if all were put into effect, due to a reduction in MEA-2 if parts were eliminated from the setup savings. This reduction, they determined, would not outweigh the conservative figure they were using for their annual quantity; so they let the total figure stand as it was at $1,528.20.

When this summation of the potential savings of their recommended minor changes was completed, they were ready to move on to the development of their recommendation sheet on their major modification.

The team members approached, at first, the preparation of this recommendation with almost childish delight and exuberance. This, of course, was due to two specific factors. First, they had deep feelings of both pride and accomplishment in this specific idea. Second, after summarizing the

JOY MANUFACTURING COMPANY    COST/ IMPROVEMENT  RECOMMENDATION
PRIORITY_____

DATE ___ 9-5-_____    REF. NO. _MEA-4_____
PRODUCT _Voltage regulator #3116·    ASSY.  OR PART _Stud, washer, gaskets_
PART  NO. _9090547-1, 4, ç 5_____    QTY. /PRODUCT _____    QTY. /YEAR ___850__

POTENTIAL  IST  YEAR  SAVINGS  $ _782.80_    | SALES FORECAST (NEXT 12 MONTHS) |  -175 PRODUCT

PRESENT                                        RECOMMENDED

— Recessed washer

— Gaskets

— Stud

1¼" flat washer

— Stud

| CALCULATION  OF  SAVING | MATERIAL | DIRECT LABOR | FRINGE BENEFIT | TOTAL |
|---|---|---|---|---|
| PRESENT | $ .997 | $ 1.194 | $ | $ 2.191 |
| PROPOSED | $ .670 | $ .600 | $ | $ 1.270 |
| DIFFERENCE PER PIECE OR ASSY. | $ .327 | $ .594 | $ | $ .921 |
| IMPLEMENTATION COST - | | MFG. $ 20.00 | ENG. $ 50.00 | |

FINDINGS & RECOMMENDATIONS: It has been found, in the course of the project
work, that a specification had been self-imposed on this design by
the engineer. This specification was that there be a seal between
the stud and the insulation panel.
      Since this specification is not necessary, it is
recommended that the configuration be modified as shown. That is,
the gaskets eliminated, the recess removed from the stud, and the
recessed washer replaced by a standard 1¼" flat washer.
      To make this change, two hours of manufacturing
engineering time would be required to change the routings and tools.
Engineering would require five hours to change the drawings and bill
of material.

APPROVED  BY _____    REJECTED _____    DATE _____
ENGINEERING  CHANGE  ORDER  NO. _____    FOR  FURTHER  INFO. _____
TEAM  MEMBERS _J.A. Doe, B.E. Egan, F.M. Smith_____    | FORM |

Figure 19-4

potential savings of their recommended minor changes they realized that,
no matter what happened, their efforts would not have been in vain.

In conflict with this buoyant spirit, however, was the realization of the
importance of all the recommendation worksheets.   With this particular
worksheet, as with the other recommendation worksheets, they were
particularly careful for they realized that the total results of their efforts
hinged on the wording and description used.   This realization came from
their understanding of the fact that the language used was the basic mate-

rial from which they must fashion all their communications regardless of any specialized jargons—also that the words were only a device to get a thought, unchanged, from one mind to another.

Recognizing both of these mental attitudes, the team members undertook the development and completion of the preparation part of the Recommendation Phase. They enthusiastically, but with deliberate thought, prepared the recommendation on their major modification of the present design (Figure 19-5).

Having thus completed the project preparation portion of their plan, they were now ready to undertake their presentation plan. The first step in this plan was for them to contact the project or product manager and make an appointment for their presentation. This they did, by telephone, and set the presentation for the following morning. The only fact that they had to bring up to date for the presentation was the inventory status of the connector; i.e., the inventory of complete units, units in process of manufacture, and the number of voltage regulators scheduled for manufacture.

When they had secured the updated information, they found it to be as follows:

1. Complete connectors in stock: ten
2. Units in process of manufacture: twenty-five
3. Voltage regulators to be manufactured: three per month

On the basis of this information, they realized that they (the company) had in stock or process $2\frac{1}{2}$ months' supply of the connectors. This, then, would allow them sufficient time to implement any idea that was accepted, either minor or major modification. They were now completely prepared for their project presentation; i.e., they had complete facts and complete costs on their project and on their recommendations. They believed that they could now motivate positive action.

## Project Presentation

Prior to their presentation meeting with the product manager, they organized their material for the presentation. In addition, they selected the individual team member who was to make the presentation.

As a team, they decided that the engineer would be the best one to convey their ideas. This they believed to be so because he had designed the original connector. Also, a number of the points to be changed had been put in the assembly by him, and their elimination could best be explained by him.

Thus prepared, they proceeded to their appointment. They approached this presentation with some fear, as all of us have a fear of the unknown, but also with assurance. The latter was due to the fact that they knew that

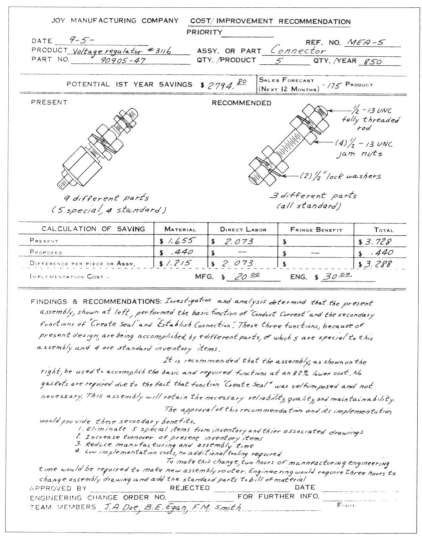

JOY MANUFACTURING COMPANY    COST/ IMPROVEMENT RECOMMENDATION
PRIORITY_____
DATE ___9-5-___    REF. NO. _MEA-5_
PRODUCT _Voltage regulator #3116_    ASSY. OR PART _Connector_
PART NO. _____90905-47_____    QTY. /PRODUCT ____5____    QTY. /YEAR _850_

POTENTIAL IST YEAR SAVINGS $ _2794.80_    SALES FORECAST (NEXT 12 MONTHS) _-175_ PRODUCT

PRESENT    RECOMMENDED

½ -13 UNC fully threaded rod

(4) ½ - 13 UNC jam nuts

(2) ½" lock washers

9 different parts (5 special, 4 standard)    3 different parts (all standard)

| CALCULATION OF SAVING | MATERIAL | DIRECT LABOR | FRINGE BENEFIT | TOTAL |
|---|---|---|---|---|
| PRESENT | $ 1.655 | $ 2.073 | $ | $ 3.728 |
| PROPOSED | $ .440 | $ — | $ — | $ .440 |
| DIFFERENCE PER PIECE OR ASSY. | $ 1.215 | $ 2.073 | $ | $ 3.288 |
| IMPLEMENTATION COST - | | MFG. $ 20⁰⁰ | ENG. $ 30⁰⁰. | |

FINDINGS & RECOMMENDATIONS: *Investigation and analysis determind that the present assembly, shown at left, performed the basic function of "Conduct Current" and the secondary functions of "Create Seal" and "Establish Connection". These three functions, because of present design, are being accomplished by 9 different parts, of which 5 are special to this assembly and 4 are standard inventory items.*
        *It is recommended that the assembly, as shown on the right, be used to accomplish the basic and required functions at an 82% lower cost. No gaskets are required due to the fact that function "Create Seal" was self imposed and not necessary. This assembly will retain the necessary reliability, quality, and maintainability.*
        *The approval of this recommendation and its implementation would provide these secondary benefits.*
        *1. Eliminate 5 special items from inventory and thier associated drawings*
        *2. Increase turnover of present inventory items*
        *3. Reduce manufacturing and assembly time*
        *4. Low implementation costs, no additional tooling required*
        *To make this change, two hours of manufacturing engineering time would be required to make new assembly router. Engineering would require three hours to change assembly drawing and add the standard parts t.bill of material*
APPROVED BY _____    REJECTED ____    DATE _____
ENGINEERING CHANGE ORDER NO. _____    FOR FURTHER INFO. _____
TEAM MEMBERS _J.A Doe, B.E.Egan, F.M. Smith____    FORM

**Figure 19-5**

this product manager was, in most instances, open-minded and willing to consider any proposition.

After the proper introduction of his team members, the engineer rapidly but factually reviewed the data and information the team had collected. This he did so that the product manager would be up to date on the project and would be making his decisions based on present facts and not personal opinion, halftruths, or hearsay.

Then, progressing according to their established plan, he presented the team's recommendation for minor change. Here he started with the recommended change on the special tube, 9090547-3; then he discussed the changes to the brass stud, 9090547-1; next the possibility of elimination of the gaskets; and finally the change in order quantity. The latter recommendation, although not affecting the design, was discussed with the product manager so that he could see the total picture relating to his product's cost.

The product manager, after some discussion, particularly on the elimination of the seal, accepted the team's recommendation for minor change. He asked for the recommendation sheets so that he could sign them and thereby start the necessary work to have them implemented. The team, however, requested that he hold off until the engineer presented their major modification. This the product manager agreed to do.

The engineer then proceeded to present the team's recommendation for a major change. In the presentation of this recommendation, as in the others, he stated only the facts and costs pertinent to the recommendation. He pointed out the benefits of elimination of drawings and special parts, of the use of all standard parts, of reduced manufacturing and assembly time, of elimination of the gaskets, and finally of the annual gross savings of $2,700.

After some discussion, the product manager asked how long it would take to implement this recommendation, what steps were necessary, and when—based on present inventories—it could be phased into the product. The team members, each discussing his own area, answered his questions.

First, tests would have to be conducted to make absolutely sure that this approach would work. This would take, at most, one week. At the same time, in anticipation of the idea's acceptance, the drawings and bill of materials would be changed by the engineer. This would take less than a week.

The team member from Manufacturing stated that as soon as the engineering changes were made and approved, a hold would be put on the manufacture of any more of the present connectors; this would take at most one day. Next, the shop routes for assembly of the new connector in the voltage regulator would be prepared, again taking less than a day. Third and last, a phase-in date by product serial number would be established, thus assuring that there would be no delay in manufacture.

The team member from Purchasing stated that as soon as the engineering changes were made, the purchasing records would be modified to increase the order quantities of the parts required and reduce the order quantities of the parts no longer required. At the same time, the Accounting Department would be notified of the change so that they could watch for and audit the change when it actually occurred.

The team as a whole stated that they believed that the recommendation for major modification could be implemented when the present inventory and in-process connectors were used up, i.e., in 2½ months. In this manner, there would be no parts to be scrapped, but the phasing in would have to be watched carefully.

With this assurance from the team and after reviewing the team's implementation plan, the product manager approved and signed the recommendation for major modification. This he did with the stipulations that it was to be used only if it passed an electrical test and if the team members personally followed its implementation.

## Recommendation Implementation

After leaving the product manager's office, the team returned to their project work area. Here they made sure that each team member knew exactly what part of the implementation plan he was responsible for. They also established a specific target date at which each step had to be completed. In order to do this, they first had to recheck the sequence of their plan. They found that their original plan had not included an electrical test; this they added.

Remembering that "the best way to be sure action is started is to start it yourself," they went into the shop and secured enough parts for three assemblies. These they took to the electrical lab for test. After discussing the product manager's order for the electrical test as well as the schedule required by the present inventory with the laboratory supervisor, the tests were scheduled for completion within two days. The lab supervisor was asked to contact the engineer at the conclusion of the tests or as soon as any problems came up.

The team also made plans to meet in one week, at which time they felt all tests should be complete and the engineering changes made. The team member from Engineering was to call prior to that time if major problems were encountered in the electrical test.

Since no problems were experienced in the electrical test, the team met as planned. All engineering changes had been made (Figure 19-6) and a hold had been put on the manufacture of the original connector. This meeting was quite short as they had only to review the remaining action steps and to agree to contact each other as each step was completed. They also agreed that if all steps proceeded according to schedule, they would meet again two months later for one final review prior to the phasing in of the new connector.

Again because of their preplanning, no problems were encountered and their implementation plan proceeded without a hitch. When they met again after two months, each team member brought with him a copy of the material generated for each action step. In addition, they had the

| BILL OF MATERIAL | | |
|---|---|---|
| QTY | PART NO. | DESCRIPTION |
| 1 | 600019-119 | Brass rod $-\frac{1}{2}-13$ UNC thd, $\times 4\frac{1}{2}$ Long |
| 4 | 600020-6 | Nut, jam-brass- $\frac{1}{2}-13$ UNC |
| 2 | 601120-6 | Lock washer, bronze- $\frac{1}{2}$ |
| 2 | 9090547-5 | Gasket, nitrile |

| | |
|---|---|
| CONNECTOR | |
| M.E.A. COMPANY | |
| BETHEL PARK, PA. | |
| | 9090548 |

**Figure 19-6**

assembly foreman attend this meeting.   After reviewing the material for each action step, they discussed the new connector with the foreman to see if he saw any problems with the phasing in cycle now that it was drawing near.   The foreman, having been forewarned of the impending change at the time of the recommendation's acceptance, did not foresee any problems and agreed to notify Accounting of the serial number of the first regulator on which the new connector was used.   In this manner, the Accounting Department could audit the change in cost and notify the product manager of the new cost of the voltage regulator.   The Accounting Department also agreed to notify the team members of the new cost of the regulator and of the audited savings to be realized from the use of the new connector.

Two weeks later, the team received back from the Accounting Department a copy of their recommendation sheet MEA-5 showing an audited annual savings of $2,794.80.   When this was received, the team had a little celebration of coffee and doughnuts to mark the successful completion of their first project.

*Success in life is a matter not so much of talent*
*or opportunity as of concentration and*
*perseverance.   — C. W. WENDTE*

## Chapter Twenty
# General Comments and Conclusions

Change can be upsetting.

It can upset old ways of doing things; it can upset people. But it is the source of the only lasting security for people today.

The man who changes with his environment—or, better still, the man who brings about change—is truly secure. Confusion and fear are not his lot; he is confident. He makes the best of himself and the best of his job.

Since change is an absolute fact, an inevitable conclusion in a growing world is that you must live with it. In order to best do this, you must learn to manage change before it manages to destroy you. One of the best ways to manage change is through the Systematic Approach of Value Engineering.

This approach involves no efficiency experts to show you how to do your job. It is constructed on the premise that you know your job and associated conditions best and are therefore best equipped to evaluate and change them.

The cost of doing business is high where routine is sacred, where change is not allowed. Routine in today's changing world is false security and is deadly. Instead of feeling secure and complacent, you must be dissatisfied

—dissatisfied to the point where you overcome the fear of change and make change occur.

The important point regarding change, however, is not to make change happen simply for the sake of change. Change should only be made to happen when it will improve the present conditions.

Throughout the Systematic Approach, one basic question permeates the whole—"Why?" This simple question, backed by the deliberate techniques of the Job Plan, strips away blind obedience to routine so that reason can be applied.

*Why?*

Learn to use that word well. If you do, you'll be way ahead. You'll have taken a major step up in the use of the Value Engineering Systematic Approach. It will aid you in developing the management of change into an enjoyable type of work.

But you don't like work, right?

Wrong. When work is enjoyable, it is pleasing to you and rewarding to your mind and spirit. Among our psychological needs is something called recognition. And recognition by our supervisors and associates is most rewarding. The Job Plan, which has been discussed in Part 1 and applied here in Part 2 is one sure method of achieving the management of change, pleasure from your work, and the desired recognition.

In dealing with the management of change, the first problem you must overcome is personal fear—the basic and fundamental fear of change. This fear of change is by no means open and clearly visible; rather, it is hidden and hard to root out. This is best explained by the following quotation from Sydney J. Harris:

> *Why does almost every person agree with the*
> *old maxim that "variety is the spice of life" and*
> *yet at the same time look aghast at any variety*
> *in ideas, ways of living, and even in dress and*
> *social demeanor?*

Throughout your application of the Job Plan of the Value Engineering Systematic Approach, you will have to keep the above quotation constantly in mind. For if you do not, your projects are doomed to failure before you start.

In the case of the team applying the concepts to the connector, it can be seen that the team members were constantly aware of the problem. The team members, it will be seen on close study, having almost fallen into the trap themselves, made sure that the others with whom they dealt did not allow the fear of change to cloud their minds. The team members, in dealing with all their contacts, made sure that the individual did not see any potential change as a personal challenge or accusation of error to himself.

In this way, they eliminated fear, the first major roadblock to change and, in so doing, left room for the individual to objectively understand that, in this particular case, something could be changed.

By accomplishing the isolation of a single change, they overcame a second roadblock—fear by association, and made it relatively easy for the individual to recommend or make a change. Change is most difficult when it is directly or indirectly associated with what an individual believes are unchangeable habits, attitudes, methods, or ideas.

In reviewing the project further, you will see that the team, for a while, fell afoul of the costly specification which required a seal at the insulating panel. It wasn't until they remembered the old adage "Machinery doesn't lie" that they pinpointed the fact that this was a self-imposed specification on the part of the designer of the original connector. It wasn't until they looked closely at the present product that this fact became clear to them, thereby eliminating this costly specification.

When working on any project, you will do well to keep this old adage in mind and constantly keep your eyes open. For, in truth, you will find that not only doesn't machinery lie but that a complete analysis of it will tell a complete and unbiased story of its general history. To the individual who looks at detail and has a questioning mind, any machinery, equipment, or product will give forth vital and productive knowledge. This knowledge, if organized and used correctly, can aid you in removing substantial amounts of cost while at the same time allowing you to maintain the necessary quality and reliability.

As you look at the completed project as a whole, you can readily see that without the proper preparation of the recommendation, the work performed on it would be lost. The preparation of any recommendations must take into account two basic points. The first point includes the facts, data, and costs to be used. These, of course, must indeed be facts, not shaded half-truths. The second point is the manner in which the facts are presented. The second point is of the greatest importance in that it controls the first. It has been said, "The results of your thoughts must be served up as a tempting refreshment which can be eaten if so desired, not as a medicine which must be swallowed whether liked or not." While the team recognized the importance of preparing and presenting their recommendations carefully, they also kept another thought in mind. This thought was, "It is often said that men are ruled by their imaginations, but it would be truer to say *they are governed by the weakness of their imaginations.*" You too, in preparing your recommendations, must keep these thoughts in clear view.

After the preparation and presentation of their recommendations, the team, to be certain, concluded their work with a follow-up to make sure their idea was implemented. It must be noted that many individuals working with this Systematic Approach believe that they need not progress any further in the Job Plan than the presentation of recommendations, at which point they consider their job done. When this procedure is followed, it has been found from sad experience that the results are almost always small or completely negative. In the greater majority of cases, it has been found that lack of follow-up permits the greater majority of the recommendations to "fall into the cracks" and either never be seen or heard of again or be rejected due to lack of support. In some cases, in order to stress this follow-up procedure, some practitioners add additional phases to the Job Plan, i.e., Implementation, Summary, and Conclusion.

The project team working on the connector not only carefully planned the preparation and presentation of their recommendations but developed a specific action plan to be sure that they were implemented. These action plans they rapidly put into operation as soon as their recommendations were accepted. Such rapid action assured them not only that their ideas would be put into active use but that the company would attain the greatest possible benefit from them. Without such plans and decisive action, their work on the connector could have been completely wasted—or at least its benefits could have been lost to the company for an undetermined length of time.

Returning again to the actual recommendation and its presentation, a critical part of the Job Plan, it is important to note that giving the proper amount of information and data is an important factor. Too much information, just like too little information, can be disastrous. When too little information is provided for the decision maker, he cannot make a knowledgeable decision and therefore has only one course to follow—rejection. After this has happened to you once or twice, the normal reaction is to overcorrect. Hence you provide too much information and data, and the results are the same—rejection. This happens because of the fact that, because of the great volume of information, the decision maker cannot and will not consider it or try to relate it to the project. Since this is the case, he must reject the recommendation for fear that what he has not considered is vital and would be that which would cause him to reject the idea anyway. It is therefore best to closely screen your information and include in your recommendation only that which is pertinent to it. The information should also be restricted to only that which will fit on the recommendation sheet. This latter point is a forcing technique one imposes on oneself, as it is more difficult to say something in a few words than in many. In this way, you force yourself to screen out the unnecessary words and data just as you have screened out the unnecessary costs. The decision maker should, of course, be informed that you do have, readily available, any backup data that he might wish to see.

Continuing this trend of thought on too much information, another fact should be considered. If it appears that you have too much information and data for one recommendation sheet, you will most likely find that you have more than one recommendation to make. When this occurs, you will find, on close examination, that you are trying to cover too broad an area with one recommendation. This in itself can be the cause of the rejection of a recommendation. It is therefore best to break your ideas down into small, manageable pieces—just as the defining of functions broke the original problem down into pieces of reasonable size—and make a recommendation on each such piece. In this manner, each recommendation stands or falls on its own merits. In this manner, a critical or major part of your solution is not rejected because of problems with a minor part of your solution. The latter, it has been found, is often the case with complex recommendations; i.e., the critical or major solutions are acceptable while the minor ones, if any, are not accepted.

Another factor to be considered in wrapping up your project for presentation is the number of recommendations you are to present. You must, whenever possible, make more than one recommendation for change on any given point. This you should strive to do so that you do not fall into the "one-idea fixation" trap—also so that the decision maker does have more than just a simple "yes" or "no" decision to make. Preferably these multiple recommendations should include both major and minor modifications for change. In this manner, no matter what the personal or political conditions, some specific change toward improvement can be made.

All your recommendations, like those of the connector project team, must be geared to the recipient. If your recommendations become stereotyped and are not directed to the particular recipient, they will not have the necessary impact and are likely to be rejected. You must learn that the recipient, the decision maker, is an individual and wants to be treated as such. If you do not treat him as such, you are flirting with disaster. For this reason, until you have learned how to work with each individual, you must proceed with great care in making your recommendations. One of the primary assisting factors here, however, is teamwork. With the use of teamwork, you will find that what you don't know about an individual someone else will be able to provide. Yes, even here at the end of your project work, teamwork continues to play a most important part in your use of the Value Engineering Systematic Approach.

The final and quite critical part of your project work is the audit of the savings to be realized. This too is part of your responsibility. For until an audit has been made of your project's savings, you are not sure that there *are* any savings. In addition, other important knowledge can be gleaned from a project audit. If the savings show up as predicted, you know that your work is complete. When the audit shows that the savings are below what was predicted, you must find out if your recommendations have been completely implemented or if your estimates were incorrect. In either case, you can take the necessary steps to correct the situation. On the other hand, if the audited savings are above those that you predicted, you must find out where you were wrong or what was done to increase the savings. If the savings were increased by additional changes, you want to know about these so that they can be considered in future work. If your estimated savings were so low due to a miscalculation, you want to know about this also for use in your future work.

Throughout this general discussion, the subject of the rejection of recommendations has been raised many times. This too, no matter how precise you are, will happen to you—perhaps more times than you might care to discuss. But you must be prepared for this so-called defeat. The rejection of a recommendation or the total work on a project can and will happen to each of us. As a matter of fact, it should be expected. For if you never fail, your aim is too low and you are not half trying. Being always successful in your recommendations simply means that you are being too conservative in your ideas. Yes, you must expect rejections, almost desire them, for then you will know that you are extending yourself to the utmost.

Of course, some of your rejections may not be caused by simple statistics; they may be caused by improper preparation, lack of information, or a clash of personalities. Because of these latter possibilities, you must review with particular care any rejection to determine why it was made. In this manner, you will also learn from these so-called defeats.

## Conclusions

The Value Engineering Systematic Approach has been applied here, in Part 2, to a simple yet understandable project. You should, with practice, be able to convert and apply this knowledge to any project, large or small, simple or complex, where you want to use it.

When you first start into the active use of the Job Plan, it is strongly recommended that you use the worksheets as they are applied here. However, as you become more proficient with the Job Plan and its techniques, you can refrain from the use of the majority of the worksheets, but you must constantly keep in mind their use and the information and data they require.

You now have a fundamental knowledge of the Value Engineering Systematic Approach and its Job Plan. You can now follow or you can lead, the decision is up to you. You can wait until you find out how others have coped with or exploited changes and then copy them, or you can think of original ideas that they have not hit on. And if you do that, you are using this methodology in the fullest sense. For change is not a sideline in the business of leadership, it is a vital and integral part of the whole idea.

Changing things is central to leadership, and changing them ahead of anyone else is creativeness.

Such creative leadership in change, the management of change, can lead to discovery—or it can even lead to invention. Creativeness and innovation in industry have never been unimportant, but they have never been as important as they are now. The reason is quite simple: it is the pace of change.

There are two areas where change must dominate your thinking: the technology and the market, what can be produced and what people want to buy, supply and demand. Technological advance is constantly bringing new possibilities into range, either new techniques, processes, and materials, or old ones at new low prices which make it possible to use them on new products. Customer demand is also constantly changing as people become wealthier and can afford new products or as advances bring products within their range.

With this new knowledge, you can become a vital, dynamic part of the growing scene. You are only limited by your will, your drive, your imagination.

# Part Three

# Case Studies

## INTRODUCTION

*Men trust rather to their eyes than to their ears.*
*The effect of precepts is, therefore, slow and*
*tedious, while that of examples is summary and*
*effectual.* — SENECA

*In order that you might excel in your application of the Value Engineering*
*Systematic Approach, it is important that you have a broad knowledge and*
*understanding of the application of this technology. The simplest means*
*of attaining this knowledge and understanding is through the study of*
*examples of its application by others.*

*The case studies used in the following pages as examples have been*
*selected from the applications of the Value Engineering Methodology by*
*many individuals throughout the world. These examples have been*
*selected from the thousands available to show you the wide variety of*
*projects to which this methodology has been applied.*

*As you consider these case studies, you will note that as different problems*
*arose, the individuals varied their application of the methodology to meet*
*the particular variation. It is important that you study these variations so*
*that you may attain the same flexibility in your application of the Value*
*Engineering Systematic Approach.*

*In most instances, these case studies are not an explanation of the complete*
*project; rather, there is just a small portion of a complete product included*
*in each example.*

247

*One of the simplest means of getting your application of the Value Engineering Systematic Approach started is to hitchhike on someone else's idea.  Therefore, as you study these examples, try to determine how the basic idea of each can be applied to your products, processes, or services.*

*Of necessity, the companies and individuals connected with these case studies must be kept anonymous.  These case studies are, however, actual, implemented projects which represent many thousands of dollars' savings to the companies involved.  These examples also, in every instance, have met the basic objective of the Value Engineering Methodology:* "The same or better performance at lower cost."

# Case Study 1
## THREE-WAY CONNECTOR CONTACTS

Marketing, after receiving a request to quote on a large quantity of three-way connectors, checked the manufacturing cost of the assembly and found that they could not provide a competitive bid. At this time, they asked the Value Engineering Department of the plant to look at the product and see if any cost could be removed. The value specialist assigned to the task found that the largest single cost items of the assembly were the brass contacts shown in Figure 1(a).

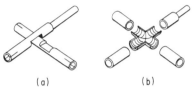

(a)            (b)

**Figure 1**

**Results:**   The information search showed that two sets of these contacts were used per assembly and that each set cost $0.838. This high cost was caused, according to the Manufacturing Department, by the fact that each of the two pieces in a set had to be machined twice in a lathe, once for each end; then it had to be milled twice to provide the mating notch and the end slots; and then it had to be soldered to the mating part. This, the value specialist was informed, required a lot of handling, machine time, scrap, and possible loss of parts, all adding to the cost.

The required basic and second-degree functions were defined as "conduct current," "provide connection," and "provide location." This was cross-checked with both the Engineering and Marketing Departments and stipulated as being quite factual.

The value specialist then queried the Marketing Department to determine if the contact configuration was critical. He was told that the only critical thing regarding the contacts was their location and end configuration. This was due to the fact that there were a number of these connectors in use and any new one put into service must be interchangeable.

With this background, the value specialist got together with Engineering and Manufacturing to determine what could be done to reduce the cost while meeting the functions and parameters.

The group decided to start at the ends of the contacts as this was a critical area from the standpoint of conducting current, providing contact, and providing connection. Looking only at the ends, they reasoned that a single end could quite readily be made on a lathe with only one setup and one operation per configuration. Continuing with this thought, they realized that only two setups would be required for both kinds of end pieces and that the drilled end pieces could be run in extremely large quantities. If this were to be done, they realized that some method of fastening the individual end pieces would have to be devised. After creating this new problem, they thought of a four-way pipe connection. As they developed this idea, they realized that they did not have to conduct fluid, only current; therefore a closed connection was not necessary. A simple formed copper stamping was designed, similar to half of a four-way pipe coupling, which would do the job. The five pieces were to be assembled and anchored by a single soldering operation.

At this point, Engineering and Manufacturing took over to make the required drawing and production routing changes and to produce the right tools. The final configuration, as shown in Figure 1(b), increased the number of parts per assembly from three to six (including the solder) but reduced the cost to $0.535. This new assembly price, plus complete interchangeability, allowed Marketing to submit a competitive bid and to secure the contract. Further, it was applicable throughout the complete product line with the same benefits accruing.

## Case Study 2
## OIL-LEVEL GAUGE

A value specialist, while walking through the plant one day, saw this oil-level gauge, Figure 2(a), being installed on one model of the stationary compressors manufactured by the company. On seeing this gauge being used, a number of thoughts immediately came to his mind. First, that this gauge

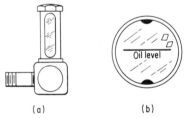

(a)                    (b)

Figure 2

is used to show how much oil is in the compressor crankcase. Second, that due to the fact that it was made of brass and glass, the purchase price was most likely quite high. Third, because of the way it was mounted, extending out from the side of the compressor, the probability of damage was great.

**Results:**   Analysis of this part showed that it was purchased at a cost of $3.02, that it was made of solid brass and glass, and that some leakage problems did occur at the points where the glass tube contacted the rest of the assembly.

Further investigation of this item with Engineering, Manufacturing, and Purchasing brought to light the fact that other types of oil-level gauges, such as that shown in Figure 2(b), were not only available but were being used on other models of the company's stationary compressors.

Investigation into this fact showed that the latter gauge could be applied to all stationary compressors at an engineering cost of $80 and a tooling cost of $20.   This gauge was being purchased at a cost of $1.20 each, which showed a 60 percent reduction in the part cost.   On the original compressor model considered, this amounted to a new material savings of approximately $500 per year.   In addition, a number of secondary savings were realized:

1. Reduced number of purchase orders due to standardization
2. Reduced inventory value
3. Reduced inventory items

## Case Study 3
## LAMP SOCKET

A task force group, starting the application of Value Engineering Methodology, decided to take this molded lamp socket as their first project.   In the course of gathering their information, they found that the lamp socket was required to seal out moisture from the base of the lamp bulb and the conduit box to which it was mounted.   Further, it was designed to isolate the bulb from shock and vibration.   Their information search in manufacturing turned up the fact that new tooling for this part was planned in the immediate future to put this item on the injection molding presses.

**Results:**   The fact that new tooling was imminent caused the team to make a rapid evaluation of the immediate problems being encountered on this project.

The team's continued information search turned up the facts that the support ring transmitted the mounting force of the screws to the lamp socket flange, that brass eyelets were put into the molded flange of the lamp socket to prevent the mounting-screw threads from cutting the molded synthetic rubber compound, and that two fiber retaining washers were used only to hold the assembly together during shipping and were thrown away when the lamp socket was mounted to the conduit box.   The information search also found that considerable hand labor was being used in manufacturing to separate and strip the twin conductor wire to two different lengths for assembly to the socket.

In the definition of functions they determined that the support ring "transmitted force."

From the above facts and functional definition they recommended to engineering that the support ring could be molded into the lamp socket flange accomplishing its function as well as the function of the brass eyelets. This

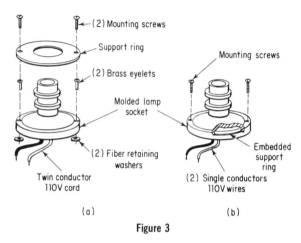

**Figure 3**

was possible due to the fact that the hole in the support ring was smaller than the hole in the flange. This meant that when the support ring was molded in the middle of the flange, the hole in it would act as a bushing and not allow the screw threads to contact the molding compound. This was accepted and incorporated into the new injection mold when it was built.

In addition to the savings in compound (that displaced by the support ring) and the elimination of the brass eyelets, another benefit occurred. When molding parts in which there are through holes, a thin membrane of compound forms across the hole due to the process of mold construction. This is normally a detriment to the product and must be removed. In this case, however, it was an advantage and was left in place; i.e., it was found that the mounting screws could be pushed through this membrane and they were thus located for shipment and installation. This eliminated the need for the fiber washers.

The team then looked at the other problem they had uncovered—the hand stripping of the twin-conductor lead. This was readily solved by recommending the use of two different-length single-conductor leads (one black, one white). These could be cut to length and stripped by machine.

When these simple recommendations were put into effect by Engineering and Manufacturing, it was found that this team, new in the use of the methodology, had caused a 14.2 percent reduction in the shop cost of the lamp socket and had reduced the inventory by two items.

## Case Study 4
## LAMP SOCKET CARTON

A task force, after studying a specific product, decided to analyze the carton in which it was packaged. The carton, as shown in Figure 4(a), was a top-opening type, made of a gloss-white carton board with nomenclature and advertising on each end. The lamp socket was packed in this carton so that it could be readily stacked for display on the shelves of the distributor by whom it was sold.

**Results:** The task force, in their information search, found that this carton had been originally designed by the Marketing Department for the purpose described above. With this data, the Purchasing Department member of the group called in the carton supplier.

When the carton supplier was apprised of the fact that the company wanted to reduce its costs and was soliciting any suggestions he might have, he was quite cooperative and requested that he be allowed to look into this situation back at his own plant. A short time later he came back with the suggestion that the carton be changed from a top-opening type to the end-opening type shown in Figure 4(b).

This change, he said, would simplify his manufacturing operations as well as reduce the amount of waste material generated in manufacturing the carton. He further stated that if this approach were accepted, he could reduce the cost of the carton by 8 percent.

The task force reviewed this suggestion with the Marketing and Manufacturing Departments. The Marketing Department approved the suggestion since it did not change the appearance of the carton once it was assembled. The Manufacturing Department approved the suggestion as they found that there was a slight reduction in packaging time when an end-opening type of carton was used.

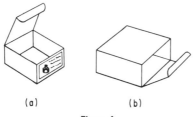

(a)                    (b)

**Figure 4**

This, however, was not the end of this case study.

A short time later, the carton supplier, after he saw that the company was indeed interested in its suppliers' suggestions and ready to put them into effect, made another suggestion regarding this carton. This suggestion was to change the carton material from a gloss white to a buff white at an additional reduction in the cost of the carton of approximately 40 percent. This new suggestion by the supplier was checked with the Marketing Department, which readily accepted it and had it put into effect.

This second suggestion by the supplier stimulated considerable interest by the Marketing and Purchasing Departments in other product cartons. The application of this carton material change, when applied to other similarly packed products, brought the total net savings on cartons to over $1,200 annually.

## Case Study 5
## PURCHASE OF CAPITAL EQUIPMENT

An appropriation request had been completed and approval requested for a C frame, nibbler-type punch press with a follower tracer attachment at approximate cost of $15,000. This piece of equipment was to be used to manufacture centrifugal fan side plates as shown in Figure 5(a). At this time, division management requested an investigation of this project.

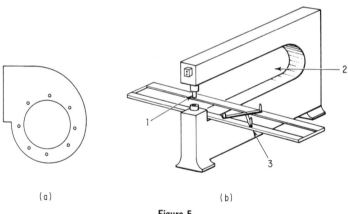

(a)                    (b)

**Figure 5**

**Results:** A functional analysis of the proposed equipment, Figure 5(b), showed that it would perform the following basic and required second-degree functions:

1. Basic function: "remove material"—punch and die
2. Second degree: "provide clearance"—C frame construction
3. Second degree: "control direction"—follower-tracer attachment

With this knowledge of the requested equipment and method of manufacture, an analysis of the present equipment and method of manufacture was undertaken. This analysis showed that the subject parts were being made on a C frame, nibbler-type punch press which provided the following basic and required functions:

1. Basic: "remove material" — punch and die (this equipment has the capacity to handle heavier material)
2. Second: "provide clearance" — C frame construction (due to larger throat depth, greater clearance was available)

This analysis further showed that the third required function, "control direction," was being provided by hand by the operator and that the present equipment was only used 30 to 40 percent of the time because of this fact. This showed the analysts that the new equipment was not being requested to alleviate a manufacturing-capacity problem and that a $15,000 expenditure was requested to acquire the additional function of "control direction."

With this knowledge, the analysts proceeded to determine whether an attachment could be designed and built to enable the present equipment to perform this third function. It was determined that this could be done for an estimated cost of $4,800 — a potential saving of $10,200. Checking further with the manufacturer of the present equipment to determine if such an attachment could be mounted on their equipment, it was learned that they had available, as optional equipment for their machine, a follower-tracer attachment. This attachment has been purchased and mounted on the present equipment at a cost of $3,000.

This represents a direct cost prevention of $12,000. This action also resulted in the following indirect cost preventions and profit improvements:

1. Elimination of scrapping and sale of present equipment
2. Elimination of installation costs of new equipment
3. Greater utilization of present equipment due to ease of operation
4. Elimination of more expensive flame cutting of parts

## Case Study 6
## LATHE-CUT GASKETS

Synthetic rubber gaskets, lathe-cut to thickness, are used by one transformer manufacturer to seal the joint between both high- and low-voltage bushings and the tank wall. The one size of gasket studied as typical was the low-voltage bushing gasket: 2.000-inches $\pm$ 0.005-inch OD by 1.500-inches $\pm$ 0.005-inch ID by 0.125 inch $\pm$ 0.005 inch thick.

**Results:** Analysis of this gasket showed that its basic and second-degree functions were:

Basic: "provide seal" — the faces of the gasket contact the bushing and the tank wall.

Secondary: "provide location" — provided by the thickness as well as the compressibility of the material.

Close examination of this particular part showed that habit and attitudes plus an adherence to close tolerances were possibly costing the company thousands of dollars extra per year.

It was found that the specification controlling all gaskets was written by the general works laboratory in 1925 in compliance with 1925 designs, and

Figure 6

that this specification spelled out a ± 0.005-inch tolerance on all dimensions. Further examination of transformer design of 1925 vintage showed that the area surrounding the bushing opening was indented to form a confining pocket into which the gasket fitted. It was also learned that if the gasket OD was too large, it would break the bushing when the bushing was tightened down to effect the seals.

When the general specification was discussed with Engineering, it was stated, "The OD must be ground to remove the 'as cured' rubber. The ground surface resists ozone attack much better than an 'as cured' surface." When discussed with the General Laboratory, it was stated, "The OD must be ground to hold a ± 0.005 inch tolerance so that the gasket will properly fit the transformer tank." Analysis of these statements shows that the Laboratory is giving an engineering answer and that Engineering is giving a laboratory answer.

Investigation showed that when each department answered for its respective responsibility, both answers were incorrect. Engineering showed that the present transformer tank no longer had a restraining pocket around the bushing opening and that the gasket could expand into open air, therefore eliminating bushing breakage due to oversize gaskets. The Laboratory showed, from numerous tests, that the "as cured" surface of synthetic rubber had greater resistance to ozone attack than a ground surface.

As a result of this correction of honest wrong beliefs, the specifications were changed to provide a tolerance on the OD of gaskets of − 0.000 inch, + 0.030 inch. This change in the one tolerance on the lathe-cut gaskets eliminated the grinding of the OD and reduced the cost of all such gaskets by 20 percent.

## Case Study 7
### SPECIAL 1/4-20 BRASS JAM NUT

Here is a case where a special brass jam nut was manufactured by the user company, special because it used the dimensions from two different jam-nut standards—the thickness from one standard, the distance across flats from a second standard. The usage of these nuts was a minimum of 375,000 per year at a cost of $13.30 per hundred.

**Results:** Analysis of this part determined the facts that in the initial planning, due to the fact that it was not standard, it was decided that this nut would be manufactured in the division's Screw Machine Department. It was further learned that it was sold to another division of the company at a price of $9.30 per hundred. The nuts, because of lack of information, were then purchased by the original division at a cost of $13.30 per hundred. With each transfer between divisions, overhead and handling costs were added.

With this information, the analyst took the brass nuts to one of the buyers in the originating division. When the subject of brass nuts was mentioned to the buyer, he immediately said: "We don't use brass nuts in our products." Here is a case where the buyer, having insufficient time, could not ascertain everything that was being used in the products of his division. When the buyer was shown, in the plant, that these nuts were used in the product in considerable quantity (375,000 per year), he became quite interested. He stated that he did not have any quotations on brass nuts but he would look into the matter.

A few days later, a manufacturer of standard nuts visited the buyer. At this time, the buyer showed the manufacturer the ¼-20 brass jam nut and asked if he would supply a quotation on it. The manufacturer stated that he could not quote, as he did not manufacture *specials*. The buyer then asked: "Well, what constitutes a standard, or what quantities would your company consider making?" The supplier said he would be interested only if the quantities were 25,000 to 50,000. When he was informed that 375,000 of these nuts were used per year, he immediately stated: "This is not a special, it has just become a standard."

**Figure 7**

It is still possible to look at this manufacturer's standard listing of brass jam nuts and find this one listed at a price of $6.30 per hundred. This was only the start, since four other sizes of "special" brass nuts were found being used in the product. These too, although not used in as large quantities, were similarly made "standard" for a full realization on the five different brass nuts of $30,000 per year net savings.

## Case Study 8
## WASTE MATERIAL

One of the major problems facing most industrial plants is the economical disposal of waste material. In a large plant, this can become a major problem. In this specific case, a value specialist assigned to the Utilities Purchasing Department was given the task of analyzing the waste disposal

Waste?

Wood

Metal

Sawdust

Boxes and Paper

**Figure 8**

problem and reducing the costs involved. Study showed that one of the major parts of the problem was the disposal of wood chips generated by the wood and pattern shops. It was found that the present procedure was to hire truckers, when possible, at a cost of $2 per truckload, to haul the chips from the plant to the city dump.

**Results:** The value specialist, after spending time on this and other portions of the overall problem, left work as usual on Friday evening. Being somewhat of a gardener, he planned to do some work in his yard over the weekend. On his way home from work, he stopped at a local nursery and purchased a couple of bags of mulch for use around his evergreens.

The following Monday morning he asked his supervisor if he could place an advertisement in the local paper. Upon receiving approval, this is basically the advertisement as it appeared in the paper:

> *For sale — clean wood chips, $1 per truckload.*
> *Contact John Doe, XYZ Company, telephone*
> *1-1000.*

Within a week, the company had a three-page list of local farmers they could call whenever they had wood chips to be hauled away.

This profitable outcome resulted from the fact that this value specialist recognized that the mulch he had purchased for his evergreens consisted basically of wood chips. He theorized from this that wood chips, at an economical price, would readily be purchased by farmers to be used for the same purpose in their fields. His theory proved correct and resulted in a saving of $3 per truckload.

# Case Study 9
## UNION SLEEVE

This union sleeve, made of brass tubing having a ⅛-inch wall thickness, was found to be part of the grounding circuit of the project being studied by a value engineering workshop seminar team. This tube was found to have a shop cost of $128 per hundred.

**Results:** The seminar team determined that the basic and required second-degree functions of this part were:

1. Basic: "conduct current"—provided by base material
2. Secondary: "provide location"—formed shoulder and length

When the team checked into the present means of manufacturing the piece to determine the reasons for the part's extremely high cost, they found that there were two basic causes. First, they found that a considerable amount of labor was required to heat and deform the end for the double-thickness shoulder. Second, they found that the scrap rate on this piece was high due to cracking where the material was doubled back to form the shoulder.

The team further determined that the sleeve was made of this material and of this thickness because of the habits and attitudes of the people involved. These people believed that this was the only tubing of this size which would take the reverse bend at the collar.

The team, in talking to company specialists in the Works Laboratory, found that pure copper tubing with a 1/16-inch wall thickness would conduct the required current and could be more easily reverse bent. They then secured material samples and had parts made for evaluation by the decision makers.

Examination of the part made from copper tube, 1/16-inch wall thickness, showed that it provided the functions of "conduct current" and "provide

**Figure 9**

location" satisfactorily and that the shop cost would be $63.42 per hundred. Besides the basic cost reduction of $64.58 per hundred, a secondary benefit was found; i.e., the scrap rate on the piece dropped to almost nothing in normal production.

## Case Study 10
## DUCT SPACERS

This general type of duct spacer is used in distribution, station, and network types of transformer coils as a spacer between the layers of wire to allow oil to circulate as a cooling agent. They are $\frac{1}{4}$ inch wide by $\frac{3}{16}$ inch thick and of varying lengths to suit the application. They are manufactured on standard

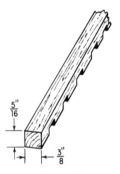

**Figure 10**

industrial woodworking equipment from kiln-dried magnolia wood. The magnolia wood is purchased by carload lot in random lengths, 6 inches wide by $\frac{5}{16}$ to $\frac{3}{8}$ inch thick. The magnolia wood is used as it does not contaminate either standard or nonflammable transformer oils.

**Results:**    A value specialist, noting the vast number of these duct spacers used, started a project analysis that was to entail 3 years of searching, experimenting, testing, frustration, and roadblocks before the final solution was found.

Analysis showed that the waste involved in manufacturing these duct spacers from the incoming material was between 55 to 60 percent or that more than half the material received went "out the back door" as sawdust, chips, or scrap pieces. It was further determined that the raw material cost of the magnolia was $18.45 per hundred board feet and that by the time this was machined into finished parts, the cost had been increased to an average of $70.55 per hundred board feet.

With this startling information in hand, the value specialist decided to try to develop a lower-cost and less wasteful method of manufacture applicable to the present material or to find a material that would meet the contamination specifications with improved manufacturing and waste reduction methods.

It was determined after careful study with the Manufacturing and Methods Departments that very little could be done to improve the product yield with the present material due to the form in which the raw material must be supplied by the vendor. Only one avenue remained open for potential cost improvement; i.e., the location or development of another material.

This task took many months of effort on the part of many people. First, some thirty-one different wood, wood products, and insulating materials were tested by the works laboratory to determine their contaminating characteristics with the standard and nonflammable transformer oils. Of these, eighteen were approved for use in both oils; but six of these were modifications of the present material and found to be more expensive, therefore they were eliminated.

Next, the remaining twelve materials were evaluated for total cost and manufacturability. Of these, two were found to be quite applicable from the standpoint of raw material cost: one a plywood, the other a wood chipboard. Evaluation of these materials from the manufacturing viewpoint showed that the chipboard would be more economical to use due to the fact that it could be purchased to the exact thickness desired.

The final step in this project was to work directly with the chipboard manufacturer to determine the best material size, shipping method, and delivery schedule. In addition, arrangements were made with the manufacturer to assure the company that no change would be made in the chipboard formulation for this end use.

With these steps accomplished, it was determined that the material saving alone would amount to well over $50,000 annually. When the material change was made, the following additional direct material and labor savings in the shop cost of the product were realized:

1. Reduced lead time—13 weeks' lead time was required for the magnolia wood while only 3 to 4 weeks' lead time was required for the chipboard. This also reduced the required on-hand inventory and storage space.

2. Reduced incoming handling costs—the magnolia wood was shipped in boxcar lots with the loads loose in the boxcar. Since each piece had to be handled individually, it required 6 man-days to unload. The chipboard, being manufactured in 4- by 4-foot pieces, was shipped palletized. This method of shipping allowed the boxcar to be unloaded by fork truck, which required 1 man-day.

3. Reduced machine and tool maintenance—the elimination of the "planing to thickness"—reduced maintenance on equipment. Due to the fact that the chipboard was easier to cut, the maintenance on saw and notching blades was greatly reduced.

In this case, persistence paid off, for the savings described above were also expanded to at least two other plants of this company.

## Case Study 11
## DIAPHRAGM BREAKER – STATION-TYPE
## TRANSFORMER

This 26-part assembly was designed to break a special 6-inch glass diaphragm in the transformer tank wall. The specifications required this action to take place at a tank pressure of 12 ±½ pounds per square inch internal pressure. The study of this assembly was recommended by both the Engineering and Manufacturing Departments.

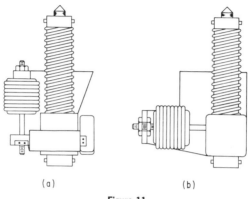

(a)                    (b)

**Figure 11**

**Results:**   This study was initially undertaken by a three-man part-time task force comprised of the design engineer, an individual from manufacturing, and the value specialist.

It was first determined that the assembly incorporated eight parts in the trip mechanism; i.e., the action is from the bellows (which is adjusted by a nut and stud), to a rod, to an arm, to a rod through the top of the casting, and then to another arm which finally releases the pin tripping the plunger. This seemed to be a rather elaborate and expensive means of performing the function of "release energy."

Investigation of the calibrating facilities determined that, in actuality, the present equipment was incapable of setting the diaphragm breaker within the plus or minus half-pound tolerance.

With this data in mind, the task force developed a 14-part assembly and recommended changes in the calibrating equipment. In addition, the specifications for tripping pressure were modified to 12 ± 1 pounds per square inch. These modifications, all of which had to be incorporated at the same time, provided the company with a substantial direct net savings as well as numerous indirect savings.

# Case Study 12
## BEARING HOUSING-SUPPORT

A Value Engineering seminar team was given a dust-collector valve to study as their project. In the Information Phase on their project, they duly reviewed the assembly and subassembly parts and their costs. During this information search, they noted that there were two bearing housing-supports listed on the bill of material, i.e., right- and left-hand gray iron castings.

**Results:**    In continuing their information search, the team found that these bearing housing-supports were used in the main assembly to provide location to the bearings which, in turn, supported and located the main shaft of the dust-collector valve. It was further established by the team that each of these assemblies required a bearing support-housing, a bearing, and inner and outer bearing seals. For the two sides, these subassemblies totaled $36 in direct material and labor cost.

In the Function Phase, the team defined the required subassembly basic and secondary functions as "provide support," "provide location," "reduce friction," and "provide seal."

In their Creation Phase work on the functions of "provide support" and "provide location," they listed steel plate for both. Taking this common idea from both creative sessions and developing it, they found that a steel plate would indeed provide the required support and location but would not "reduce friction" or "provide seal."

Their problem attack now centered on these latter two functions. In this part of the problem attack, they secured and searched a number of bearing manufacturers' catalogs. In each of these they found listed as a standard

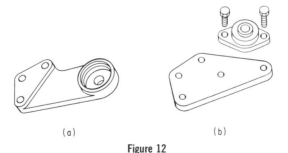

(a)                              (b)

**Figure 12**

item a sealed, self-mounting bearing. When the solution to the functions of "reduce friction" and "provide seal" was combined with their solution to the functions of "provide support" and "provide location," they realized they had a workable solution.

They realized that, for right- and left-hand sides, the self-mounting bearing could be mounted on either side of a common piece of steel plate as shown in the picture. This solution to the original problem reduced the total housing subassembly cost by 33 percent to $24 per pair. Since only minor engineering changes were required and no tooling was needed, the annual net saving of approximately $3,100 began with the first year.

## Case Study 13
## CONTACT SEGMENTS

While walking through the assembly plant, the value specialist noticed one of the production personnel hand-filing all edges of the copper contacts shown. This aroused considerable interest since he knew that eighteen of these were used within each complete assembly for an annual usage of approximately 10,800 pieces. He found that this hand-filing operation was being conducted on every piece and that the total shop cost was $1.58 per segment. He also determined that each contact segment weighed 8 ounces (a cost of approximately 20 cents per ounce or ten times the cost of raw copper at the time).

**Results:** The value specialist found, in a discussion with the foreman, that the present method of manufacture of these parts entailed turning and boring copper tubing to the proper contour, sending it to the Plating Department to have the inside diameter plated for electrical contact, returning

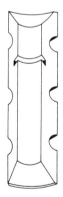

Figure 13

the tubes to the machine shop where they were laid out, stamped with sequential numbers, and cut into six segments on a milling machine. This milling-cutting operation, by its nature, produced a burr on all edges which had to be removed by hand-filing. It was further learned that because of this method of segmenting the tubing, the individual parts had to be kept in sets; and if one segment were lost, the remainder of the set had to be scrapped.

With this information in hand, the value specialist went to the Engineering Department. His first query of the engineer was to have him estimate the cost of the segments. The engineer stated: "I'm guessing high, but I believe that they cost no more than 35 cents apiece." When informed of their actual cost, he had no objections to a detailed investigation and evaluation of the parts and total assembly.

This investigation resulted in a number of interesting circumstances and potential roadblocks. Going out to different suppliers, both forging and casting, the value specialist was unable to obtain quotations for the contact segment because of tight specifications on current-carrying capacity. This specification more or less required that the segments be made of oxygen-free copper. During a further discussion with a manufacturer's representative, the value specialist was advised that a forging company he represented might possibly make the part to specification.

Drawings and part specifications were immediately sent to the forging company via their representative. This company, not knowing the user's shop cost per piece, answered the request for quotation by stating that the tooling cost would be too high and could not be amortized and that the piece price would also be quite high.

At this point, the value specialist "saw red." He telephoned the forging company and requested that they supply a quotation stating the tooling cost and the piece price. When the quotation was received, the piece price was 43 cents each and the tooling cost was $1,200 for a forging die and a trimming die. This showed a $1.13 saving per piece which meant that the tooling could be amortized, actually in about three months.

This forging company was given the job and the annual savings amounted to better than $12,000 annually. Besides the basic dollar saving per year, it was found that the new forged contact provided three additional benefits:

1. Final testing of the forged contact showed that it could carry a maximum of 18,000 amperes (whereas the old contact could only carry 15,000 amperes), thus providing a better factor of safety.

2. Manufacturing determined that a much simpler method of silver plating could be used on the forged contacts. This provided additional savings.

3. The most significant additional benefit from this change was that the forged contacts were completely interchangeable, greatly reducing loss due to scrapping.

## Case Study 14
## BRAKE-PEDAL ASSEMBLY

This brake-pedal assembly became the project of a value specialist as a result of a request from a shop foreman. The shop foreman requested that this assembly be looked into due to the fact that it comprised four individual parts which in turn required six production orders, which, because of parts shortages, caused assembly delays.

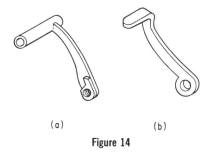

(a)                    (b)

**Figure 14**

Results:    Although this was a simple assembly, an immediate study was started because an investigation had been requested by a shop foreman.

The information search brought out the facts that the assembly less the shaft cost $5.04, and that it was typical of a number of pedals used on this and other major products. It was also found that sixty of these particular brake pedals were used per year.

The value specialist, working informally with Engineering, Marketing, and Manufacturing, looked into ways and means of accomplishing the required functions; i.e., "transmit force" and "provide location." After a number of false starts, such as investigating the use of castings, forgings, or a standard pedal, one of the informal team members suggested that there might be a possibility of making the pawl and arm in one piece.

Engineering investigated this idea and stated that this could indeed be done if the material for the arm were increased from 3/8 to 1/2-inch-thick steel. When this had been tested, it was realized that the only semicritical part of the total assembly was the hole in the arm and the location of the flat area (formerly provided by the pawl) with relation to the hole.

From this realization it was a simple step to suggest that when the part was burned out, sufficient stock be left on for the pedal itself and that the part be heated and bent, in the burning shop, to form the pedal. A prototype was made and proved entirely satisfactory. This answered the shop foreman's original problem by reducing the number of parts to two in place of the original four, and it reduced the number of production orders from six to three. While accomplishing this, the cost of the pedals was also reduced 70 percent to $1.52 each.

This concept also reduced the work load in the following departments: Machine and Structural Shops, Material Control, Warehouse, Accounting, and Material Handling.

## Case Study 15
## QUOTATION BINDER

The marketing manager came into the value engineer's office in a rage. His rage was occasioned by an incident that had just occurred in the office of a major customer. He explained to the value specialist that while he had been waiting to see the customer, he happened to look into the waste basket. Lying in the basket was one of his company's quotations. Holding back his anger, he asked the secretary what had happened. He was immediately informed that that was not his company's quotation, just the binder, which was too thick and would take up too much file space.

**Results:** The value specialist, after calming the marketing manager down a bit, started to ask some basic questions. His first question was, "What is the purpose of quotation binders?" The answer he got was that the binder provided basic company advertising and that it prevented the competition from seeing what the quotation contained if it was left on the customer's desk. The second question asked was, "How much does the quotation binder cost?" The immediate reply was, "I don't know, I just don't want them thrown away, leaving our quotations free for anyone to see

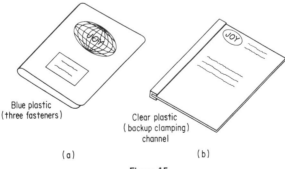

Blue plastic
(three fasteners)

Clear plastic
(backup clamping)
channel

(a)                    (b)

**Figure 15**

or to get lost." The value specialist promised to look into the matter and the marketing manager left the office.

The value specialist then contacted the supply warehouse and found that each quotation binder cost the company 79 cents and, because they were special, the binders had to be ordered in minimum lots of 5,000. He was also informed that the company used, on the average, 4,000 per year of this type.

The value specialist then determined, and cross-checked with the marketing manager, that the quotation binder performed two functions, i. e., "provide protection" and "provide advertising." It was also realized that the "provide protection" function was twofold in that the quotation binder provided both physical and visual protection.

After a short discussion with the supervisor of the supply warehouse and some investigation with his suppliers, it was found that a standard binder could be secured that would accomplish the function of "provide protection" (physical) at a cost of 13 cents.

In a later discussion of this point with the marketing manager, the other two functions were readily accomplished by the letter of transmittal on company letterhead, a letter always sent with each quotation.

It was realized that when a clear plastic binder with a snap-on back was used and the letter of transmittal was stapled in the binder with the quotation, all the required functions would be met; i. e., "provide advertising" and "provide protection." It was further realized that a small secondary benefit would accrue; i. e., it would take the company secretaries less time to assemble the quotation as the pages would not have to be punched and individually placed in the binder.

## Case Study 16
## FORGED LOOP

The task force team, studying the intermediate section of a conveyor system, started a depth analysis of the forged loop, shown in Figure 16, simply

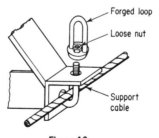

Forged loop
Loose nut
Support cable

**Figure 16**

because they had considerable difficulty defining and justifying its function in the assembly. Their investigation determined that the forged loop was part of an assembly comprising a right-angle bracket, a nut, and a J bolt. Analysis showed that by turning the forged loop, the nut was moved down on the J bolt, pulling it against the support cable, which in turn pulled the cable against the angle bracket. This forcible location of the cable between the J bolt and bracket held an intermediate conveyor section in place on the support cable. From this knowledge, the team defined the forged loop's function as "transmit force."

**Results:** With this information secured, the team further determined that the forged loops were purchased at a cost of 22 cents each. At this point, the team was ready to drop any further investigation of the piece because, as one team member put it, "Twenty-two cents, that's only peanuts."

This thought was rapidly dispelled when the nagging thought of the part's odd function in the assembly of "transmit force" was coupled with the fact that the annual usage was found to be a minimum of 48,000 pieces or a total expenditure of over $10,500 per year. This spurred the team on to proceed with the steps of the Job Plan, as much for satisfaction and practice as for what they thought they might eliminate from the part's cost. From the Information and Function Phases, the team proceeded into the Creation Phase. In this phase they developed, as would be expected, a long list of ways and means of accomplishing the function "transmit force."

During the functional development portion of the Evaluation Phase, they realized, as sometimes happens, that they didn't know how much force had to be applied by the loop to the nut or, for that matter, why it had to be transmitted from the loop to the nut.

This realization sent them back into the Information Phase and thereby back to Engineering and Marketing.

This second session with Engineering and Marketing revealed that when this design was first conceived, a certain condition existed. This condition was that the conveyor maintenance man in the mines, where this conveyor is used, carried a rod or bar as his major tool. As he would walk along the conveyor, he would insert this rod into the forged loop and give it a push, thereby tightening the assembly. Further discussion of this point brought out the fact that this condition no longer existed. As a matter of fact, it was determined that the maintenance men now carried a standard crescent wrench (one of the items the team had on its creative worksheet to "transmit force").

Looking at this new condition, the team realized that with the forged loop in place, the maintenance men would have to take hold of the crescent wrench by the business end and use the handle as a bar to transmit the required force. When these facts came to light in the interdepartmental discussion, Engineering and Marketing suggested that the forged loop be eliminated from the assembly, their reason being that the maintenance men could then use the crescent wrench as it was meant to be used.

Here, as a result of a nagging thought or constructive discontent plus a desire to secure all the facts, the forged loop was completely eliminated from the assembly for a 100 percent saving on this part. So what initially looked like peanuts turned into more than $10,000 net savings plus a reduction in purchase orders, inventory items, and inventory cost.

## Case Study 17
## MINE-FAN TAIL CONES

Analysis of the mine-fan line showed that the tail cones used ranged from 3 to 5 feet in diameter by 6 to 14 feet in length, dependent upon the fan size. It was further determined that these tail cones were fabricated from cut and rolled steel plate welded to a structural-steel framework. Besides being costly to manufacture, they were found to be extremely heavy and cumbersome to handle, especially in field maintenance operations.

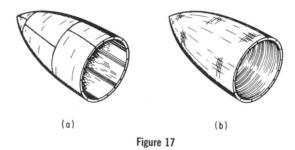

(a)                    (b)

Figure 17

**Results:** A detailed analysis determined that the basic function of the tail cones was to "control airflow." With this function plus the stated problems in mind, a solution was sought.

Cooperative investigation between Engineering, Purchasing, and Value Engineering showed that these tail cones could be produced by a sprayed fiberglass technique. Samples were secured, tested, and found to perform the required functions satisfactorily. Tail cones made by this process were found to be considerably lighter in weight and therefore much easier to handle in the plant and in the field.

Although tooling—a spray-up form—was required for each tail cone size, it was found that the tooling cost was more than amortized by the saving on the first part of a particular size purchased. An average savings of more than 60 percent was then realized in the purchase of each subsequent part of that size.

In addition to these direct savings, a number of secondary savings and benefits were realized. It was found that the painting and associated operations were no longer required, that there was a distinct reduction in assembly and shipping costs, and that greater freedom of tail cone design and form was possible.

## Case Study 18
## MOLDED NEOPRENE POWER CONNECTOR

The investigation of this case study was occasioned by a complaint from the customer that tape used to seal connector end caps was coming off due to aging. The failure of the tape adhesive prompted Engineering to seek the assistance of Purchasing and Value Engineering in order to find more reliable tape. See Figure 18(a).

**Results:** The team of Engineering, Purchasing, and Value Engineering, instead of pursuing the problem of finding a more reliable tape, asked the fundamental questions: "What is the function of the tape?" "Why is it required?" "Will something else accomplish the required function?"

These searching questions brought out a number of facts. First, the function of the tape was "provide seal." Second, this function was required due to the fact that an end cap (as shown) was used to close the end of the connector insulating cover and the tape was used to seal the joint between the end cap and the connector's main body. Third, the power connector had always been made this way. Finally, not all of the information regarding this connector's specifications, requirements, and manufacturing procedures was in the team's hands.

When the latter material was secured, it was determined that the parts of the connector that conducted electricity had to be protected against moisture when in operation. It was further determined that the present manufacturing procedure was to mold the neoprene main body (using a removable hexagonal steel mandrel), remove the mandrel after molding, reheat the finished part to 250° F (in an annealing furnace), insert a hexagonal copper conductor, insert the end caps, and, finally, apply tape to the joints.

Analysis of this manufacturing procedure in conjunction with the specifications led the team to believe that the procedure and the assembly could

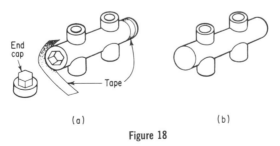

(a)                              (b)

Figure 18

be simplified. After an intensive creative thinking session, the following recommendation was made.

The mold should be modified to eliminate the cavity and clearance for the end plug, leaving a plain end plate. This would allow the direct molding in of the hexagonal conductor with closed ends, eliminating the need for the two end caps and the troublesome tape.  See Figure 18(b).

The customer readily approved this change, as it met all of the specifications and requirements while providing a more reliable part.

This change, the result of looking deeper than the original problem, resulted in a 17 percent reduction in product cost; the elimination of the manufacture, inventory, and assembly of the end caps; the elimination of the end-cap mold and its maintenance; and the elimination of the purchase, inventory, and assembly of the tape.

## Case Study 19
## MOTOR GUARD

A Value Engineering seminar team working on the detailer rod assembly of a candy-coating machine found this motor guard subassembly to be part of their project.  The guard is manufactured of four pieces of stainless steel which are welded together and then hand-finished and polished. Shop cost of this guard was $20.

**Results:**   The team, in analyzing this subassembly as part of their total project, found that it covered the top of the 40-watt, totally enclosed motor used to drive the detailer rod.  During the Function Phase of the workshop seminar, they defined the motor guard's basic function as "provide protection."

Later on, while discussing other aspects of the project with the Marketing Department, it was learned that the initial candy-coating machines were shipped without this motor guard.  This small piece of information whetted their curiosity and caused them to seek further information regarding the motor guard subassembly.

This quest brought out the fact that after the initial shipment of these machines, a series of complaints was received.  Each complaint stated that the detailer-rod motor was overheating and should be replaced.  The company personnel involved knew that this was an honest wrong belief; i. e., they knew that this type of 40-watt, totally enclosed motor would get

Figure 19

just about as hot as a 40-watt light bulb, which is hotter than usual motor operating temperatures, without harming the motor.  They further recognized the fact that it was the practice of maintenance personnel to touch motors with their hands.  When this was done and the motor was found to be hotter than expected, it was considered to be overheating and burning up. The personnel of the equipment manufacturing company, recognizing these two facts, designed the motor guard to keep the customers' maintenance personnel from readily putting their hands on the motor. When these motor guards were installed on the equipment, the complaints stopped.

When the team had secured and analyzed this data, they recognized that they had defined the function of the motor guard on the basis of its name rather than its actual purpose. They then changed the difinition of the basic function from "provide protection" to "prevent complaints."

This definition of the basic function showed them an entirely different problem. The team's solution to this new problem was to recommend the elimination of the motor guard and its replacement with a 1-by 2-inch self-adhesive nameplate which read, "This motor normally runs hot."

This recommendation was accepted and put into effect. The nameplates cost 25 cents each, and initial art work cost $20. This $19.75 net saving per unit provided an annual saving of approximately $500.

## Case Study 20
## AIRPLANE RECEPTACLE SHIELD

The investigation of this formed sheet aluminum part was undertaken because of two basic factors. First, in the manufacture of the part, there was a high scrap rate in welding the thin material. Second, and partially resulting from the first, was the high cost of $1.15 per piece. See Figure 20(a).

**Results:** Investigation of these interrelated problems by a team comprising personnel from Engineering, Manufacturing, and Purchasing disclosed that the material was first cut to shape, then formed, and that, finally, the joint was welded. This latter operation was the point at which the greatest manufacturing problems were being encountered.

During the normal course of the investigation, Purchasing submitted prints to various suppliers for quotation. This was done so that a make or buy evaluation could be made.

As a result of this request, one of the suppliers submitted his quotation on the part per the print, and he also submitted an alternate quotation. This alternate quotation was to shear and form the shield from an aluminum extrusion which was to be the required oval shape of the finished part. See Figure 20(b).

The team, recognizing that the basic function of "provide protection" would be adequately met by this alternate approach, rapidly evaluated the quotation. They determined that this approach would not only eliminate the welding and associated high scrap rate but would also, at a price of 35 cents each, be a 69 percent reduction in cost.

The supplier was called into the plant for final discussion before final placement of the tooling and parts orders.

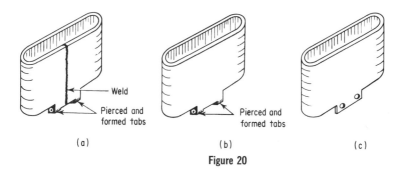

(a)                    (b)                    (c)

**Figure 20**

As a result of this consultation and study of the part and final assembly prints by Purchasing, Engineering, and the supplier, one additional modification was adopted. This was to eliminate the formed-under tabs by piercing and fastening the shield to its base directly through the side of the shield. This second modification of the shield further reduced its cost to 29 cents, making a 75 percent overall reduction in cost. See Figure 20(c).

## Case Study 21
## COMPRESSOR MOTOR BASE

Engineering undertook the investigation of the motor base portion of the compressor motor base and oil tank assembly, Figure 21(a), as part of their standardization program. This investigation was to determine if a universal motor base could be designed to accommodate all sizes of compressor drive motors, thereby ultimately reducing the number of required drawings and associated inventory.

**Results:** Initial analysis of the motor base showed that this subassembly comprised six basic parts and that its functions were to "support weight" and "provide location." Due to the rigidity required in the motor base to accomplish its two functions, it was found that it was constructed of precut industrial I beams and steel plate welded into a single unit.

The investigators, in trying to determine the welding time required, learned from Manufacturing that the motor base and oil tank were welded as one subassembly requiring 15.2 hours of welding time. This information led them to broaden their investigation to include the oil tank. Investigation of the oil tank disclosed that it was made up of nine additional basic pieces of industrial I beam, steel plate, and pipe; that its basic function was to "contain fluid," and that second-degree functions were to "support weight" and "provide location."

It was immediately recognized that the functions of "support weight" and "provide location" for both the motor base and the oil tank were the same; i.e., the measurement parameters of weight to be supported and location distances were identical or interrelated. With this as background knowledge, Engineering undertook a creative effort to see if this commonalty of functions could be used to some advantage.

As a result of this creative effort, the combined oil tank-motor base design, Figure 21(b) was developed. This design, comprising six basic pieces of formed steel plate and pipe, readily accomplishes all the required functions as well as the initial purpose of the investigation; i. e., design of a universal motor base.

The new design provided a number of additional benefits. The total cost was reduced by 23 percent and the welding time reduced by more than 50 percent. Fewer drawings were required, with an ultimate reduction of associated parts inventory. A major secondary benefit of this design was the increased aesthetic value; i. e., its smoother blending into the design of the compressor and other associated subassemblies.

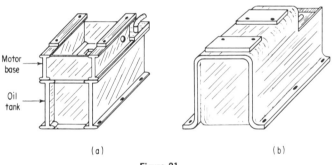

Figure 21

## Case Study 22
## CABLE-GUIDE ASSEMBLY

The cable-guide assembly shown in Figure 22(a) is used to guide the transport cable by which a piece of road construction equipment moves itself. This type of motive power is required only occasionally. Further, this type of motive power is installed on only 30 percent of these equipments. Field problems of rapid wear because of the rollers bending and/or seizing stimulated an investigation.

**Results:** A team comprising representatives from Marketing, Engineering, and Manufacturing was formed to evaluate and eliminate the field problems.

The team's fact-finding investigation disclosed that the seizing and rapid wear were caused by lack of lubrication by the equipment operator, a fact

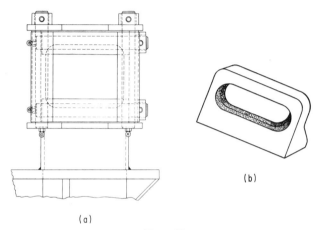

(a)

(b)

Figure 22

over which the plant had no control. They also determined that about forty of these assemblies were manufactured per year. Examination of the components of the assemblies determined that each of the four roller sub-assemblies comprised seven parts and that the support bracket was a weldment comprising six pieces of plate and tubing. This meant that thirty-four individual parts had to be processed through the shop to make the assembly at a direct material and labor cost of just under $40.

From an analysis of the use of the assembly, they determined that the required basic function was "create location" and that a major second-degree function was "reduce wear." Next, they developed a number of creative ideas on each of these functions.

From their list of ideas on the function "create location," they selected the idea "a loop or ring," which they believed was the lowest-cost idea and a place at which to start their redevelopment process. The statement of this idea immediately brought forth the roadblock "A loop or ring will wear just as rapidly as the bent or seized rollers."

Recognizing that they were not as yet at a point of considering the function "reduce wear," they evaluated the loop or ring idea. This evaluation showed that a loop or ring would create the required location just as effectively as the four-roller assembly.

They then moved on to consideration of their creative ideas for "reduce wear." In examination of this list to find an idea which would blend with that of "a loop or ring," they came to "harden or heat-treat." Since this process was being used on other plant products to reduce wear, they reasoned that it would work here as well.

Working with the foundry personnel and the metallurgist, a hardened cast-steel ring such as shown in Figure 22(b) was developed. Once the concept was deemed feasible, the drawings and patterns were made at a cost of approximately $100. The cast, heat-treated, and finished loop has a direct material and labor cost of just under $7 for a per-piece saving of over 80 percent.

A number of secondary benefits are also derived from this change. These included a substantial reduction in parts inventory, shop orders, and purchase orders. Likewise, there are less drawings to maintain and fewer field problem reports to process.

These direct and indirect savings were made possible by the team's realization that they could do nothing about the lack of lubrication in the field by the equipment operator. They therefore turned what looked like a disadvantage into an advantage in developing their lower-cost approach.

## Case Study 23
## COMPRESSOR SCROLLS

Each compressor manufactured at this plant incorporates two to four cast-steel scrolls similar to the one shown in Figure 23. The cast steel has properties of 60,000 pounds tensile, 30,000 pounds yield, and 24 percent elongation. Numerous sizes of these scrolls are used for different compressor sizes.

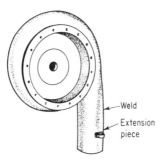

**Figure 23**

The casting buyer, due to his basic knowledge, was sure he could purchase these scrolls at a lower cost if the material were changed to gray iron.

**Results:** Based on his feelings about this costly item, the buyer requested and received numerous quotations on these parts using gray iron. These quotations showed that the use of gray iron would reduce the scroll cost by approximately 70 percent.

With his basic knowledge of materials confirmed, he then secured the assistance of Engineering, Manufacturing, and Marketing for an in-depth study of the possibility of using gray iron castings. Engineering, through evaluation and calculation, determined that gray iron would not be satisfactory, but that pearlitic nodular iron could be used.

Armed with this information, the buyer requested and received quotations on the scrolls using pearlitic nodular iron. An evaluation of these quotations showed a reduction in the savings potential to approximately 55 percent. This material has properties of 60,000 pounds tensile, 45,000 pounds yield, and 12 percent elongation.

At this point, two roadblocks were encountered. First, "The customer doesn't want cast iron in the machine." Second, "Cast iron can't be welded."

The first of these roadblocks was thoroughly investigated and evaluated. It was determined that the customers' prime interest was product integrity and quality. As long as the customer could be assured of these, the material used made little difference.

The second roadblock was overcome by consulting the plant's welding material supplier. He brought in technical assistance to explain to and teach the plant's welders the techniques of welding pearlitic nodular iron.

With these roadblocks overcome, free sample castings were secured from spare patterns. These sample castings were machined, tested, and found quite satisfactory, whereupon all the patterns were moved to the new vendor. A minor tooling cost to modify the patterns for his use was incurred at this point.

This change from cast steel to cast pearlitic nodular iron provided a direct saving of 57 percent in direct material cost.

In addition, numerous indirect benefits were realized: new knowledge of welding techniques and different material; decreased machining; freight paid by vendor; and, because of the new knowledge, ideas for other, future projects.

Since a project of this magnitude required 1½ years from start to finish, total and continuous teamwork was required. The only function in the plant not directly involved was Industrial Relations.

## Case Study 24
## PACKAGING AND TRANSPORTATION

Sixteen large machines were ordered from a United States plant by one of its international subsidiaries in Great Britain for sale to one of its major customers. Included in the cost of each of these machines, and thus in the price to the customer, was the normal cost of handling, packaging, and transportation. These costs were approximately $3,500 per machine. **Results:** Close investigation of the normal methods disclosed that each unit would be loaded onto a truck or railroad flatcar at the United States plant and transported to a New York warehouse for crating. At the warehouse, the machine would be unloaded and crated for overseas shipment.

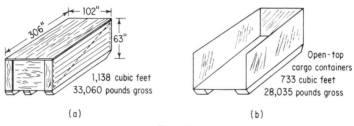

102"
306"
63"
1,138 cubic feet
33,060 pounds gross
(a)

Open-top
cargo containers
733 cubic feet
28,035 pounds gross
(b)

**Figure 24**

After crating, it would be loaded onto a barge for transport to the cargo ship. At this point, it would be loaded on the cargo ship for transport to Great Britain. Upon arrival at Great Britain, it would be unloaded from the cargo ship onto a truck or railroad flatcar and transported to the plant. At the plant it would be unloaded, uncrated, and prepared for delivery to the customer. This normal method entailed six different loadings and unloadings which would cost approximately $3,500 each, plus the cost of transportation and handling to and in the British plant.

Recognizing the high cost involved in these repetitive handlings and transport moves, a joint investigation was undertaken at both plants. These joint investigations uncovered a number of very significant facts. First, that there were readily available a number of companies in the cargo container business. Second, that these companies' containers were of sufficient size to handle these machines, which had a gross weight of slightly over 28,000 pounds. After securing competitive quotations, one of these land-sea container services was selected for shipment of the sixteen machines.

The use of the land-sea container method entailed the following steps. When the container arrives in the United States plant, the equipment is loaded and blocked into it. It is then transported directly to the cargo ship where it is loaded directly aboard. When the ship reaches Great Britain, it is unloaded and transported to the plant. At this point, it is removed from the container for preparation for delivery to the customer. This land-sea container method entails only four different loadings and unloadings which cost approximately $1,550 per unit, a saving of 55 percent.

This saving is accomplished because of the following facts. First, with the use of land-sea containers, the shipper pays only for the total weight or cubic footage shipped; in this case, 733 cubic feet. Second, because of the use of containers, no "heavy lift charges" are incurred, as when a crate is used. Third, a 5 percent reduction on ocean freight is realized when land-sea containers are used.

## Case Study 25
## DISTILLED WATER

It has been the plant practice to purchase distilled water, in returnable carboys, for use in electric trucks and in blueprint and photographic laboratory equipment. One of the plant's personnel, seeing this water being unloaded, questioned the reason for buying distilled water.

Figure 25

**Results:**    The reason he asked the question was that he knew that there was a still located in the metallurgical laboratory. His idea, therefore, was to secure from this still the pure water needed. Although a sound one, his idea proved to be impractical due to the fact that the laboratory still did not have sufficient capacity to meet all the needs.

At this point in the project study, a basic question was asked, "How pure does the water have to be for use in industrial batteries?" No one knew the answer. Knowing that facts were necessary, one member of the cost improvement team contacted a battery company in Boston. The battery company was questioned on this point and, having been told the plant's location, said to use local tap water. The battery company explained that this answer was due to the fact that tests had shown the local water to be quite pure. Checking further, the team also found that the same answer applied to water for the blueprint and photographic laboratory equipment.

This simple but significant attitude of questioning every item of cost resulted in an annual saving of over $250. These direct savings and several indirect benefits were accomplished for very little investigation and no implementation cost.

# Index